EVOLUTIONARY FAITH

*Rediscovering God
in Our Great Story*

Diarmuid O'Murchu

ORBIS BOOKS

Maryknoll, New York 10545

Copyright © 2002 by Diarmuid O'Murchu

Published by Orbis Books, Maryknoll, New York 10545-0308

Manufactured in the United States of America

Library of Congress Cataloging-in-Publication Data
O'Murchu, Diarmuid.
    Evolutionary faith : rediscovering God in our great story / Diarmuid O'Murchu.
      p. cm.
    Includes bibliographical references and index.
    ISBN 1-57075-451-9 (pbk.)
    1. Evolution – Religious aspects – Christianity. 2. Theology. I. Title.
BL263 .O2 2002
213 – dc21
                                       2002003390

With love and gratitude I dedicate this book to
Sr. Frances O'Kelly, IBVM
Teilhardian scholar, visionary woman, faithful friend,
whose persistent faithfulness drew forth the author
slumbering within my psyche

Contents

Introduction

Although we are inhabitants of a mere speck of dust floating in a vast universe, the very vastness is itself an indispensable condition for our being here to wonder at it. —John Polkinghorne

If we knew the unwritten story of our past, especially the prehistoric past, its fascination would cut the history of kings and queens, wars and parliaments, down to proper size.
 —John McLeish

A S A CHILD in the 1950s, I grew up in a remote rural village in the south of Ireland. We had no electricity, automobile, refrigerator, or television. I remember the first time my mother bought a battery-powered radio; I was about ten years old. News bulletins occasionally referred to events happening in Dublin, London, or New York; those places felt as if they were a million miles away. Even in my teenage years, not in my wildest imagination could I envisage myself visiting London, never mind living there.

It seems to me that very few of us, either in the Western world or elsewhere, truly appreciate the cultural shifts that happened throughout the 1960s and thereafter. They were earth-shaking and earth-shattering. We began to question the nature and function of institutional structures and paradigmatic ways of understanding in a way that had not been done for quite a long time. And inevitably, we witnessed an enormous variation of response, leading to uncertainty, chaos, confusion, and a whole range of new polarizations.

Some of those who, like myself, had been nursed in the idyllic insularism of rural Ireland came through the 1960s and 1970s more or less unscathed by the cultural impact happening all around us. In my own case, I was largely unaffected by the student revolts of the 1960s; my elders told me that I should have nothing to do with such bizarre behavior, and I took them at their word. By the mid-1970s, however, skepticism was taking root in my life and a growing distrust of those who had sought to protect me from the "evil influences of the secular world."

And it was not just the secular world, but also the religious one. I had read two books by the priest-paleontologist Pierre Teilhard de Chardin: *Hymn of the Universe* and *The Divine Milieu*. Truly, my heart burned within me; everything I read resonated with a depth and conviction I had not known for many years. And when my respected elders showed various degrees of disapproval of what I was reading, our ways began to part. For me, a whole new world was opening up and everything in me was telling me to go for it.

For many years I grappled with what I would have to abandon if I were to follow my heart's desire. Would I have to give up my inherited culture, my faith, my church? And then, quite by chance I met another searching soul mate. She used a different vocabulary, not the language of abandoning the faith or leaving the Church, but feeling the call to outgrow previous allegiances. That made a great deal of sense; for me it was a type of synchronistic moment.

This distinction resonates as I travel internationally and encounter many people from my home country of Ireland. Ireland very quickly becomes the subject of conversation, and often I learn more from them than they do from me. And I find myself having strange reactions, even feelings of annoyance. I no longer see myself as a citizen of Ireland; I am now a citizen of Planet Earth. That I consider to be my primary domicile, and when I travel internationally, that is what I want to converse about. Ireland feels like a springboard that launched me into the wider world; I cherish what Ireland has done for me, and I always will, but I also know that I have outgrown that aspect of my identity. My planetary and cosmic identity is what matters now — and for the future.

My Evolutionary Creed

I share this brief autobiographical introduction to set the scene for the topics I explore in this book. I find myself in a radically different place from the scientist Steven Weinberg, whose sense of creation is that of a cold, hostile place where we humans forever battle for survival and sanity. That never has been my sense of creation. While the world around me certainly is not perfect, and at times manifests some cruel anomalies, it nonetheless has a genuine feeling of home, and for me is the ultimate space for love and meaning.

Evolutionary questions stretch the mind and, more so, the imagination. One begins to think big, and conventional ways of understanding seem very restrictive at times. I feel a need to formulate a new creed in which religious and scientific insight blend together and thrive through creative dialogue. My emerging creed goes along these lines:

- I believe in the creative energy of the divine, erupting with unimaginable exuberance, transforming the seething vacuum into a whirlwind of zest and flow.

- I believe in the divine imprint as it manifests itself in swirling vortexes and particle formations, birthing forth atoms and galaxies.

- I believe in the providential outburst of supernovas and in the absorbing potential of black holes.

- I believe in the gift of agelessness, those billions of formative aeons in which the paradox of creation and destruction unfolds into the shapes and patterns of the observable universe.

- I believe in the holy energy that begot material form and biological life in ancient bacterial forms and in the amazing array of living creatures.

- I believe in the incarnation of the divine in the human soul, initially activated in Africa over four million years ago.

- I believe in the "I Am Who Am," uttered across the aeons, pulsating incessantly throughout the whole of creation and begetting possibilities that the human mind can only vaguely imagine at this time.

- As a beneficiary of the Christian tradition, I believe in the power of the new reign of God, embodied and proclaimed in the life of Jesus and offered unconditionally for the liberation of all life-forms.

My Lack of Faith

Being human, I also have my doubts, my agnostic and atheistic moments, and there are many things in my inherited faith that no longer resonate with my newfound vision:

- I find it hard to concur with the rationalism of science, claiming that one day we will uncover the whole rationale of creation and then be able to control the mind of God.

- I disassociate myself as much as possible from those who claim that humankind is the measure of all things. I no longer believe that humans are the masters of creation.

- I no longer accept that the universe consists of dead, inert matter; in fact, I never really believed it.

- I find it hard to accept that life evolved for the first time about four million years ago; I suspect that it has been doing so since time immemorial.

- I do not believe that we are the first intelligent creatures to inhabit creation. We belong to an intelligent universe that for many millennia has known what it's about. It seems to me that our intelligence is derived from the intelligence of the greater whole.

- I consider the heady debate between "creationists" and "evolutionists" to be so irrelevant and irreverent that I largely ignore it.

- I no longer believe in the anthropocentric myth of the end of the world. There is every likelihood that we humans will destroy ourselves, but not creation. Creation has an infinite capacity to cocreate.

- I have grave doubts that the story of evolution can be reduced to one cycle, commencing about twelve billion years ago and culminating in a big crunch some five to ten billion years from now. It's all too neat for the creativity of divine becoming.

My hope is that this book will create sparks — maybe even explosions — that will generate enthusiasm and energy for further exploration. The story of evolution belongs to no one person, group, or specialization; it belongs to all of us who participate in it. It needs all our collective wisdom and, above all, the creative dialogue that can ensue from that enterprise. With that quality of involvement we can begin the long journey home to the planet and cosmos where we truly belong.

Part One

OUR GREAT STORY

Adventure is what moves a process beyond triviality and monotony toward more highly nuanced forms of order. The cosmos reveals itself as an adventure of continual experimentation with novel forms of order. Hence, being part of this cosmos already means being a participant in a momentous adventure story.

—John F. Haught

Chapter One

Evolution: The Narrative Told Afresh

Until the 1970s investigators leaned to the view — expressed most eloquently by Jacques Monad — that evolution is due mainly to accidental factors. But as of the 1980s many scientists have become convinced that evolution is not an accident, but occurs necessarily whenever certain parametric conditions are fulfilled.
— Ervin Laszlo

What then surely is most new about our modern understanding of life is the idea of evolution, for it enables us to see life not as an eternally repeating cycle, but as a process that continually generates and discovers novelty. — Lee Smolin

THIS BOOK FEELS like an expedition into an unknown land, yet one that feels strangely familiar. The book arises not out of any particular intellectual pursuit or academic need. It is being born out of a type of hunger, a need to explore the big questions that face our world today, questions that deserve consideration and attention at a more spiritual level, rather than being forever subjected to the harsh, piercing light of scientific analysis or socioeconomic reductionism.

Evolution tends to be explained in one of three dominant ways: the scientific, the religious, or the mythological. Scientific research tells us a great deal on how the universe began and unfolded over some twelve billion years, and within that context, science tends to cherish the Darwinian "survival of the fittest" as an important clue to our understanding of the entire process. The religions share a broad agreement on the idea that God created the world and everything in it, sustains its unfolding at every moment, and eventually will bring it to an end according to God's mysterious but wise plan.

Both science and religion aim at observable, verifiable truths, using different but related methods. Neither gives much attention to my third line of pursuit, the mythological. As popularly understood, myth belongs to the realm of the fanciful and the speculative, popularized stories that explain away rather than explain what the world is about. Alternatively, some social scientists — anthropologists, for example — have attempted a rehabilitation of the notion of myth, suggesting that many ancient and primitive stories embody deep and enduring truths. The truth of the stories rests not in whether or not we can verify the facts, because often we do not have the relevant information with which to do that; we access their truth more through intuition and imagination than through rational discourse and logical argument.

Throughout the present work I draw on a range of different insights from both science and religion (theology), but I am attempting to blend them into what might begin to look like a myth for our time. This is an onerous undertaking far beyond my learning or expertise, but I hope that it serves as a humble beginning that others no doubt will modify, correct, embellish, and build upon.

Evolution as Story

I adopt a strategy of story as my primary mode of interpretation and exploration. I believe that there is something enormously profound in a child's fascination with a good story, and therein is a connection with truth that rational wisdom can rarely if ever provide. The story of an event or an experience embraces a great deal more than the facts that comprise the story; it unravels and exposes the meaning behind and beneath the event or experience. The observer becomes a participator, and consequently we are each changed by every story that engages us.

Story opens up an expanded, engaging world. Good stories leave us with unanswered questions and tease us into further exploration. Every story, no matter how mundane, rubs shoulder with mystery — the mystery of life, but also that sense of mystery that convinces us that there is more to life than just the discoveries and facts of rational learning.

I wish to suggest that evolution itself is the story par excellence, the great narrative within which every story unfolds, luring the participator into the ultimate questions of meaning and purpose. The story will seek to honor the discoveries of both science and religion, but frequently I will use standard terminology with an openness and fluidity required by the narrative approach.

Throughout the book I use three terms interchangeably:

Evolution. In scientific literature this word tends to be used in a Darwinian sense, indicating the gradual emergence of species over time largely determined by the survival of the fittest. In popular writing evolution usually refers to the unfolding of cosmic and planetary creation over billions of years. I tend to use the word in the latter context.

Coevolution. To the best of my knowledge, this concept was introduced in 1965 by the American biologists Paul Ehrlich and Peter Raven. It has been adopted by several theorists committed to the view that cosmic evolutionary development is governed primarily by innate, self-organizing processes, and not by external mechanistic forces (e.g., Jantsch 1980; Kauffman 1995; Laszlo 1993; Margulis 1998; Sahtouris 1998).

E-mergence. The Santa Fe Scientific Institute in New Mexico favors this notion. An E-mergent phenomenon occurs when whole systems at one level of organization merge to become parts of the systems of a new organizational level. In this process the new systems have different properties from those of their parts prior to their merger (see Lewin 1993, 178ff.). This notion is quite similar to that of coevolution.

Spelling this word (and its variations) in hyphenated form, as I do throughout the text, helps to illustrate the fresh nuances being explored in this book. The capital *E* stands for "energy," the primal substance, scientifically and theologically, from which everything comes into being; and *mergence* denotes the mergers that forever are taking place whereby diverse wholes on one level become coordinated parts of new wholes on the next level — what Teilhard de Chardin described as creation through differentiated union.[1]

What I wish to honor above all else is the unfolding story that comes from within the evolving process itself. This is not a book in which an author is trying to address the story of evolution in a new light. It is an attempt at allowing the universe to tell its own story as it has been narrated over several billion years. Consequently, much of my attention will be on the billions of years preceding organic life, whereas Darwinian evolution often focuses on the organic phase and subsequent developments.

The Conventional Story

Conventionally, "evolution" refers to the study of life-forms developing through a gradual, continuous process of change, from earlier, simpler forms to subsequently more complex ones. Usually, scholars deal with "organic" evolution, referring to living beings, from the first bacteria right up to our contemporary human life-form. "Inorganic" evolution describes the unfolding of the universe itself from its presumed initial state of unorganized matter.

The idea of the gradual unfolding of the universe was explored by the early Greeks, especially by Thales, Empedocles, Anaximander, and Aristotle, who envisaged everything evolving according to universal ideal forms. Due to the restraining influence of the church, no evolutionary theories developed during the first fifteen centuries of Christendom. Adopting a literal interpretation of the Book of Genesis, the church viewed creation as a one-time event that would retain its basic structure more or less unchanged until the end of time.

It is difficult today to envisage the enormous influence of the Christian church on our understanding of evolution. For much of the past two thousand years, the plan of creation outlined in the Book of Genesis was what primarily influenced both scientists and theologians. For much of that time, too, Europe was considered to be the center of the known world, and the European way of seeing things dominated all other perspectives. Consequently, the evolutionary insights of other religious and philosophical systems were either ignored or superseded.

Things began to change in the sixteenth century when Nicolaus Copernicus challenged the long-held belief that the earth lay at the center of the universe. The idea met with enormous opposition, not least from the church, which claimed to hold a monopoly of truth even on astronomical matters. But the discoveries of Johannes Keppler (1571–1630), using data on planetary motions assembled by the Danish astronomer Tycho Brahe (1546–1601), further enhanced Copernicus's original perception. Meanwhile, the Italian scientist Galileo Galilei (1564–1642) established that the force of gravity, not some mysterious divine force, activates movement and flow in the universe at large. Finally, Isaac Newton (1642–1727) laid the foundations of classical science, proposing that the universe worked in clocklike fashion under the guiding hand of God.

None of these scientific geniuses speculated on the course or meaning of evolution. However, they weakened the monopoly of ecclesiastical control, creating space for an intensive period of research and exploration. From the beginning of the seventeenth century, evolution became a topic of substantial scrutiny, culminating in the groundbreaking work of Charles Darwin and his classic, *The Origin of Species,* published in 1859.

Darwin chose to describe evolution in terms of inheritance, random variation, natural selection, and the survival of adapted species. When Darwin published the detailed evidence in support of his proposal in 1859, he did not know how the variation of traits could arise in living things, or how specific traits could be passed on from one generation to the next. Between 1856 and 1871, the geneticist Gregor Mendel provided the missing clues: inheritable factors, now known as genes, pass on organic information to subsequent offspring. This information is stored, transmitted, and expressed by DNA molecules. The metaphorical description has changed somewhat in recent decades, with the now "selfish" gene (Dawkins 1976) understood to be the driving force behind the competitive struggle for the survival of the fittest.

In scientific terms, the Darwinian-Mendelian emphasis on gradual unfolding governed by adaptation and the survival of the fittest has dominated scientific research until the present time. In its current neo-Darwinian status, the theory goes like this:

> Genes multiply by making more copies of themselves: they vary by mutation; they evolve by competitive interaction, the better versions increasing in number at the expense of less useful variants. And in addition to all this, genes make organisms as a means of exploiting different environments over the face of the earth so that they can increase and prosper. Better organisms made by better genes are the survivors in the lottery of life. But behind the front that we see as the living, behaving, reproducing organism is a gang of genes that is in control. It is they alone that persist from one generation to the next and so evolve. The organism itself is mortal, dying after a mere generation, whereas the genes are potentially immortal, the living stream of heredity that is in the essence of life. (Goodwin 1996, 1)

Scientists like the Darwinian interpretation. The evidence is observable, measurable, and quantifiable. More importantly, it fits well with the widely held scientific conviction that life, whether organic or inorganic, is a rather brutal process driven by mindless forces, a type of battleground where only the strong and the resilient win out. Whether or not Darwin himself saw it as starkly as that is an issue on which commentators are not agreed.

What is unfortunate is that other scholars of equal stature proposed alternative theories of evolution that rarely have been given due recognition. These include people such as Henri Bergson (1859–

1941), John Baptiste Lamarck (1744–1829), and Pierre Teilhard de Chardin (1881–1955). Much more serious is the almost total omission of the wisdom from the Far East furnishing a comprehensive view of evolution far more integrated and profound than our Western approaches; this strand is eminently represented by the great Indian philosopher and mystic Sri Aurobindo (1939, 1963). Collectively, these alternative visions represent a more creative and penetrating view, and their insights are central to the theological understanding of evolution explored in the present work.

Bergson proposed that evolution is driven by a creative energy that he called the "élan vital." For Bergson, this was a divine force forever engaged in overcoming the power of dead matter. Lamarck, on the other hand, did not view matter in this negative light, suggesting that nature was endowed with a tendency toward complexity and perfection arising from a process of spontaneous generation. Organisms developed new traits in response to environmental change, building up a repertoire of acquired characteristics passed on from one generation to the next. The work of Lamarck often is considered to be the first systematic study leading to a theory of evolution.

The Jesuit paleontologist Pierre Teilhard de Chardin infuriated both the scientific and theological communities by inferring that matter itself was sacred and was characterized by an unceasing process of becoming for which he identified five main stages: geogenesis, biogenesis, psychogenesis (mind-power within humanity), noogenesis (consciousness within the whole of creation), and christogenesis (which for Teilhard is the equivalent of cosmogenesis, the omega point of convergence, the final unification of all creation under God as head). Sri Aurobindo (1872–1950) developed an evolutionary theory very similar to that of Teilhard, emphasizing that the process is essentially one of spiritual unfolding, with each stage transcending but including its predecessor.

In the ensuing debate, fueled particularly by the scientific and dogmatic desire for hard fact, many scholars miss the ultimate goal that both Teilhard and Aurobindo had in mind: to comprehend the nature of consciousness as the key element in a spiritual understanding of the evolutionary process. The Darwinian understanding still commands enormous credibility and tends to be vociferously defended in the face of challenge or disagreement.[2]

However, the focus has shifted considerably in recent decades. Today, the inorganic rather than the organic grips the mind and heart of humanity. What we now call the "new cosmology," with the focus on the intriguing evolution of cosmic and planetary life over twelve to fifteen billion years, has altered several perceptions and understandings. The big picture rather than attention to the minute details is what engages the contemporary imagination.

Some suggest that we are dealing with a paradigm shift of the type noted by Kuhn (1970). Apart from an enlarged vision, we are dealing with a new methodology, precisely the one that facilitates the sharing of ideas across several sciences and brings to the table of dialogue visions that for long have been construed as irreconcilable opposites — for example, science and religion. And the dialogue is not just between humans. Like the mystics of every age, we need to converse also with the creation itself. We are outgrowing the subject-object relationship and embarking upon a new intersubjectivity. It is not just we who tell the story; creation itself is a narrative experience, telling its own story across the aeons of evolutionary unfolding.

The Story Told Afresh

Ours is a culture dominated by literalism and materialism. The hard facts are presumed to reveal the whole truth. And once the facts have been established, they often take on an unwieldy dogmatic assertiveness. In today's world the pursuit of clarity and factualism tends to leave the human spirit impoverished, restless, and thirsting for deeper meaning. We hunger for a bigger picture, because as an evolutionary species, that is what we have known for most of our time on this earth.

For the long aeons of human evolution we have approached reality in a very different light. Innately we unravel meaning by communicating, verbally but also nonverbally and over time; many of our stories relate to what it means to be at home in the surrounding creation. More than anything else we are a people who tell stories; the narrative infrastructure is indelibly imprinted in our inner being. It is our greatest resource for meaning and purpose. It long predates all the religious scriptures and dogmatic treatises, and it will long outlive all the monumental tomes that populate the scholarly centers of learning today.

Story is a pivotal clue to the human search for meaning in life. More importantly, it also is the clue to understanding the course of evolution itself in its cosmic, planetary, and human unfolding. I suggest that it is not by accident that all the great religious leaders of humankind communicated their message through the medium of story. In fact, for thousands of years before the formal religions, humans told their own sacred stories, and many of those stories were every bit as theologically profound as anything we humans narrate today. The verbal format of the story goes back at least one hundred thousand years — the date usually given for the evolution of human speech — but the energy of story, and the social bonding generated through storytelling, probably are a great deal older than that.

As a creative species, we humans rarely have been lacking in imagination and innovation. Long before our capacity to tell stories verbally, we told them actively. Robson (1987) reviews evidence for the claim that we developed a highly sophisticated manual mode of communication several millennia before adapting to vocal speech; we communicated with our hands long before we spoke with our tongues. Out of the surrounding landscape we also carved beautiful and useful artifacts, such as the famous Berekhat Ram sculpture, discovered in the Golan Heights of Israel by excavator Naama Goren-Inbar in 1981 and believed to be at least 250,000 years old.[3] We communicated and related through symbol, gesture, and a vast range of nonverbal interactions. Finally, we now know that as far back as one hundred thousand years ago, we droned and drummed, chanted and danced, meditated and prayed.

In fact, it may have been in dancing, chanting, and drumming that we spent most of our time in dialogue with our creative God. Long after the development of the verbal mode, we continued to pray and worship in highly symbolic and creative ways. What many of the great religions call miracles may in fact be the acted-out counterpart to the verbal medium. Miracle stories are primarily *stories,* and the transforming power is in the story and not necessarily in some type of miraculous action. Wisely indeed do some contemporary biblical scholars suggest that Jesus used two dominant modes of storytelling: parables of word (the parables), and parables of action (the miracles). In other words, the power for transformation is in the story rather than in rare miraculous events.

And it is precisely when we honor the miraculous in the creation around us, and in the cosmic coincidences that proliferate throughout the course of evolution, that story takes on a deeper meaning. We no longer are telling stories about the earth and the cosmos; rather, we are engaging with the story that *is* evolution in both its earthly and cosmic significance. At this juncture, the ability to listen is every bit as important as the desire to speak.

Theorists such as Lovelock (1979, 1988), Margulis and Sagan (1995), Eldredge (1999), and Swimme and Berry (1992) illuminate this new narrative horizon. What seems radically new is in fact a very ancient wisdom, long known to the great mystics and sages. Instead of the prevailing paradigms, ranging from "dead inert matter" to "survival of the fittest" to "gradualism" to "intelligent design," we begin by acknowledging that the earth and the surrounding cosmos are in fact alive (precisely how they are alive will be explored in subsequent chapters). And if they are alive, we should allow them to tell their own story, instead of we humans assuming that we know what their respective stories really are about.

Swimme and Berry (1992) attempted to facilitate this grand narrative in their book *The Universe Story*. The mysticism that makes this enterprise possible is not just a spiritual quality; it also is a scientific one, incorporating indeed many of the rigorous skills of observation and research. Seeing and listening are the perennial skills required for this undertaking. The astronauts who peered down at the earth from outer space could well have held rigidly to their scientific training, which insisted that they should not allow their emotions to govern their perceptions. They chose to transcend that guideline — Einstein also suggests that we often should transcend it — thus embarking upon a different wisdom and with it a radically different view of the earth as a living organism.

Stories engage the whole psyche, indeed, the whole personality. And the purpose of every story is to break open our conventional views of reality, to orient us to a larger reality with a more holistic aperture for truth. Every good story overwhelms. One often is baffled by the intensity of the mystery — a feeling that gradually yields to the encompassing sense that the mystery within which we are all held is fundamentally benign. This yields a very different view from that of scientific skepticism (frequently associated with scholars such as Daniel Dennett and Richard Dawkins), which views evolution as a random, blind, impersonal process devoid of purpose or ultimate meaning.

Symbiosis: How the Story Hangs Together

Walter Brueggemann (1993) claims that we are a species engulfed in cultural amnesia, haunted by a primal longing to come home once more. We have been forced to forget who we really are and what our existence within creation is all about. We are out of kilter with our surrounding world.

No longer are we able to acknowledge how things hang together. No longer can we identify the big picture in which everything has its place and its purpose. We have lost our sense of what the story is about in its primordial meaning. And it is not just a matter of reinventing the story; rather, it is about acquiring that openness and transparency whereby we can allow ourselves to be enveloped by the story that has invented us. To quote Elisabet Sahtouris (1998, 45),

> This is what we are learning to understand—that the Gaian life system has evolved in such a way that it takes care of itself as a whole, and that we humans are only part of it. Gaia goes on living, that is, while her various species come and go. We used to believe that we were put here to do whatever we wanted to with our planet, that we were in charge. Now we see that we are natural creatures which evolved inside a great Earthlife system. Whatever we do that is not good for life, the rest of the system will try to undo or balance in any way it can. That is why we must learn Gaia's dance and follow its rhythms and harmonies in our own lives.

We are the progeny of a storied universe. We are a dimension of a story that has been told for aeons past. And we are now the privileged participants in that story becoming conscious of its own unfolding. All indications are that we are evolution growing into a new quality of self-awareness, which we call consciousness. We are not just another chapter or a specific section of the story; rather, story is embedded in the fabric of our being and becoming. Story, I suggest, is the surest way to resolve the great philosophical search for our true identity.

Above all else, ours is an identity of belonging. We belong to a story unfolding over billions of years. Our brains carry remnants of ancient mammalian structures, and every fabric of our being is related to the ancient bacteria, those wonderful life-sustainers that have been given such a bad name in the medicine of sickness and pathology. And as we move into the dim and ancient past, we encounter those initial explorations of supernovas expelling carbon out into the open spaces. Today, we encounter that same carbon in nature's biodiversity. Our ancestors include the ancient stars. In a symbiotic universe, nothing stands alone; everything is interrelated.

Among contemporary scholars, Lynn Margulis (1998) is considered to be a pioneering voice for the evolutionary developmental theory known as "symbiogenesis." Symbiogenesis refers to the coevolution of several microbial organisms in a kind of sentient symphony. Contrary to the Darwinian notion of different species competing to adapt and survive against alien environments, Margulis suggests that nature operates on a subtle but powerful cooperative endeavor while engaging the creativity of several life-forms at any one time. Smolin (1997, 188) endorses this view when he writes,

> When we are dealing with a self-organized system, we cannot afford to look only on one scale.... It is only by finding a viewpoint which allows us to see that something interesting is happening on all possible scales, from the smallest to the greatest, that we are able to really comprehend the whole of any interesting system.

Essentially, therefore, our story is not about evolution, but coevolution. It is a story with several actors and many intriguing plots. And most of the actors and the plots long predate the human phase of participation. The hardest lesson to learn for the human participants is to realize that without the big and inclusive picture of this complex and intriguing landscape, we are in danger of misunderstanding our fundamental role within it. Consequently, we are in danger of misconstruing our engagement with it, with possibly deadly consequences both for ourselves and for the natural world we inhabit.

The story of coevolution is indisputably a story of cooperation and collaboration, and as Singer (2000) advocates, this needs to be adopted henceforth as the primary thrust of social and political policy. On our own, none of us can make it. We isolate and alienate ourselves from a life-process to which we radically and intimately belong. By opting to go it alone, by setting ourselves over and above as masters, rulers, governors, and other questionable anthropocentric roles that we have adopted, we do not merely set ourselves at variance with the coevolutionary process; more precariously, we set in motion a process of disintegration of which we ourselves become the primary victims.

As we seek to relocate our own identity within the evolutionary story, we can scarcely escape the painful and embarrassing anomaly that our alienation from creation generally is a cultural fixation of our own making. In setting ourselves up as the "masters" of creation, we have seriously misconstrued our own role in the overall process, and this in turn has seriously deranged our perceptions and understandings of universal life and its great evolutionary story.

By withdrawing our cultural projections — our need to dominate and control — we become more transparent and receptive to the greater reality, to its meaning and its mystery. We begin to appreciate the other as other; we become receptive to the greater story, more at home in the place that has been home to us and to so many other species for billions of years. We begin to understand our planet and universe for what they are in their own right. And as we begin to integrate all that, we are likely to find ourselves appropriating quite a different understanding of what God and the divine life-force are all about.

As we engage more deeply with the great story, we detect a progressive continuum, and we note it at every level from the macro to the micro. The nature of God's creativity in the world becomes even more transparent and convincing when we honor the innate creativity of nature itself. The process manifests its own magic, an innate inner meaningfulness. Ervin Laszlo (1996, 25, 27) provides the following description:

> We find a truly elegant continuum. As we move from microscopic systems on a basic level of organization to macroscopic systems on higher organizational levels, we move from systems that are strongly and rigidly bonded to those with weaker and more flexible binding energies. Relatively small units with strong binding forces act as building blocks in the formation of larger and less strongly bound systems on higher levels of organization. These in turn become building blocks in still larger, higher-level, and less strongly bonded units.... On a given level of organization, systems on the lower level function as subsystems; on the next higher level of organization, systems jointly form supra-systems.

The structure is orderly, elegant, and innately poised toward self-renewal (autopoiesis), yet it thrives on complexity and therefore frequently defies human rationality. The process never can be comprehended purely on the level of rational thought or analysis. Hence comes my suggestion that we adopt story as our primary means of interpretation, investigation, and discernment.

Moreover, across the entire spectrum of evolutionary unfolding we need to keep in mind the scientific principle that "the whole is greater than the sum of the parts," while also keeping in the forefront of our consciousness that the whole is contained in each part, as illustrated vividly in holography. Rather than isolating any dimension of reality, cosmic or local, and seeking to explain its meaning in isolation — that is, in its unique individuality — we need to seek out the larger whole to which it belongs and explore its uniqueness in terms of its relationships within the greater whole.

We belong to a universe of creatively interacting systems, a giant network of interplay and possibility forever drawn toward novelty and innovation (which is what natural selection makes possible). In the creation around us there are no isolated objects; everything belongs to creative interactive systems. We miss the deeper meaning if we stay with the product and ignore or bypass the evolving process. Nothing is static or stable (a favored concept of classical Newtonian science); each moment characterizes the unfolding dynamics of a highly creative universe.

As the Story Unfolds

In concluding this chapter, I wish to highlight some key assumptions that underpin the reflections of this and subsequent chapters.

Scope. Most textbooks on evolution highlight the evolution of biological life as outlined by Charles Darwin and his followers. In fact, many books begin their exposition with the evolution of the earth and earth life about four billion years ago. In the present work I want to reclaim and prioritize the big picture with the inherited legacy of the twelve-billion-year cycle known to us, and I also want to include the possibility that this is only one of several cycles our universe has been through.

Scientists have discovered many fascinating aspects about the origins of the universe, relating particularly to the Big Bang and its impact during the first few minutes of the universe's existence. There are still many things to be discovered and explored. The scope of scientific research, while informative and immensely useful in the technological world, is limited by what we humans define as objective reality. But the story of evolution, and our own human way of experiencing things, is bigger than that. Story is one medium that helps to expand the horizons of exploration.

Context. We need to outgrow our debilitating anthropocentric reductionism whereby we tend to focus attention on what it means *for us*. The universe does not exist for us; it is out beyond us in the elegance of its own story, both past and future. We need to appreciate it for what it is in itself, and not simply for what it means for us. We are not the sole reason, or even the main reason, why creation exists. More accurately, it exists for its own growth and becoming, for the elegant work of its own symbiogenesis, of which we are an integral part.

The evolutionary story, therefore, requires that we listen attentively to the evolving process transpiring over billions of years. Our failure to attend to this expansive vision may well be the major cause of the alienation and estrangement that we often experience in our daily lives.

Movement. Although we largely have transcended Newton's notion of absolute space and time, in which things effectively never changed, the sciences still resort liberally to closed, mechanistic concepts that favor values such as stability and permanence. I find it strange that one of the great transmechanistic discoveries of the twentieth century, quantum theory, tends to be described as "quantum mechanics." Adopting language of this nature can in itself inhibit our potential for creativity and fresh discovery.

Recent developments in cosmology favor more the notion of life's processes being open-ended, not rigidly defined, and transparent to surprise and mystery. Fixity has given way to mobility, with metaphors such as "movement," "dance," and "turbulence" being widely adopted.

Paradox. It is the nature of the human mind to unearth the secrets on which everything in life is based. But the more we search, the more we realize how much we yet have to discover. Moreover, our rational, analytical research often leaves us with more perturbing questions. And sometimes there follows a type of compulsive pursuit that is well articulated in this ravaging statement by Francis Bacon: "We must keep torturing nature, 'til she reveals her last secrets to us."

The present work advocates that we learn to live with mystery and that we develop the wisdom and skill to befriend paradox. We then begin to see with different eyes, intuit with a different heart, and tone down that compulsively driven anthropocentrism that may well be our greatest source of alienation in the world today.

Synergy. Science seems to have a strange fascination with the second law of thermodynamics and its prediction of the ultimate dilution of all life-forms. Religion, too, has a type of fixation on the cataclysmic end of the world, whether described in the theological categories of apocalypticism or of eschatology.

We live under a dark cloud of enduring pessimism, one that has jaundiced our whole understanding of evolutionary growth and development. The course of evolution provides enduring evidence that life is nourished and sustained by symbiosis, cooperation, energies working in unison. Disasters and failures, tragedy and catastrophe, never have the final word; in fact, they often foster the preconditions that lead to a new evolutionary outburst.

Meaning. To use the word "meaning" in a book on evolution is a risky adventure. Those of scientific persuasion might feel that we are diluting the neutrality and objectivity of science; those of a religious persuasion might feel that I am stretching religious horizons to include secular and material concerns that belong to the mundane rather than to the sacred. But the search for meaning cannot be hemmed in, and in the contemporary world, many people seek, and believe they will find, meaning in the natural world and in its evolutionary unfolding; and for growing numbers of people, that meaning carries spiritual weight and significance.

Evolution, explored through the medium of story, stretches even our understanding of the notion of meaning. As the story unfolds, we detect something akin to a "will for meaning," not just in humans, but also in creation at large. It surfaces in the oft-noted perception that in a strange and mysterious way, evolution generated the conditions in which life could emerge on earth. It also underpins concepts like autopoiesis (self-organization) and the Gaia theory (explored in later chapters).

Spirituality. By far, this area probably will provide the most original insights of the book, and perhaps the most controversial as well. My conviction that spirituality has a much broader and deeper meaning than religion is explored in previous works (O'Murchu 1997b; 2000). That same conviction underscores several key ideas that follow.

I am applying spirituality not just to humans, but also to all aspects of creation and evolution. I suggest that spirituality denotes "Spirit-power," whether understood theistically or otherwise. It seems to me that this power is most creatively at work in the quantum vacuum, that indefinable and unfathomable reservoir that empowers the whole process of evolution and creation. We will explore its meaning in chapter 3.

Consciousness. If Spirit-power is the ultimate force field that generates and maintains the creativity of the cosmos, then, as Ken Wilber (1998) argues, the evolution of consciousness becomes the gateway to the wisdom that drives the entire enterprise. In recent decades we note a shift in our understanding of consciousness, away from viewing it as merely a human endowment and toward seeing it as something that permeates every realm of the created, cosmic order (see chapter 11). We humans are conscious creatures because we are the progeny of a conscious universe. We help bring to conscious awareness the consciousness out of which our own self-awareness is born.

The secret to what consciousness is all about rests within the story of evolution itself. As we will see in subsequent chapters, the whole story of evolution is about the awakening of consciousness. It is the inner "intelligence" of coevolution that pushes life toward greater complexity and creativity.

Something of this new evolutionary vision can be gleaned from the response offered by Margulis and Sagan (1995, 49) to the age-old question "What is life?" They write,

> Life as God and music and carbon and energy is a whirling nexus of growing, fusing and dying beings. It is matter gone wild, capable of choosing its own direction in order to indefinitely forestall the inevitable moment of thermodynamic equilibrium — death. Life is also a question the universe poses to itself in the form of a human being.

Humans pose many questions about the past: How did it all begin? Where did we come from? Does the pattern convey meaning or not? We are somewhat fixated on the past. And because of our cultural programming, we tend to judge the truth of things in terms of what has worked in the past.

As reflective human beings with hopes and dreams in our hearts, our most profound questions are not about the past but about the future. Whereas the past indicates where we have come from, it is the future that inspires and motivates us. In fact, it is the future that lures us forward, propels us into being creative, dynamic creatures. And the reason is based not on some illusive or escapist spiritualism, but on, I suggest, the very driving force of evolution itself. Evolution is biased toward the future. It is the future rather than the past that gives evolution its foundational meaning.

Before unraveling the impact of the future upon us (in the next chapter), I conclude the present chapter, having noted the impressive contribution of Charles Darwin along with his central significance for the main body of scholars and scientists. I also note the limitations of the Darwinian model for the emerging evolutionary paradigm, eliciting growing attention and commitment from cosmologists in many parts of the world today.

•

It is time to outgrow...

the narrowly defined, competitively driven understanding of evolution, favoring the triumph of our successful biological species, with a tendency to overshadow the significance of cosmic and planetary unfolding over the vast aeons of inorganic evolution.

It is time to embrace...

the grandeur, complexity, and paradox that characterize evolution at every stage, a story that continues to unfold under the mysterious wisdom of our cocreative God, whose strategies always have, and always will, outwit our human and religious desire for neat, predictable outcomes.

Chapter Two

Evolutionary Theology: Meaning from the Future

Unlike the previous static views of the world, evolution invites us to picture nature as the unfolding of a promise, a promise that has been internal to the universe from its inception.
— John F. Haught

Before the evolution of life ... the portals of the future remain wide open.
— Louise Young

WE ASSOCIATE STORIES with past events; indeed, the storyteller often embarks upon the story with the line "Once upon a time...." Evolution, too, has a past rich in narrative embellishment. Yet, for much of this book, it is not the past that will weave our narrative tapestry. It is the future more than anything else that will adorn our vision and inspire our hope.

Telling stories inspired by the lure of the future is an ancient strategy of sages, philosophers, and great religious leaders. Unfortunately, the prevalence of rational thought and quantifiable analysis in recent centuries has largely subverted the power of stories inspired by an alternative future. All the parables of Jesus, although describing past or contemporary events, challenge the hearer into creative action because of the power of the alternative future they envisage. Hope builds eternally on stories inspired and animated by the open-ended future.

Both science and theology tell the story of creation in terms of what already has taken place, facts that we can establish and verify, achievements we consider to be foundational for everything that ensues thereafter. The litmus test of reality often is judged by how it relates to the past. Has it got solid foundations? Is it faithful to tradition? Does it honor time-sanctioned modes of operation?

The past is real, because we humans can observe, quantify, and control it. We set the criteria, and reality becomes what we choose it to be. We tell the story from our point of view, and often we assume that it reflects the ultimate meaning of everything else in our world.

It is at this juncture that the human-made story and the evolutionary story begin to part company. Human rationality and evolutionary creativity end up on a collision course. The constraints of human reasoning jar with the creative freedom of evolution. Evolution always has outpaced the human mind, and indications are that it always will.

Our Pessimistic Future

In the popular press, science and religion often are depicted as irreconcilably opposed. Ironically, the respective proponents, who appear to be at loggerheads, often are operating out of some quite powerful collusions, especially on matters that impact heavily upon human perception. This is particularly so when we review the doomsday sense of the future promoted by both fields of learning.

Both science and religion view the long-term future with a great deal of gloom and doom. Whether it is the scientific "big crunch" or the theological "end of the world," each depicts a pessimistic future both for creation and for humanity. Faced with the fear generated by such a problematic future, we human beings tend to veer to one of two extremes: manipulate the future to our advantage in the hope of defying the calamitous outcome, or throw caution to the wind because in the end our efforts will come to nothing anyhow. Both orientations are deeply flawed, and the tragedy is that both are based on assumptions that make little or no evolutionary sense.

In our human terms, the future often does look gloomy and unpredictable, but we view reality in very short time spans. As a young Christian, I grew up with the impression that nothing of significance happened in the world before the coming of Jesus some two thousand years ago. Before that time the world was in the grip of dark, satanic forces. In that same context, the two-thousand-year time span feels enormously long, indeed almost incomprehensible to the human imagination. In evolutionary terms, it is a mere second.

We misconstrue the past, and that makes it difficult for us to view the future in a more cogent and creative way. The culture of control, whether overt or subtle, drives us in a direction that often lacks trust, imagination, and creativity. This often is revealed in statements such as this: "Are we somehow to be freed from the tyranny of entropy, and is the universe to shine forever as the resplendent creature of God — a *new* heaven and earth?" (Robert John Russell, quoted in Worthing 1996, 157–58). Why must we consider entropy to be a form of tyranny? Tyranny for whom? And if we can re-create the universe as a "resplendent creature of God," what God have we in mind? And how can we be so sure that this is what God would want us to do?

The story of evolution seems to suggest that entropy is an integral dimension of the unfolding story. Surely, the time has come when we need to learn how to befriend entropy as an innate and necessary part of life's evolving pattern. We need to move to a larger and more inclusive vision. We need to cultivate a sense of trust in the power of the evolutionary process. It has gotten us places in the past twelve billion years; I suspect that it will achieve even greater things in the next twelve billion!

At several levels we need to bring an air of realism into what both scientists and theologians have to say about the end. This, too, is necessary if we are to respect the creative unfolding of evolution itself. The pattern of evolution will continue to beget radical newness at those creative and critical junctures when the old is no longer useful. Those unique and persistent forms of innovation and creativity that characterize the evolutionary process guarantee that the future deserves more serious attention than either science or religion has given it in the past.

Lured by the Future

What drives evolution more than anything else is the allurement of an open-ended future. In the words of the philosopher Karl Popper,

> It is not the kinds from the back, from the past, that impel us, but the attraction, the lure of the future and its attractive possibilities that entice us; this is what keeps life — and indeed, the world — unfolding. (Quoted in Crawford 1997, 53)

Life is forever yearning toward greater creativity, complexity, and becoming. There are always new possibilities inviting exploration and proffering hope. The future evokes fresh excitement and the desire to weave new pathways. The future never ends.

Our rational human minds focus on the past because we can quantify and control its impact upon us — or at least we think we can. But we have only a limited control over the future. The future always is out beyond us, bigger than our plans and promising more than we can ever imagine in each present moment. And despite the scientific prognostication of an ultimate cosmic heat-death and the religious prophecy of an apocalyptic demise of the world, evolution is likely to outwit all our theories and continue to unfold novel possibilities into an open-ended future, probably one of infinite duration.

Because science and religion rely so heavily on evidence gleaned from the past or the present, they are largely unable to offer a meaningful analysis of the future. That requires a different body of wisdom. What today we call "spirituality" may well prove to be the wisdom that enables us to come to terms with the challenge of living in a universe whose future is essentially open-ended. Spirituality, in this context, refers to the power of spirit that inspires and animates all creation, a life-force aptly described in the Christian scriptures as a creative energy that blows where it wills (John 3:8).

John F. Haught (1993, 2000) proposes that it is religion, specifically the Christian faith, that develops the notion of the future as the dimension that impregnates life with hope and meaning. The God of faith is a God who promises, and those promises are credible because they are fulfilled, specifically in the life and ministry of Jesus. This is one of theology's great gifts to the religion-science debate.

Haught acknowledges that although religion (particularly Christianity) offers hope on the basis of a promise awaiting fulfillment, religious practice rarely couches this aspiration in a meaningful or engaging way. Instead of seeking to attune religious devotees to the challenge, hope, and engagement required by such a vision, we tend to advocate a paralyzing fear in the face of a future that is about judgment, reward, and punishment in an idyllic world outside and beyond the present creation. Even for those who do not follow a religion, this fear casts its debilitating shadow far and wide.

From a religious point of view, Haught is seeking to retrieve a long-subverted wisdom, and while this is an admirable undertaking, I am unconvinced that it is a truly authentic starting point. In evolutionary terms, we need to honor the more ancient and enduring story. God did not begin the spiritual renewal of creation with the introduction of major religions; neither should we.

Long before humanity evolved, and long before formal religion emerged (in Hinduism, about five thousand years ago), the future already was luring evolution into expanding horizons of complexity, creativity, and novel possibility. Every new development — stars, supernovas, galaxies, bacteria — paved the way for others to follow; one can detect a type of logical consistency in each subsequent development. But quite rightly scholars have long questioned the "logical consistency," noting that many of the original breakthroughs came as total surprises, almost as a gratuitous gift from some anonymous source. This, I suggest, is where the lure of the future is most transparent.

New life-forms do not simply come into being when all the conditions are right. Often they unfold long before their expected time. Genetic mutation and natural selection are not just random processes; new possibilities are being invoked, often against tremendous odds. And we do not need to invoke some "God of the gaps" to explain the new upsurge. There is a deep and powerful creativity at work within the evolving process itself.

Religion provides useful clues to name and appropriate this dynamic sense of future, but we need to claim it primarily as a characteristic of the evolutionary process itself. The creative divine energy has been at work since time immemorial. It outpaces and outwits all our anthropocentric theories. I suggest that it always will. The ingenious "mind" behind the whole thing is precisely what leaves us restless and always searching for deeper answers. Truth always is before us, rather than being based on the certainties from behind. We are the beneficiaries of a creative cosmos with a radically open-ended future.

To describe this creative future as endowed with a sense of "promise" embraces religious wisdom in a way that enhances and enforces some of science's greatest discoveries. In all the major religions, God promises — not just a reward in a life hereafter, but a fullness of life in an open-ended future that is more enduring and all embracing than any "here" or "hereafter." This is the resilience of life that science never has been able to explain adequately. The fascinating coincidences are sometimes suggested as evidence for God's involvement in the evolutionary process; they certainly awaken a sense of awe and mystery, but I suspect that they are no more than a tiny glance at the depth of mystery that characterizes creation. We never are, and never will be, able to explain adequately this divine creativity; to do so would effectively strip the future of its radical promise and possibility.

Evolutionary theology is not that worried about the "God question" in itself. Its main concern is that we engage creatively with those several disclosures of God (revelations) that we encounter throughout the unfolding story. If we could begin to appreciate and appropriate something of this divine cocreativity and integrate it into our daily lives, then the chances are that we would come to terms more readily and coherently with what the divine is all about. In our cerebral pre-occupation of trying to sort out who and what God is, we may well be missing the actual encounter with the living God happening right before our eyes in the midst of creation itself.

So what does the divine evolutionary promise entail? That sounds like another anthropocentric question. Does it matter whether or not we can analyze it in fine detail? Might the challenge not be that we should engage with our evolving universe as fully as possible, and in that process we will begin to know *experientially* what the promise entails?

We would quickly discover that many things in our world today, scientifically and religiously validated, do not offer promise in any compelling sense. We would have to confront the painfully destructive state of affairs whereby people and planet are plunged into the darkness of meaningless suffering and debilitating despair — not by God, but often by wrong human interference. Yes, we do find it difficult to engage with life as promise. We largely have betrayed our call to be people of promise, that is, to honor and promote creation's own wishes to offer a meaningful future to all creatures.

The modern dilemma around the promise inherent to evolution, therefore, is not so much about God as it is about ourselves. We are the ones who religiously claim to be the primary beneficiaries of God's promises to creation. That is our first perceptual and idolatrous error. The promise is to all and for all; it is global and universal in its dynamism. We share it in proportion to our uniqueness and giftedness, but we hold no monopoly over it. It does not belong to us; it belongs to creation at large.

The promise is made and offered in radical freedom. It is a driving force within the process of evolution itself. When we humans try to appropriate it to ourselves, it is then that we mount the greatest obstacles to the realization of its fulfillment. When we seek to control and manipulate it, we end up deluding ourselves and alienating every significant other, including our home planet and the cosmos. We become the first victims of our anthropocentric arrogance.

Liberating Possibility

The British theologian John Macquarrie (1966) adopts the metaphor of "letting be" to describe the divine becoming at the heart of creation. The creative process happens in radical freedom, often appearing random and chaotic to the human eye. But it is a "letting be" undergirded by the energy of promise. It is a "letting be" endowed with purpose and a sense of direction. It may not have a beginning or end point, but it is a story in the process of being told, and the deep meaning is within the story itself.

Before we can adopt a stance open to new freedom and hope, we need to shed that sense of cosmic pessimism that bedevils the scientific imagination and often diminishes the sense of the numinous that religion is meant to awaken. It often seems more rational to embrace the postmodernist world of nihilism and the absurd than to remain steadfast in hope, especially when we are surrounded by so many scars of tragedy and despair. We tend to confuse the state of the world with the state of the human mind. Most of our bewildering problems are not the outcomes of a mindless world in the grip of selfish genes; rather, they are the inventions of human beings, acting out of blind ignorance and an addictive fascination with the masculine will to power. The satanic powers that haunt us may well be projections of our own collective spiritual and intellectual darkness, as suggested by Marc Ellis (1997).

Our most urgent need today is a new sense of what our universe is about. That more than anything else is what can liberate us from the forces that bind and paralyze us. We must attune ourselves once more to the cosmic womb that begot us. We are the progeny of a life-form larger than ourselves. We have raped and ruptured that womb and in the process have catapulted ourselves into a hell on earth. Evolution never intended things to be like this; we have chosen it to be this way. We have the freedom and responsibility to alter our circumstances.

The conversion at stake is not a religious one, although a wholesome type of religion undoubtedly will help. As I have argued elsewhere (O'Murchu 2000), religion itself may be a major part of the problem. The challenge right now, the liberation that is at hand, is cosmic and planetary. We either choose to come home to the cosmos to which we belong and to the planet that nurtures and sustains us, or our destiny on earth will continue to be one of alienation and self-destruction, with the almost inescapable eventual extinction for *Homo sapiens*. There are urgent choices to be made, but much more urgent is the change in consciousness without which we are unlikely to make life-enhancing options.

The perceptual shift — perhaps the first step in the conversion process — is to understand our universe in terms of blessing rather than of curse. Haught (1993, 90) identifies three features, what he describes as persistent elements of revelation, characterizing the unfolding course of cosmic evolution: gratuity, extravagance, and surprise. Instead of viewing reality around us as dead, inert matter, there for us to conquer and control, we need to move to a much more humble and receptive mode whereby we learn to appreciate that all is gift, something sacred to be safeguarded, protected, and cherished. This attitude and outlook make a great deal more sense as we accommodate the growing awareness of an alive universe, an organism that requires a relational response rather than an object to be used for our selfish ends.

If everything is perceived as gift, given for the sheer joy of giving, then the quality of our receptivity has huge implications for the future of evolution itself. We are not going to change the course of cosmic or planetary evolution, but we can change the pathway of our own E-mergence, predisposing ourselves to a more benign and beneficial participation in life's grand endeavor.

The shift in awareness from viewing the world as an object to be conquered to seeing it as a gift to be received begins an expansion of mind and heart. When I gift somebody with my time, my concern, my love, or simply my act of duty, I break down something of that bartering sense of reality that generates adversarial conflict and opposition. Things and people are valued for their inherent goodness and not for some external worth.

And the very gesture of gift giving can assume proportions larger than just an interpersonal exchange. Nature itself gives generously — mineral resources, food, and medicines, for example. In our commercial, consumerist world we have lost virtually all sense of this cosmic generosity. There is a kind of extravagance in life that knows no boundaries. Sometimes we are more aware of its shadow than its light, as in the extreme suffering we humans impose upon people and planet alike.

Our culture of acquisitiveness and consumerism leaves us at a loss on how to cope with extravagance; all we can do is exacerbate our efforts to conquer and control it. We have forgotten how to celebrate the abundance that surrounds us, within and without, and because we are unable to celebrate it, we cannot bring ourselves to share it, with generosity of spirit, to the advantage of others.

For most of our time on earth, we humans seem to have had an intuitive sense of the inherent giftedness of everything in a planet of abundant resources. We are accumulating evidence that for much of the Paleolithic era humans believed in God as a mother of prodigious fertility (see Christ 1997). Currently, scholars are beginning to think that the agricultural revolution initially ensued from this religious-cultural sense. Unfortunately, it is the shadow side of that same revolution — the culture of acquisitiveness and consumerism — that blinds us today from being able to appreciate and appropriate the extraordinary abundance of life in the universe.

I already have alluded to the element of surprise in the evolutionary process, and it will be a recurring theme in subsequent chapters. Nothing is fixed or rigid in our universe. We live with unpredictability, uncertainty, openness, and novelty. The dynamics of Darwinian evolution — genetic mutation, conscious choice, natural selection — are not fixed and determined. Rightly, they are described as random processes, but it is randomness with a bias toward novelty, often characterized by unexpected and surprising outcomes. It is this element of surprise more than anything else that gives an underlying sense of meaning to the evolutionary process.

Embracing the Shadow

Not everything in the story makes sense (to us), and there is no reason why it should. The fact that we cannot make sense of it all does not mean that it's senseless. It simply means we do not fully comprehend. And that being the case, our theological attempts to rescue ourselves from anomie — adopting notions like original sin, reincarnation, redemption — need a fresh articulation, one that will honor the insights of contemporary cosmology. The chaos of the evolving story in no way points to a fundamental flaw requiring some type of divine intervention from without, or a recycling series of human liberations to obtain salvation (nirvana). The chaos is inherent to the radical freedom, the precondition for creative possibility ensuing from the God of unlimited promise.

We tend to confuse promise and perfection. It is we humans who have invented a need for perfect outcomes and solutions. We must not project that same need onto God. The story of evolution suggests that for God, chaos, unpredictability, and messiness are not problems as they are for us. The promise rarely comes in a neat package — unlike the way the outcomes of science and theology tend to be parceled. The promise tends to be about novel possibility activating potentiality, enhancing complexity, and awakening fresh hope.

The language of promise and fresh hope is intolerable for many people precisely because our views of reality are so distorted. In setting ourselves up as the ultimate conquerors of all that exists, we have engulfed ourselves in a dungeon of darkness and confusion from which the world can look gloomy indeed. And we try to assuage our pain by continuously inventing recreational gimmicks to distract us from the monstrosities we have created.

We will not resolve our dilemma by escapism or denial. We need to reclaim and re-member what our lives are meant to be about. We need to reclaim the cosmic and planetary context of our existence. We need to put back together again those several cultural fragmentations inflicted in the "battle" with reality. We need to outgrow our anthropocentric isolation. We are not a superior species, and we were never intended so to be. Unique, yes; superior, no. Superiority has no place in the evolutionary story; everything is unique to the degree that it becomes integrated with everything else. It is in the survival and thriving of the relational matrix that every aspect of life realizes its full potential and truly becomes itself.

Evolutionary Theology

According to Peter C. Hodgson (1994, 3), theology today "is rather like sailing. It is in contact with powerful fluid elements, symbolized by wind and water, over which it has little control and by which it is drawn and driven toward mysterious goals. The only truth we know is the truth we create as we sail the seas." Theology needs to reclaim some of that cosmic drama and excitement, and the evolutionary story is poised to offer several seminal insights.

Evolutionary theology works with one major assumption: *the Originating and Sustaining Mystery has been totally involved in the unfolding process of creation from the very "beginning."* In the words of John Haught (2000, 36),

> Evolutionary theology, unlike natural theology, does not search for definitive footprints of the divine in nature. It is not terribly concerned about "intelligent design," since such a notion seems entirely too lifeless to capture the dynamic and even disturbing way in which the God of biblical religion interacts with the world. Instead of trying to prove God's existence from nature, evolution-

ary theology seeks to show how our new awareness of cosmic and biological evolution can enhance and enrich traditional teachings about God and about God's way of acting in the world. In other words, rather than viewing evolution simply as a dangerous challenge that deserves an apologetic response, evolutionary theology discerns in evolution a most illuminating context for our thinking about God today.

There never has been (and never will be) a time when the divine was not fully involved. Consequently, every E-mergent experience of creation reveals something of the divine creativity. This is not to say that we humans, or other creatures of nature, grasp the full impact of these several revelatory moments. As Karl Rahner once suggested, we receive revelation partially, in accordance with our ability to receive it, at various moments in our evolutionary unfolding.

I do not see theology as dealing just with the mystery of God; rather, it strives to make sense of the mystery of life, and if we embrace the evolutionary landscape explored in this book, then, in my opinion, we cannot avoid or escape the God question. All our attempts at ultimacy (whether scientific or religious, ancient or modern) are the subject matter of theology as I now understand it.

Evolutionary theology invites new perspectives on meaning and understanding. Conventional, closed, and fixed understandings give way to enlarged horizons, open possibilities, and quantum leaps of liberating imagination. The faithfulness of the Originating and Sustaining Mystery awakens faith not only in the human heart, but also in the heart of creation itself. Faith invites faith, and a lack of response becomes in effect an act of despair.

Evolutionary theology is not something about which we write or speak. Like the explosive energies of the evolving process itself, evolutionary theology "happens." God never ceases to be, and the very being of God is not about passive presence but about active engagement. For long, theology has claimed that God cannot but act. It is the very nature of creativity to create.

The evolutionary process always is one of coevolution in which everything interconnects in the dance of cocreation. We all are invited to be participators, and for much of evolutionary time indications are that we humans engaged in this process in a truly symbiotic way. After some millennia of a misguided response — the patriarchal phase of divide and conquer — we now find ourselves confronted with fresh options. Once again, our creative God invites us to embrace a larger reality.

Does this mean that everybody is a theologian? Yes, it does. God reveals indiscriminately and with prodigious generosity. Some will appropriate the revelation through the study of theology or some other exploration of ultimate meaning. An indigenous person may appropriate it through a convivial relationship with the land. A little child staring into her mother's eyes and intuitively knowing that she is loved unconditionally is responding as profoundly as any theologian ever did. An old man sitting in an armchair and reflecting in gentle gratitude on the story of his lifetime is doing theology in its fullest sense. And so is the politician seeking a peaceful and just outcome to the tribal conflicts that ravage many African countries. All are touching into the energy of the ultimate mystery.

And what does revelation mean in this context? Primarily it denotes the exuberant creativity of God in galaxies, planets, stardust, bacteria, people, and life-forms not yet created. From our human point of view, creation is the primary source of revelation in the sense that this is where we access the creativity of the divine as manifested throughout the ages. It also is the sphere in which we encounter the suffering face of God, in the ravages endured by suffering peoples and in the torture imposed upon creation at large.

In this new theological landscape one criterion is foundational to all others: *we need to be where God has been, and will be, as our absolute priority.* God has been at work in evolution right from the beginning. That same prodigiously creative God always is ahead of us in the future, which beckons us forth. That deep ancient past and that alluring future of promise and new hope are the hermeneutical horizon, governing every present moment of theological discernment.

The Promise Fulfilled

For many people, faith is sustained because of the promise of a life to come, one guaranteed in the Christian story through the death and resurrection of Jesus, in the Islamic faith through a faithful following of God's will, and in the Eastern religions through the attainment of nirvana. Each religion offers a specific rendition of this faith in the future, which, foundationally, belongs to the great story of evolution itself. Evolution thrives not only on past success, but also on future hope. And as many of the religions remind us, this is a hope that will not deceive.

Within the evolutionary process itself is a faithfulness, a sense of unrelenting promise, that there will be a future, that this future will evince hope and confidence (while continuing to be baffling and bizarre at times from the human point of view), that our universe will continue to grow in complexity and explode in the elegance of mystery, and that meaning will continue to outpace meaninglessness.

For some, these convictions inevitably lead to faith in God and an affirmation of the existence of a divine being. For others, the process of evolution itself is felt to be sufficiently compelling and meaningful, and therefore they do not need to postulate the idea of God. Both positions embody a deep sense of faith and take away something of our anthropocentric urge to manage and control the divine creativity. In ways, an evolutionary theology comes very close to classical Buddhism: Let's allow God to be God; we have more than enough to do to rid the world of meaninglessness (suffering). Let's take that task seriously by spiritually and intellectually embracing our universe in its full evolutionary grandeur. And then the God question is not likely to be a major problem anymore.

Whether we view it from the stance of formal religion or from an evolutionary perspective in its own right, the promise of fuller life shines like a glowing beacon above and beyond all those human preoccupations that weigh us down, and all the human projections that suffocate the mystery that surrounds us. With or without us, the universe has a future, as creative and elegant as it has been over past millennia, and indeed even more elegant as complexity and creativity weave unprecedented patterns for the future.

Our future depends on evolution's future. Evolution's future is guaranteed. Ours can be, too, if only we would take evolution seriously and adjust our lifestyle accordingly.

•

It is time to outgrow . . .

our tendency to exonerate the past with certainty and security, to dogmatize its definitive, unchanging nature, often turning tradition into an unwieldy ideology of oppression and encrustation.

It is time to embrace...

the future thrust of evolution toward increased complexity and renewed creativity, a future endowed with hope and promise as new possibilities unfold unceasingly and the innate mystery becomes more transparent to human intelligence.

Part Two

SYNERGY

Life on earth is not a created hierarchy but an emergent holarchy arisen from the self-induced synergy of combination, interfacing, and recombination.
                                        —Lynn Margulis

Chapter Three

An Emptiness That Overflows

*In this crucible of the modern world, only the mystic will survive.
All the others are going to disintegrate; they will be unable to
resist either the physical strictures or the psychical strains.*

— Raimon Panikkar

*The dynamic vacuum is like a quiet lake on a summer night, its
surface rippled in gentle fluctuations, while all around, electron-
positron pairs twinkle on and off like fireflies. It is a busier
and friendlier place than the forbidding emptiness of Democri-
tus or the glacial ether of Aristotle. Its restless activity is utterly
fascinating!*

— Hans Christian Von Baeyer

O F ALL THE INCREDIBLE THINGS in this world we inhabit, none is
more baffling than the space that surrounds us. And in its cosmic
proportions it becomes even more incomprehensible. On February 23,
1987, some of the debris from a supernova explosion arrived on the
earth, an explosion that had taken place some 150,000 years ago. It
took all that time to travel the vast abyss that constitutes the universe
that we inhabit.

In one sense, our eyes do not deceive us. Stand on a mountaintop
and let your eyes stretch as far as they will. But instead of focusing on
material objects, give your attention to the space that surrounds you.
It looks empty and vacuous. It feels as if nothing is going on in it. Yet
it is real and is full of subatomic particles all bristling with energy and
potentiality. The emptiness is anything but empty. What constitutes its
fullness is the subject of this chapter.

Now, the scientist enters our story and embellishes it with some
amazing discoveries. At least 95 percent of the known universe is
empty space. The ancient Greeks knew this and postulated that the
emptiness was full of an illusive intangible substance called "ether."
Three thousand years later, the scientist Thomas Young still held to the

idea of the ether and used it to explain how light waves travel in space. But by the end of the nineteenth century, scholars began to doubt its existence, and eventually Albert Einstein discarded the notion entirely.

While Einstein had demolished what was merely an abstract concept, Ernest Rutherford dealt a deadly blow to the substance of matter itself. The Greeks had suggested that matter consists of atoms, grain-like objects that could be measured and objectified, but Rutherford established that atoms consist of over 90 percent empty space, in which a minuscule nucleus and a few pointlike electrons dance an arcane minuet.

Empty space without; empty space within. Was there any such thing as real substance? Was the story of creation itself based on some great illusion?

The great vacuum, thus cleansed, remained empty for a quarter of a century, but it began to fill up again. This time, the ingredient was neither matter nor ether, but a baffling, mysterious force buzzing with energy and hidden activity. Terms such as "vacuum fluctuation" and "vacuum polarization" entered the scientific vocabulary.[4] But most controversial of all was the growing awareness that what filled the great vacuum was the same "stuff" that materialized as planets, rocks, bacteria, plants, and humans; it was believed to be the seedbed and source of all form and structure in the universe. Far from it being a useless emptiness, we came to understand, it is a pregnant fullness.

It often is referred to as the "creative vacuum" or the "quantum vacuum." In scientific terms, it is one of the most exciting and baffling aspects of the emerging evolutionary story. The physicist Brian Swimme (1996, 91–93) adopts a homely image, making this otherwise complex notion accessible:

> In order to bring the idea home, cup your hands together, and reflect on what you are holding there. What are the contents cupped by your hand? First in quantitative terms would be the molecules of air — the molecules of nitrogen, oxygen, carbon dioxide, and other trace gases. There would be many more than a billion trillion. If we imagine removing every one of these atoms we would be left holding extremely small particles such as neutrinos from the Sun.
>
> In addition there would be radiation energy in the form of invisible light, such as the photons from the original flaring forth of the universe.... In order to get down to nothingness we would

have to remove not only all the subatomic particles; we would also have to remove each and every one of these invisible particles of light.

But now imagine we have somehow done this, so that in your cupped hands there are no molecules left, and no particles, and no photons of light. All matter and radiation have been removed. No things would be left, no objects, no stuff, no items that could be counted or measured. What would remain would be what we modern people refer to as the "vacuum," or "emptiness," or "pure space."

Now for the news: careful investigation of this vacuum by quantum physicists reveals the strange appearance of elementary particles in this emptiness. Even where there are no atoms, and no elementary particles, and no protons, and no photons, suddenly elementary particles will emerge. The particles simply foam into existence.... Particles emerge from the "vacuum." They do not sneak in from some hiding place when we are not looking. Nor are they bits of light energy that have transformed into protons. These elementary particles crop up out of the vacuum itself — this is the simple and awesome discovery.... Being itself arises out of a field of "fecund emptiness."

The ground of the universe then is an empty fullness, a fecund nothingness.... The base of the universe seethes with creativity.

Fecund emptiness is the source of everything that exists. It is where the story of evolution begins, and it also is the reason why we cannot speculate with any degree of accuracy on how the whole thing will end, if indeed it ever will end. We have no way of knowing or measuring the amount of creative energy contained in the vacuum. The story itself strongly suggests that the supply is infinite. The life that ensues, in its several forms — organic, inorganic, and other modes that may not yet have evolved — is likely to continue forever.

How Did It All Begin?

Scientists point to a moment in time when the story of evolution begins. They call it the "Big Bang." What existed before the Big Bang is of little or no concern to the conventional scientist. I suggest that it is of enormous importance for those among us seeking to unravel the meaning of the new evolutionary story of our time, and this includes a growing number of scientists and theologians.

The fecund emptiness, described above, predates even the Big Bang. Mystics and sages, particularly from the Far East, long have suggested an origin to the universe that requires a more mystical and poetic rendition. They favor a story line of this nature: In the beginning was silence, a restless stillness, pregnant with potency and meaning, as the Creative Spirit brooded over the Void, the quantum vacuum, empty, receptive and waiting to explode into expression and form. The Spirit is without beginning or end, and so is everything that comes into being under the in-spirited power of the originating life-force. In more scientific terms, the scenario goes like this:

> According to this startling new picture, in the beginning was Nothing. No space. No time. No matter or energy. But there was the quantum principle, which states that there must be uncertainty, so even Nothing became unstable, and tiny particles of Something began to form. (Kaku 1998, 352)

The Big Bang is a powerful metaphor, one of the most ingenious conjured up by the human imagination. I suggest, however, that as a metaphor it is not about a one-time event but about an unceasing process that has occurred, and will occur, many times in the story of evolution. Metaphorically, we are touching upon the novelty, the surprise, the unexpected, the strange twists and turns that characterize the evolutionary process in several of its creative outbursts. On the other hand, the religious notion of *creatio ex nihilo* (creation from nothing), while it might help to safeguard an exalted understanding of God, does little to open us up to the wonder of the quantum vacuum. In the desire to safeguard the uniqueness of God, we are in danger of bypassing the uniqueness of God's creation, which is the pathway to divine enlightenment for many contemporary spiritual seekers.

Science describes in great detail what happened in those instantaneous seconds after the Big Bang. Quarks, leptons, and several other subatomic particles foamed into existence, followed shortly thereafter by chemical substances such as hydrogen, helium, lithium, and deuterium.

This is a wonderful explosion of exotic elements, a proliferation of possibility that certainly needs to be remembered, celebrated, and honored in a story that will animate and inspire generations yet unborn. Behind — or beneath — the various elements lies another enduring phenomenon, another feature of the creative vacuum, which we commonly call "energy." Innocent though it may sound, it is in fact the connective tissue from which we weave the entire tapestry of our evolutionary story.

What Is Energy?

While many scientists define what they mean by entropy (how energy is used or wasted), they refrain from precise description of what energy signifies. Paul Davies (1987, 68) describes it as "an imaginary, abstract concept" but almost immediately goes on to suggest that we need to invoke the notion of beauty to truly understand what energy means. The physicist Lee Smolin (1997) writes about "flows of energy," while the biologist John Joe McFadden (2000), following the line adopted by most scientists, looks at how energy is stored (in food, sunlight, electricity, etc.).

Eric J. Chaisson (2001), a scholar with an adventurous evolutionary spirit, breaks new ground in asserting that energy (more precisely energy flow) is the connective tissue and enduring force of all evolutionary growth and change. Energy, he claims, is more basic than either entropy or information to explain and explore the driving forces of evolution:

> More than any other term, energy has a central role to play in each of the physical, biological and cultural evolutionary parts of the inclusive scenario of cosmic evolution; in short, energy is a common, underlying factor... in our search for unity among all material beings. (Chaisson 2001, 133)

The theologian Peter Hodgson (1994) grapples extensively with the meaning of energy, and he concludes that we are dealing with something akin to a primal, erotic, alluring, relational force. It is beyond precise definition, and Hodgson, like Chaisson, believes that it permeates every sphere of existence. It is tangible but not quantifiable. For those who believe in God, energy is a primary characteristic of divine creativity; indeed, it might well be the most tangible evidence of God's creativity at work in the cosmos.

The philosopher of religion Grace Jantzen (1998) helps to illuminate our exploration. She highlights that our culture is engulfed in necrophobia, an irrational fear of everything to do with death. We invest many personal resources in warding off our fear of death, leaving us with a depleted energy to engage in life's real concerns. To counteract the deleterious impact of mortality, Jantzen seeks to reclaim a fresh sense of "natality" (i.e., the creative energy we associate with birthing). Natality could well be considered to be a theological counterpart to the scientific notion of the quantum vacuum. To describe this new concept, she quotes from the theologian Sharon Welch (1990, 178):

> Divinity is not a mark which is other than that of the finite. Grace is not that which comes from outside to transform the conditions of finitude. Divinity, or grace, is the resilient, fragile, healing power of finitude itself. The terms holy and divine denote a quality of being within the web of life, a process of healing relationship, and they denote the quality of being worthy of honor, love, respect and affirmation.

Energy is not something that is merely stored, nor is it simply the driving force of action. It is a given reality, apparently with unlimited resourcefulness, and in the unfolding of evolution's great story it exudes as a subtle, vibrational force giving shape and direction to all being and becoming. Scientists touch upon this all-pervasive quality of energy precisely at the point where they suspend conventional wisdom and allow the fascination of the quantum vacuum to expand their imaginations.[5]

Far from being merely a mechanical notion, energy is an all-embracing, cosmic force that defies all our definitions and categories. Perhaps, our ancient ancestors had a deeper appreciation of its meaning than we, the learned ones, of the contemporary world. When animists attribute the energy of God to the wind, the sun, the storm, and the surging sea, are they not in touch with the immediacy that we describe today as the creative vacuum? That being the case, are we not also confronted with the need for a radical assessment of how we understand and describe the creativity of God?

Thus far, the evolutionary story is somewhat illusive and mysterious; to some it may feel vague and tantalizingly nebulous, as indeed any story can be until we intuit the emerging message. In a world in which we prize what we can measure, quantify, use, and consume, it is difficult for us, intellectually and emotionally, to stay with what is beyond our immediate grasp. Yet, if we truly want to respect and cherish our evolutionary story, somehow we must honor these indefinable features of our great cosmic narrative. In a word, we must learn afresh to befriend the cosmic mystery within which we, and all life, are held, forever open to new possibility.

This is where science and religion often part company. Scientists cling to the objective truth of experiment and verification, while religionists consider God and the divine power to be the ultimate explanation for everything that exists. In our multidisciplinary age, this dualistic division between science and religion undermines the richness of both sets of wisdom. The distinctions that keep them apart enhance neither clarification nor mutual understanding. The unfolding cosmology of our time requires the complementary insights of both science and religion in aiding us to pierce the depths of wisdom and understanding.

Both science and religion seek explanations for the way things arc, and why they have come into being. They search for the wisdom behind the realities rather than within them. When we attend closely to the evolving story, we begin to intuit that meaning rests within the realities that we encounter. In a sense, mystery haunts us, and it will keep haunting us until we engage it in new intellectual, scientific, and religious ways. This may well be one of the supreme challenges, and indeed awesome responsibilities, of attending more responsively to the evolving story of our universe.

The reader may be wondering where humans fit into this grand scheme of things. Thus far, the story is largely about impersonal issues such as emptiness and energy. Humans in general are not much concerned about such mundane things. Or are they?

Here is where the story becomes important once more. What sustained our ancient ancestors through thick and thin? What gave them vision, hope, and faith in the future? Deeply immersed in the creative forces erupting around and within them, they began to comprehend the enveloping sense of mystery and they explored its significance in myth and storytelling. They do not seem to have been trapped in the dualisms that often cripple us today, and their intuitive understanding of the divine power likely contained a wisdom and depth that many of our contemporaries would envy. Long before our ancestors became labeled with the primitive ignorance suggested by nineteenth-century rationalism, they were the beneficiaries of a wisdom that growing numbers of our contemporaries hunger for once more.

Creative Energy and Our Understanding of God

In the faith development of our ancient ancestors there is little evidence for a fatherly, governing figurehead, divine or human. That image largely belongs to the last five to six thousand years. Prior to that time, the prevailing image is that of a spiritually active life-force. And that "Spirit-power" is considered to be the "one" that activates the creative energy from within the process of evolution itself, luring creation into shape and form. For Peter Hodgson (1994, 279), "Spirit is an immaterial vitality that enlivens and shapes material nature. . . . Energy is simply that mysterious power that is active and at work in things, and that power is God as Spirit."

Elizabeth Johnson (1992, 124) strongly endorses this same view when she writes,

> Since what people call God is not one being among other beings, not even a discrete Supreme being, but mystery which transcends and enfolds all that is, like the horizon and yet circling all horizons, this human encounter with the presence and absence of the living God occurs through the mediation of history itself in its whole vast range of happenings. To this movement of the living God that can be traced in and through experience of the world, Christian speech traditionally gives the name Spirit.

God as Spirit is the oldest and profoundest understanding that humans have of the divine. For our ancient ancestors, life was not always easy, wholesome, or even meaningful. Nonetheless, the enduring belief in Spirit-power evoked a sense that creation is essentially blessed and not fundamentally flawed. The creative power of the Spirit-filled vacuum has inexhaustible reserves of grace and goodness. Despite all the paradoxes and contradictions, creativity wins out. It has happened so often in the evolutionary story; the fidelity of the past itself guarantees hope and promise for the future. The story has a consistency and a sense of congruence that ultimately defy irrationality.

In the course of these reflections, two important concepts are beginning to coalesce: energy and Spirit-power. For our ancient ancestors, they were often experienced as one. The energy that drove wind, sea, and water was also the divine energy, a nurturing gift, a life-force, awesome and frightening at times, but always close at hand. As we delve scientifically into our understanding of energy's nature and theologically into a deeper understanding of the traditional notion of God as Spirit, we begin to intuit that we are touching upon the same foundational reality.

In evolutionary terms, I am suggesting that if we, like our ancient ancestors and the indigenous peoples of our own time, honor the emerging story of evolution itself in its rich and complex unfolding, then we cannot avoid the divine cocreative energy that is at work throughout the breadth and depth of creation. And this divine inspiring energy does not emanate from some external heavenly realm, but from within the depths of the creative process itself. The creative energy is unambiguously an "inspirited" and inspiring life-force.

For both science and religion, our story opens up horizons that challenge several time-honored notions. In conventional science, energy tends to be measured in units. In the new physics, energy is understood to be a vibrational (stringlike) force, embracing at any one time several relational possibilities. Energy manifests itself in connections and in relationships. Consequently, the evolutionary story is not just about cosmology; to be more precise, it is about cosmogenesis.

What Is Cosmogenesis?

"Genesis" is an English word used to describe the beginnings or origins of various things. In the West, its biblical significance tends to take precedence over its colloquial meaning. The story about the creation of the world in the opening chapters of the Hebrew scriptures has become a type of public knowledge, one familiar even to those who do not follow the Jewish or Christian faiths.

In the course of the twentieth century, the word began to take on an enlarged meaning. Teilhard de Chardin (1959; 1964) extended its use to include a process of origination, which happened not just at the beginning, but also throughout the evolutionary process of creation. Thus, he speaks of "geogenesis," life unfolding and growing in geological and geographical terms; "biogenesis," the unfolding of life in biological terms; "psychogenesis," the mental dimension that enhances life's evolution; "noogenesis," an innate intelligence, not necessarily divine, that governs life's unfolding (e.g., DNA); and "christogenesis," which for Teilhard marks the culminating point in which all the evolutionary strands are gathered into the omega point.

Swimme and Berry (1992) revisit the notion of cosmogenesis (closely related to Teilhard's christogenesis), along with the accompanying idea of the "cosmogenetic principle." The latter is reminiscent of Einstein's "cosmological principle," which states that all places are alike in the universe: from every direction, microwave background radiation left over from the original fireball comes to us in nearly identical packages. The cosmogenetic principle postulates that the way things unfold follows a broadly similar pattern throughout the entire universe. On the large scale of universal order, form-producing powers prevail everywhere.

Cosmogenesis claims that the power to become is universal and universally enduring in every sense. In biological terms (epigenesis), it is the nature of life to replicate and further its own development (cf. Jantsch 1980). Swimme and Berry claim that we have been overwhelmed by the negative image of the second law of thermodynamics, which focuses on the depletion of all life-forms, with the universe eventually culminating in the extermination of heat and light themselves. We need not simply to restate a balance, but to reclaim what the long aeons of evolution affirm categorically: despite the forces of destruction, which undeniably exert enormous and widespread influence, life survives and, indeed, thrives. It is this will to life that underpins the process of cosmogenesis and pushes both the scientist and theologian to grapple with the enduring nature of being and becoming at every level of existence.

In a word, cosmogenesis refers to those unfolding patterns that reveal a tendency for everything to grow and develop. Nothing is static, nor do life processes simply repeat a once-and-for-all blueprint. There is a tendency toward repetition within nature (explored by Rupert Sheldrake 1988; 1991), but something new and fresh is added each time. The "something new" often is described as an increase in complexity, revealing other features that have entered our story in relatively recent times.

The Self-Organizing Universe

Cosmogenesis belongs to the evolutionary story itself. It is not an external force impacting upon the world we know and experience. It is all about life's natural propensity to come into being, grow, change, and mature. All life-forms, whether inorganic or organic, are endowed with an innate propensity to grow and develop and bring to fruition inner potentials for creativity and possibility.

Undoubtedly, this process often is thwarted, or at least so it seems to the human eye. But that may be because we are looking in the wrong places or, more accurately, looking in the wrong way for the supporting evidence. We humans have great problems with the basic untidiness of the evolutionary story. It is not a perfect story — far from it — but precisely because it is not perfect, it is forever experimenting with and exploring its own growth and development. And yet it is not totally random. Somehow or other it moves on, often against heavy odds. This is precisely what the process of cosmogenesis is capable of achieving.

Classical science looks on everything in life as if it were a machine. But in the domain of the living there is little that is solid or rigid. Whereas a machine is geared to the output of a specific product, a biological cell is primarily concerned with renewing itself. In 1973 the Chilean biologists Humberto Maturana and Francisco Varela named this capacity for self-renewal "autopoiesis," referring to the characteristic of living systems to continuously renew themselves and to regulate this process in such a way that the integrity of their structure is maintained. Autopoiesis, this power to self-organize, is what has seen life through many a major catastrophe.

The inherent capacity for self-organization in no way diminishes or undermines the notion of God's involvement in evolution's great story. We are embarking upon a radical re-visioning of how we understand the divine to be at work in creation. Most significantly, we are abandoning the idea of an outside manipulator (engineer) in favor of an animating force from within, not because it gives us humans more power, but because the evidence of evolution requires us to make that adjustment.

Here we encounter what may well be the central challenge of this book. When we honor and appropriate the big picture of the evolutionary story, and begin to appreciate and understand its sense of innovation and creativity, then we ourselves begin to see and think differently. The creation that is forever changing also changes us. We begin to realize that the inherited wisdom of both science and religion often was too narrow for the breadth and depth of our creative spirits. The evolutionary story sets free a new sense of what creation is about, and when we truly come to understand it, we too are liberated from perceptions that limit and inhibit our vision.

Unfortunately, the dualism between science and religion still stymies our minds and spirits. It divides things up in a superficial and destructive way. It often eschews the enveloping sense of mystery. What is more disturbing is the collusion whereby both sets of wisdom (science and religion) enforce perceptions and values that distort and distract us from the inspiring vision of the evolutionary story.

The British biologist Brian Goodwin (1996, 29–30) provides an intriguing and disturbing example. He indicates how the popularized version of Darwinian evolution strangely resonates with the traditional Christian doctrine of sin and atonement. In both cases we witness a kind of battle for survival in which, allegedly, humans emerge as victors. One wonders how there could be any victors in such a distorted view of reality:

Darwinian Principles	*Religious Principles*
Organisms are constructed by groups of genes whose goal is to leave more copies of themselves. The hereditary material is basically "selfish."	Human beings are born in sin and they perpetuate it in sexual reproduction. Greed and pride are basic elements of that flawed, sinful condition.
The inherently selfish qualities of the hereditary material are reflected in the competitive interactions between organisms, resulting in the survival of the fittest.	Humanity, therefore, is condemned to a life of conflict and perpetual toil in the desire to improve one's lot in life.
Organisms constantly are trying to improve and outdo weaker elements, but the landscape of evolution keeps changing, so the struggle is endless, as in Steven Weinberg's "hostile universe."	Humanity's effort at improvement is jeopardized by the imperfect, sinful world in which we have been placed. The struggle never ends.
Paradoxically, human beings can develop altruistic qualities that contradict their inherently selfish nature, by means of educational and other cultural efforts.	But by faith and moral effort, humanity can be saved from its fallen, selfish state, normally requiring the intervention of an external, divine influence.

Precisely because both science and religion are preoccupied with the flawed state of evolution, and of life in general, and because proponents on each side feel that they must do everything possible to set it right, the whole enterprise is fundamentally misconstrued.

Why depict evolution as fundamentally flawed? It may look flawed to us humans, but there is little to suggest that it is flawed in the eyes of that deeper wisdom that keeps the whole thing in being. As already indicated, the process of cosmogenesis is not perfect; if it were, there would be no surprise, no ingenuity, no room for novelty, and creativity largely would be suppressed. What makes the process both exciting and sacred is precisely its incompleteness.

The Divine Life-Force

Several rich concepts weave in and out of this chapter. Energy abounds, creativity explodes, complexity reorganizes, relationships unfold, and chaos demolishes order but strangely tends to beget reorganization. It is difficult to avoid the conclusion that the whole thing is saturated in meaning. And traditionally we call the source of that meaning "God." As our story unfolds, what is God beginning to look like? What sense of God does the evolutionary story conjure up? I offer some brief reflections to conclude the present chapter.

Through the cracks and fissures, God peeps in. But God also looks out from the same liminal spaces. As the mystics put it, the one you are looking for is the one who is looking. This "one" feels very personal at times, and the name "God" feels appropriate. Nonetheless, we also need to acknowledge the negative reactions to the word that prevail in our time.

Traditionally, the word "God" is associated with a male, distant, judgmental figurehead commanding allegiance from an objective distance, often described as "on high." The image suited, and still suits, the predominant patriarchal culture in which formal religion is so deeply embedded. It carries connotations of power and domination that in many people's experience are felt as overwhelming, despite all the attempts to highlight the underlying notions of covenant, love, compassion, and the like.

Frequently in this book I use terms such as "divine," "divinity," and "divine life-force." My intention in these is to keep our understanding open, porous, and transparent to larger meaning. Whether the life-force is personal or impersonal is a debate I tend to avoid. My sense is that it is neither, and yet it somehow transcends both. But to consider the divine to be a person, in the sense in which we typically understand personhood, feels to me like a form of reductionism that could easily undermine the wonder of God throughout the length and breadth of creation (including the human).

I feel that we are on a more authentic and creative ground if we honor the views of our ancient ancestors (and today's indigenous peoples) for whom the divine was an inspirited life-force inhabiting everything in creation while simultaneously transcending it. Both the intimacy of the personal and the awesomeness of the mystery are safeguarded. In the words of John's Gospel (4:4), "God is spirit, and those who worship God must worship in spirit and in truth."

When we see life through the lens of the evolutionary story, it seems to me that we encounter a continuum of Spirit-power in action. Everything in creation, from subatomic particles to galactic structures, and every life-form we know reveals an elegance and creativity that defy rational explanation. Somehow or other, definitive proof no longer is necessary, and even when proof becomes available, I am not sure that it convinces in any kind of an enduring way. Those who experience the grandeur of creation know that it is undergirded by mystery; those who have not known that experience are unlikely to be convinced by rational argument, supernatural or otherwise.

Prodigiously Creative

Finally, the image of the divine that I favor most, but which I use rather sparingly throughout the book, is that of the "Originating and Sustaining Mystery." The notion of "originating mystery" I borrow from Albert la Chance (1991). I like the emphasis on "originating" rather than on "original." The former denotes the abundant and prodigious creativity that the peoples of Paleolithic times seem to have attributed to the divine life-force as they understood it, primarily as the great Mother Goddess, and it also honors the originality and vivaciousness with which God creates, not just once, but throughout time and eternity.

It also feels necessary to include "sustaining." The divine engages the creative process at every stage of cosmic, planetary, and personal unfolding. The divine befriends what is happening both in the chaos and in the order, in the distortions and in the breakthroughs, in the death and in the rebirthing. The notion of befriending also has important connotations. It honors the nuance of the nurturing mother, animating and empowering, so that new life can be released and the process of liberation can continue to unfold.

The "mystery" is important if we are to honor the paradoxes that I allude to several times throughout this book. The evolutionary story embodies several contradictions and incomplete scenarios. Those seeking evidence for a rational God do not meet with much reassurance. Extravagance, imagination, wildness, and proclivity characterize so many unfolding sequences. And yet there are long epochs during which one wonders if anything at all is happening or if the whole thing has not come to a bizarre and tragic end. But it never does, and I suspect that it never will. This is mystery writ large.

As human beings, we need to play around with images to make sense of anything in life, and all the more so in our engagement with the notion of God. Our inherited religious images are useful to get us started, but it seems that for many of our contemporaries they prove to be obstacles rather than catalysts to release the power of the creative Spirit. All the dominant images are culturally conditioned, geographically restricted (Hinduism with Indian subculture, Christianity with European subculture, Islam retaining several features of Arabian culture of the Middle Ages), and heavily influenced by the patriarchal desire for unmitigated power.

We need to outgrow the small God who perhaps served us well at one time in our lives. Reductionism diminishes the awesomeness of divine creativity, both in science and in theology. The God who outpaces all our constructs and who unceasingly lures us to radically new places and new ways of being is the God of our great evolutionary story. This is not about inventing a new religion. It is about reappropriating the archetypal divine story that creation itself has been narrating long before we humans ever inhabited that creation. It is about realigning our perspectives and perceptions.

Nature has no problem with the enveloping sense of the great mystery. Perhaps it would not be much of a problem for us either, if we could learn to honor the great story to which we intimately and inseparably belong.

And from within the depths of that story, we may, in fact, hear a different set of reverberations inviting us to a more mystical sense of prayer and worship in which we let go of our human need for control and learn to flow within the embracing sense of benign mystery. Two short passages from contemporary writers issue a similar invitation to adopt an inner space in which our capacity to listen and to receive becomes more refined and astute:

> Discussing God is not the best use of our energy. If we touch the Holy Spirit, we touch God, not as a concept but as a living reality. (Thich Nhat Hanh, Vietnamese monk and mystic)

> I suggest that we start by holding our God lightly, letting her go and evolve rather than guarding a tight-fisted faith. This way we can be more flexible in our world view, shifting as we must with new knowledge and insight. If our God/ess is not big, elastic and embracing enough to make the change, then I wonder what we mean by the divine. (Mary Hunt, American theologian)

•

It is time to outgrow...

our anthropocentric desire to measure and quantify every aspect of existence; to dismiss as irrelevant those aspects which we cannot measure or control according to our human-made norms; and to attribute primary significance only to that which can be objectively observed and quantified.

It is time to embrace...

the radical openness that characterizes our universe, and the mysterious fullness that inebriates the whole of reality; the seething energy surfacing from the quantum vacuum, forever begetting novelty and vitality in a universe poised for unlimited innovation, creative possibility, and divine exuberance.

Chapter Four

Aliveness as an E-merging Property

Earth is dirt, all dirt, but here we find revealed what dirt can do when it is self-organizing under suitable conditions with water and solar illumination. This is pretty spectacular dirt.

—Holmes Rolston III

The earth is still so radioactive ... that its core is kept hot by continuing nuclear reactions, and many atoms all over its surface — in rocks and trees and even in our own bodies — are still exploding. In our own bodies it has been estimated that three million potassium atoms explode every minute. —Elisabet Sahtouris

O UR STORY ENTERS a new phase of exploration — long before the scientists got there. All this energy that we have encountered pushes the horizons of comprehension beyond several traditional limits. It begs questions about the very aliveness of creation billions of years before we gathered hard evidence for the existence of organic life. The nature of this aliveness and its impact upon evolution are what our story now seeks to explore.

Energy surrounds us within and without, and everywhere it seethes with creativity. Yet it does not overwhelm or absorb us. Spirit-power works with a gentle but pervasive influence. It works through a process of transformation. We seem to be describing the very makeup of life itself. Is our universe alive? That is the question that will engage us in the present chapter.

In its conventional meaning, "life" is something that we associate particularly with human beings. According to many renditions of the great cosmic story, humans are assumed to be fully alive, while all other creatures possess a quality of aliveness that is unique but inferior to that of humans. When we view life in this hierarchical fashion, we rapidly move in the direction of seeing the material universe as dead, inert matter. From an environmental and ecological viewpoint, this understanding is considered to be dangerous and destructive, and it may already be contributing to many of the major environmental crises that we face today.

Placing humans at the top of the ladder is not what the evolutionary story does. The story was unfolding with incredible elegance for billions of years before we ever evolved. And even after our own appearance on the scene, some four million years ago, for most of our time we seem to have harmonized with the unfolding story, contributing with sensitivity and care to nature's emergent process. It is only in the past few thousand years that we assumed an arrogant, overpowering stance and began to tell a story that promoted our own development at the price of the greater whole. It is now abundantly clear that this strategy does not enhance the quality of life for either humans themselves or the planet we inhabit.

Paradoxically, the Darwinian understanding of evolution enlarges this otherwise limited and restricted horizon of understanding. We know that organic life first evolved some four billion years ago and for an estimated two billion years consisted of tiny organisms called bacteria. But all scientists agree that bacteria were alive. And the story of evolution in its conventional sense takes off from there, as if nothing important had been happening before that time. Now, with our added discoveries of the quantum vacuum and the energy that permeates the universe, we are at a new juncture, one that requires us to rethink our understanding of what it means to be alive, and to define afresh what life is all about.

Scientists are reluctant to describe or define life. For many, it is a topic best left undefined. It is something that happens when everything else unfolds according to "the laws of nature." It has a specific biological meaning, often identified with genetic makeup, that we can trace back some four billion years. Scholars suggest that life within the biological story remains essentially indefinable because the dynamics of Darwinian evolution require it to be so. But those dynamics are open to other interpretations, and with that possibility comes a fresh sense that biological life, too, has a story to tell, every bit as elegant, creative, and dramatic as the great cosmic story itself.

In this chapter I want to trace the unfolding story of life, and I want to honor the story in all its breadth, depth, and grandeur. I want to highlight aspects of the story in which vibrant forms of creativity invite our attention, reflection, and discernment. I also want to honor its complexity, which at times may feel complicated. The complexity itself is precisely the evidence that seems to suggest that the notion of aliveness extends beyond the organic forms of the past four billion years, and that our home planet and the universe at large also possess a distinctive sense of being alive. Let's review some of the evidence.

The Lively Universe

Everything in existence springs forth from the cosmic womb of unlimited possibility. This is the realm of creative Spirit, weaving the story of creation's unfolding across aeons that our human minds can scarcely comprehend. Even within the mathematical formulas of the scientists there is, in the language of Stephen Hawking, "fire in the equations." The physicist Lee Smolin (1997) poses the question, "Why is the universe hospitable to life?" and he responds, "Because it is filled with stars." There are stars exploding, stars "on fire," stars that are windows into the soul of the universe itself. Smolin (1997, 27) explains his central insight:

> Light is the ultimate source of life. Without light coming from the sun, there would be no life here on earth. Light is not only our medium of contact with the world; in a very real sense it is the basis of our existence. If the difference between us and dead matter is organization, it is sunlight that provides the energy and the impetus for self-organization of matter into life on every scale, from the individual cell to the life of the whole planet and from my morning awakening to the whole history of evolution.
>
> We will never know completely who we are until we understand why the universe is constructed in such a way that it contains living things. To comprehend that, the first thing we need to know is why we live in a universe filled with light. Thus the problem of our relationship with the rest of the world rests partly on at least one question.... Why is it that the universe is filled with stars?

Stars are the primary sites for transformations of energy and matter in the universe. In each star, as the elements are forged, gravitational and nuclear energy are converted into light and radiation and sent into the universe. And the secret power of stars is in their heat; they are much hotter than anything else that exists, and they are able to maintain themselves as constant sources of light and heat for long periods of time.

Consequently, the notion that ours is a warm, living earth inside a cold, dead cosmos is fundamentally false. A cold, dead universe would contain no stars, no living planets, and it would be totally inhospitable to life. Life is begotten from stardust, radiant in light and heat. An amazing symbiosis between the heights above and the depths below is encapsulated in the miracle of life. In the words of Paul Davies (1998, xix), "While I have no doubt that the origin of life was not in fact a miracle, I do believe that we live in a bio-friendly universe of a stunningly ingenious character." John Joe McFadden (2000, 83) echoes that sentiment: "It seems a bright beginning for life to know that the stuff of all of us was made in stars and scattered throughout space by supernovae. We are, quite literally, stardust."

For life to exist we need a variety of different atoms that can combine to form a large number of molecules of different size, shape, and chemical makeup. In biochemical terms, we need a large quantity of carbon compound, built with copious amounts of carbon, hydrogen, oxygen, nitrogen, and traces of many other atoms. All these elements, except hydrogen, are forged in stars. All the chemical elements out of which we, the plants and animals, are made are produced in the stars that populate our nighttime skies. Holmes Rolston III expresses it vividly:

> No mechanism for life has ever been conceived that does not require elements produced by thermonuclear combustion. The stars are the furnaces in which all but the very lightest elements are forged, exploding as supernovae and dispersing this matter, subsequently re-gathered to form planets and persons. Humans are composed of fossil star dust. In this historical perspective, astronomical nature is the precondition of the rational self, of the spiritual self. (Quoted in Hefner 1992, 189)

Carbon is the crucial element. Without carbon, life as we know it would be impossible. Carbon atoms can link together to form extended chain molecules, or polymers, of limitless variety and complexity. Proteins and DNA are two examples of these long chain molecules. Carbon is a story unto itself, elegantly woven into the unfolding evolution of all life-forms.

Carbon emanates largely from the explosions of stars and supernovas. From the death throes of star life is born the energy form that impregnates all living things. Once again we find evidence for the recurring cosmic paradox of death and resurrection (more on this in chapter 6). And then there is that cosmic pilgrimage of billions of years before carbon atoms inhabit spirited bodies like our own. Biochemistry and biology help us to unravel the process.

But we must not rush into the scientific facts. Context and story must be honored as the resources that keep us exposed to the big and deep vision. When it comes to the story of life, we need to keep the edges fuzzy and the boundaries permeable. Let's try to honor the creative Spirit, who always is several steps ahead of us. There is more to life than biochemistry or biology. It is a foundational energy prone to replicate with increasing complexity and incomprehensible durability. At best, we get glimpses into its nature, but never the total picture.

Our exploration of what it means to be alive begins with the big picture of exploding stars and carbon dust disseminated throughout the cosmos. Light, heat, and dust are contributing factors. Water is another important ingredient, and that follows several billion years later. We now are approaching the biological threshold.

Enter Biology

Sometime around four billion years ago, the gas and dust from a great star explosion gathered into a spherical spin made of twelve different kinds of atoms. As it condensed, it grew heavier and spun faster. The heat of pressure and nuclear reactions inside it melted the packed matter into a fiercely burning liquid. But the outside of this fiery sphere, touching cold space, cooled off as a thin, crusty skin. The earth's skin was made of rock, a crust of rock around a molten core.

The young earth spun so fast that daylight lasted only five hours. At first, when the earth's crust cracked here and there, the liquid inside oozed out as lava. The lava separated either into heavy atoms that formed more crusty rock, or into water that hissed up as steam, or into lighter atoms that floated over the surface as gases. It appears that the water steaming off the hot crust stayed high above the early atmosphere but eventually formed clouds and condensed into rain. Water was born, and its rains poured down long and hard, gathering on top of the heavier rock. The great seas had come into being.

Meanwhile, as the earth's crust grew thicker, new streams of lava broke through with greater force. Volcanoes erupted, spewing their fiery insides high into the atmosphere. As the lava cooled and the hot ashes settled, mountains were formed. For an estimated hundred million years, gigantic thunderstorms exploded across the earth's surface. High-voltage sparks were passed through the mixture of gases existing in the early terrestrial atmosphere. Energy was enjoying an explosively erotic feast.

As yet there was no oxygen, only a mixture of gases that, had the earth not come alive, eventually would have settled into something like the atmosphere of Venus and Mars today. Neither too hot (like Venus) nor too cold (like Mars), the earth generated the right temperature amenable to the emergence of molecular life. However, water also was a crucial factor. It was produced with sufficient abundance to act as a chemical carrier for the newborn planet, possibly along lines similar to the bloodstream in the human body. The stage was set for biological life to unfold.

Charles Darwin suggested that life began in some warm, little pond containing a mixture of ammonia, phosphoric salts, light, heat, and electricity.[6] From this humble brew, over immense periods of time, life unfolded as an adventure of great chemical complexity and spiritual potentiality.

Today, microbiologists are shifting attention from theories about the origins of life (e.g., those of J. B. S. Haldene in the 1920s; Harold Urey and Stanley Miller in the 1950s) toward the focus on the nature and evolution of the primordial life-forms. The earliest-known living organisms scientists call prokaryotes or monerans. These were cells without a nucleus, the first bacteria, which to this day remain basic to all life, although on their own they cannot generate living organisms.

Over two billion years later, evolution took another gigantic leap. Ever more specialized bacteria got together within the same walls, where they could mobilize their resources to survive and thrive. In doing so, they evolved a radically new kind of cell which came to be known as eukaryotes or protoctists. These were cells endowed with a nucleus, aptly described as the first builders, using their multicellular capacity for mutuality and cooperation of a nature previously unknown in creation. This new cooperative strain, so fundamental to the whole course of evolution, has been named in our time as "symbiogenesis" (Margulis 1998; Margulis and Sagan 1995; Lovelock 1979; 1988). Cooperation rather than competition is what features most prominently in evolution's great story.

The Essence of Life

Thus far, we have been exploring the evolving story of life, the inspiring and inspired process exploding in stars, dispensing its wealth through chemical energies, birthing galaxies such as the Milky Way and planets such as the earth. Sunlight is endowed with an incredible propensity to enhance the expansion of life. It supports the nurturing properties of organic microorganisms such as bacteria and enables multicellular creatures to grow and thrive. And from that elegant and diverse tapestry of life-forms, we humans eventually emerge, endowed with consciousness and the capacity to reflect on the wonder of it all.

It is a long, complex narrative full of surprises, occasional failures, and several paradoxes, baffling, mysterious, and mind-blowing. And we have not reached the end yet — if indeed there ever will be an end. Other creatures, perhaps unimaginable to our minds today, will evolve in due course. There are no limits to the power of creative Spirit.

So, what is the essence of life? What is its hidden secret? I suggest that the secret is in the story itself. And in a sense, there are no secrets. All is revealed in the evolving process. We humans often are driven by a compulsion to understand things in minute detail. It enhances our felt need to be in control, but not necessarily our need for intellectual or emotional comprehension. Perhaps, the evolutionary challenge is not in understanding the dynamics, but in befriending the evolving process. When we learn to flow with the evolutionary process and to trust its creative movement, then, I suspect, the eyes of our hearts will be opened as never before. We will have moved beyond the need for control. Intuitively, we will sense and know that a wisdom greater than ours propels the onward movement.

But that requires enormous trust in a world in which people find it difficult to trust one another, never mind trust the life-forces at work in creation. We are creatures ensnared in crippling fears against which we defend ourselves by the relentless pursuit of absolute certainty. To attain that certainty, we move in the direction of dissection and analysis. We break things down and cut them up. And then we feel that we know where we stand with reality. Perhaps, that's as much as we can manage at this stage of our evolution, being still a relatively young and rather immature species, as Elisabet Sahtouris (1998) reminds us.

Although this is proving to be a deeply dissatisfying space for growing numbers of our species, we do need to honor the glimpses of wisdom and truth that have been attained through "rigorous research." Insight often surfaces at unexpected moments and in surprising ways, and the scientific search for the essence of life has produced some exciting and inspiring discoveries.

In the scholarly world of our time, life is construed as a chemical process activated and sustained through the interactions of genetic information. Frequently, "information" is invoked to explain the nature of genetic behavior. Beatrice Bruteau (1997, 104) describes information as the order that we observe among material things but that is not itself a material entity. Following this line of thought, theologian John F. Haught (2000, 70ff.) suggests that information subtly weaves creation into interconnecting patterns, then gathers these into still more comprehensive wholes, and always slips silently out of our grasp. It hides itself, although it fulfills the evolutionary tasks of integrating and renewing the life-forces that make evolution possible in the first place. Mainstream science views the information transfer in terms of nucleic acids (RNA and DNA), proteins, and other complex molecules.

Today, scholars focus attention on our genetic makeup, with the genes themselves often described as blind, impersonal forces ruthlessly seeking their own survival and propagation — a view most commonly associated with the British biologist Richard Dawkins. His is often considered to be an extremely mechanistic and materialistic viewpoint. Nonetheless, in his book *The Selfish Gene* (1976, 215), we read this rather unexpected statement:

> We have the power to defy the selfish genes of our birth.... We can discuss ways of deliberately cultivating and nurturing pure, disinterested altruism — something that has no place in nature, something that has never existed before in the whole history of the world. We are built as gene machines ... but we have the power to turn against our creators. We, alone on earth, can rebel against the tyranny of the selfish replicators.

Altruistic human behavior can alter the tyrannical power of the genetic world, but if Dawkins could adopt a less mechanistic cosmology, he also would realize that nature has several other facilities to engage and redirect the postulated selfishness of the genome. There are other ways of understanding gene behavior, as illustrated graphically by Steven Rose, professor of biology at the Open University in the United Kingdom. Mutations can change the quality of genes, and natural selection can change the frequency of these genes. As Rose (1997) highlights, the process is totally dependent upon the interactive context of cells, organisms, and environments — a view endorsed by other reputable researchers of our time such as Ursula Goodenough (1998) and Adrian Woolfson (2000). In the final analysis, the context is the wise and intelligent universe, within which everything evolves, grows, and flourishes.

Life: The Properties and the Process

The Darwinian approach is largely concerned about organic evolution, taking its evidence almost entirely from the biological sciences. What is missing in this approach is the cosmic and planetary context, which the larger story seeks to honor. And we seek to honor it not merely for its inherent value, but more importantly because it modifies significantly how we view the unfolding process and understand afresh the dynamics on which the creative process thrives.

As popularly portrayed, Darwinian evolution is characterized by intense competition whereby more adaptive forms tend to win out at the expense of weaker variants. We draw abundant evidence from the animal world and give scant attention to the unfolding trajectory of the cosmic and planetary realms releasing prodigious creativity for billions of years before either animal or human ever evolved.

Swimme and Berry (1992), in their original and provocative rendition of the universe story, highlight three pervasive and enduring features of evolution on the cosmic and planetary scales: differentiation, autopoiesis, and communion.

"Differentiation" refers to the diversity, variation, and heterogeneity that we see all around us, highlighting how things differ from one another even within the same class or species. In a word, everything is uniquely different, irrespective of its strength or weakness. No two atoms are identical. This variety is enhanced by an essential newness — what Swimme and Berry call "an outrageous bias for the novel" — that characterizes the unfolding of life at every level. Continuous innovation rather than consistent preservation is what we witness throughout the story of evolution.

"Autopoiesis" describes that propensity within all life-forms to self-organize and self-renew, a power from within that does not simply maintain homeostasis (balance), but engenders the enduring creativity that begets sustenance and growth. It is described by Swimme and Berry (1992, 75) as "the power each thing has to participate directly in the cosmos creating endeavor."

Hans Jonas (1996, 170ff.) suggests that we might ascribe to matter a "tendency" toward inwardness. He suggests that there is no plan or logos in the early universe, but there is a "cosmogonic eros": "Right from the beginning, matter is subjectivity in its latent form, even if aeons, plus exceptional luck, are required for the actualizing of this potential."

"Communion" is the goal of all movement, personal and planetary alike. Communion is the power within the evolutionary story that forever draws things into mutual interdependence. Relationship is the essence of existence; nothing makes sense in isolation. Everything that exists, animate and inanimate alike, is begotten out of a relational matrix. Communion is the cosmic destiny of all beings in a universe structured within the embrace of the curvature of space-time.

Together, these three fundamental energies provide the "lifeblood" on which evolution unfolds and thrives. To quote Swimme and Berry (1992, 73),

> Were there no differentiation, the universe would collapse into a homogeneous smudge; were there no subjectivity (autopoiesis), the universe would collapse into inert, dead extension; were there no communion, the universe would collapse into isolated singularities of being.

Revisiting Darwin

We now can revisit Darwin's theory of evolution and conceptualize afresh some of its key elements. Biologists tend to regard the foibles of organic evolution as prescriptive for all forms of evolution. In other words, the Darwinian belief that all life originated with one source and evolved according to the haphazard process of chance mutations and natural selection holds unquestioned status in many fields of contemporary science.

A great deal has been written about Darwin's own apparent belief in an ultimate divine source as the origin of life — a perception that tends to be overrated both by those virulently opposed to a religious viewpoint and by those ardently committed to it. Those who oppose or suspend religious considerations consider the forces of chance and necessity to be foundational to evolution, and some go on to suggest that this either obviates or rules out the need for God. Take, for instance, this statement from Stephen J. Gould:

> Odd arrangements and funny solutions are the proof of evolution — paths that a sensible God would never tread but that a

neutral process, constrained by history, follows perforce. (Quoted in Nelson 1996, 171)

On the other hand, several scientists, religious believers, but also a number of avowed atheists, adopt the notion of a perfect God — the creator of "intelligent design" — whom we expect to do things in a perfect way, as *humans* understand the concept of perfection. Once again we note a strange collusion between the scientist and the theologian. Why can't a divine force operate in a manner congruent with "odd arrangements or funny solutions"? Why does God have to be perfect, and perfect according to whose criteria and by what standards? Why does God have to be restricted to our expectations and perceptions? Why do our human projections have to dictate the ultimate nature of reality?

Whatever the religious beliefs of Darwin himself may have been, the vigorous atheism popularly associated with his followers is a dangerous and misleading generalization. Followers of Darwin offer several interpretations of his seminal insights. Beyond the narrow mechanistic adaptation are other insights, which enlarge and expand upon the conventional understanding. For instance, in the light of the evolutionary dynamics highlighted by Swimme and Berry, concepts that have been reserved to the sphere of biological life-forms now can be extended to include the larger evolutionary picture, as illustrated in the table below:

	Differentiation	*Autopoiesis*	*Communion*
Fundamental Energies	DIVERSITY heterogeneity complexity variation	SUBJECTIVITY interiority self-organization inner-centeredness	MUTUALITY interrelatedness interdependence connectedness
Foundational Behaviors	GENETIC MUTATION nourishing source of diversity	CONSCIOUS CHOICE niche creation	NATURAL SELECTION tendency toward interrelatedness
Philosophical Namings	CHANCE (Creativity)	CONSCIOUSNESS (Wisdom)	NECESSITY (Providence)

"Genetic mutation," which often seems to ensue from pure chance, is the foundational behavior of nature that makes possible and enhances differentiation. "Natural selection" may also be understood not so much as a desperate option that had to be made to guarantee survival, but rather as a form of adaptation needed to facilitate a meaningful form of communion toward which all life-forms gravitate. In this context, necessity is not so much a blind determinism as an innate tendency for a greater good. Finally, there is "niche creation," a form of conscious choice of those pathways that lure the attention of the exploratory creature(s). This autopoietic tendency is described by Swimme and Berry (1992, 135) in these words:

> We say conventionally that the environment is fixed...but it is also true to say that the species itself "fixes" the environment by choosing out one of a potentially infinite number of niches to inhabit. We say conventionally that the fixed environment selects the species, but it is also true to say that it is the species that selects the environment. And in so doing, the species chooses its own evolutionary pathway.

The table on the previous page offers a résumé of the dynamics involved in the process of cosmogenesis, with key concepts of Darwinian theory reconceptualized to provide a fresh synthesis. This résumé suggests that instead of modeling the grand sweep of evolution on a biological (animal) pattern, the biological pattern itself reflects the creative unfolding of the greater reality. The ancient story is the primary datum; the conventional Darwinian model is a derived vision.

Life in Context: Theological Horizons

Evolution is a story of several strands weaving a complex and elegant tapestry. Information insinuates itself into the universe. It does not interrupt ordinary physical routines, as described by science, but instead makes use of them in its ordering activity. Information quietly orders things while honoring the paradoxical and often chaotic features of the evolutionary story.

The information that we describe is itself begotten from within the womb of an alive universe. Long before the sophisticated discoveries of the computer sciences, our intelligent universe unraveled the complexities of evolution's requirements, forging the creative possibilities that surround us today. Everything that exists, or that ever will exist in the future, emanates from the prodigious womb of cosmic possibility.

In part 5 I will propose "consciousness" as the more dynamic description for the type of information that informs life's unfolding. Meanwhile, we invoke another generic concept to complete the reflections of the present chapter and to unveil some relevant theological insights. "Wisdom" is the new character that is about to enter our story.

Compared with knowledge and information, wisdom sounds rather innocuous and of questionable scientific worth. It is one of those congenial, subtle concepts that we admire and admonish precisely because it never bothers us too much. It carries connotations of being prudent, informed, discreet, and discerning, but not necessarily intellectually or academically rigorous. It is a nice word, to be used with discretion!

The surprising discovery is that creation uses wisdom with prodigious proclivity. Long before we humans came on the scene, evolution had woven a wise and wonderful tapestry — elegant, complex, and incredibly resilient. Some modern scholars, such as Barrow and Tipler (1986), espouse the notion of the anthropic principle, claiming that it was all happening for the sake of us, intelligent beings. But, as indicated above, the intelligence was there long before us, embracing but also transcending the wit and ingenuity of the human mind.

The innate wisdom of creation (autopoiesis) is manifest in a unique way in nature's propensity for self-organization (see Jantsch 1980; Kauffman 1995). The self-organizing dynamics, however, rarely follow the cause-and-effect procedure that makes sense to us humans. So we are often baffled and confused by the apparent illogicality of the whole thing. To the human eye, it seems anything but wise.

Even theologians are baffled by this mysterious force, and in their attempts to decipher and describe it they tend to adopt images and metaphors measured to human wisdom and perception. They short-circuit the mystery, the power to meaning. We note the scant attention that scholars attribute to the Wisdom literature of the Hebrew scriptures, a corpus of sacred writing that seems to attract significantly less attention than the reports of the fiery and warlike achievements of kings, priests, and prophets.

The great Eastern religions seem much more focused on the pursuit of wisdom. In many cases, however, preoccupation with techniques for enlightenment distracts the devotee from the underlying mysticism. The techniques themselves, with detailed procedures and observations, instead of leading to wisdom, frequently undermine it.

In recent years, Christian scholars such as Peter C. Hodgson (1999) have begun to revisit the Wisdom literature of the Hebrew scriptures, rediscovering a relevance that reaches far beyond the Christian religion itself. Two things strike the reader of this material: (1) it carries a strong ecological undercurrent, and (2) the language is distinctly feminine and largely devoid of the violence that dominates much of the Hebrew scriptures.

Describing the Wisdom literature, Kathleen O'Connor (1988, 59) writes,

> At the center of the Wisdom literature stands a beautiful and alluring woman. She is Lady Wisdom, or as I prefer to call her, the Wisdom Woman. The primary mode of being of the Wisdom Woman is relational. In all the texts where she appears, the most important aspect of her existence is her relationships. Her connections extend to every part of reality. She is closely joined to the created world; she is an intimate friend of God; she delights in the company of human beings. No aspect of reality is closed off from her. She exists in it as if it were a tapestry of connected threads, patterned into an intricate whole of which she is the center.

The Wisdom Woman is, above all else, a force for connection and relationship. Her aliveness and well-being thrive on her ability to link with others, right across the spectrum of personal, planetary, and cosmic reality. Her wisdom both arises from and contributes to the generic sense of mutuality.

The evolutionary story being told in our time evokes these three concepts — aliveness, wisdom, and relationality — with renewed vigor and meaning. And nowhere are they more creatively developed than among some leading theologians of our time. Peter Hodgson draws liberally on the Wisdom literature, offering new insights on a theology of the Holy Spirit. He writes,

> Spirit is an immaterial vitality that enlivens and shapes material nature. It is the *energeia* that infuses all that is. . . . It is the relationality that holds things together even as it keeps them distinct, it is a desire or eros at once intellectual and sensuous. . . . Spirit is nothing without relations; it is precisely relationality, the moving air that permeates and enlivens things, the open space across which the wind of Spirit blows. (Hodgson 1994, 280, 284)

Wisdom (*sophia*) defines the kind of Spirit that God's Spirit is: not a possessing, displacing, controlling force, but a persuading, inviting, educing, communicating agency, acting not merely in human interaction but throughout the whole of cosmic reality. Theologically, we can say that the fullness that fills the quantum vacuum is indeed the creative energy of Spirit, permeating and animating potentiality with a gentle, subtle, almost evasive power that we call wisdom.

Denis Edwards (1995; 1999) claims that the self-communication of God is activated in and through creation. Creation is the context in which the revelation and creativity of God are made possible and without which the divine creativity would not be known to us. Contrary to long-standing notions about the sinfulness and limitations of fallen nature in humans and in the surrounding world, Edwards invites us to view creation as wisely transparent and receptive to the revelation of God, made manifest in a unique way for Christians through the coming of Jesus.

Both Elisabeth Schüssler Fiorenza (1984; 1994) and Elizabeth Johnson (1992) explore the mission of Jesus and the story of Christian theology in the light of the Wisdom literature. As a special embodiment of wisdom, Jesus, too, adopts a strategy based on storytelling (parables and miracles), inviting all who follow into a radically new way of relating beyond the dominant and oppressive structures imposed by the powerful upon the poor and marginalized. Jesus expands the inherited Judaic world into an inclusive partnership of universal love and justice, described in the Gospels under the rubric of the "kingdom of God."

What is truly revolutionary in this new vision is the reconceptualization of what it means to be a person, no longer dictated by the isolated, independent, and dominant values of atomistic science or individualized religious autonomy. Persons are considered to be relational creatures whose identity, individually and collectively, belongs primarily to the context of their relationships. For Jesus, therefore, espousal of the vision of the new reign of God is not merely about commitment to a radically new way of activating love and justice; rather the new reign of God becomes the relational matrix from within which Jesus assumes and develops his personal identity. Peter Hodgson (1989, 209–10) describes this new departure in vivid terms:

> Jesus was "incarnate" not in the physical nature of Jesus as such, but in the gestalt that coalesced both in and around his person — with which his person did in some sense become identical, and by which after his death, he took on a new communal identity.... For Christians, the person of Jesus of Nazareth played, and continues to play a normative role in mediating the shape of God in history, which is the shape of love in freedom.

Jesus' personal identity merged into this shape in so far as he simply *was* what he proclaimed and practiced. But Jesus' personal identity did not exhaust this shape, which is intrinsically a communal, not an individual shape.... The *communal* shape of Spirit is the true and final gestalt of God in history.

According to this understanding, God's presence in our history and in the evolution of creation at large is that of a Spirit-power, wisely shaping and forming the interconnected web of relationships that holds everything in being. The divine is first and foremost a wisdom-force, forging unceasingly the relationships that sustain and enhance life. In our Christian story, that relational process is encapsulated in the concept of the new reign of God, traditionally described as the "kingdom of God."

The wisdom that imbues the sacred writings of many great religions, the wisdom that Christians perceive to be embodied uniquely in Jesus of Nazareth, is that same wisdom that gave birth to stars, pulsars, planets, and people. Although I have drawn mainly on the Christian story, I want to acknowledge that the wisdom story is bigger than Christianity and indeed exceeds in grandeur and elegance all the insights of the great religions. It is the prodigiously creative energy of being and becoming. It is the heartbeat of the evolutionary story in its elegant, timeless, and eternal unfolding.

Evolutionary theology requires us to honor the big picture where God in time begins prior to the evolution of the major religions as we know them today. The wise and holy God was at work for billions of years before religious consciousness began to develop. And that same creative wisdom will continue to beget radically new possibilities, forever defying and challenging the outstanding theories and inventions of the human mind.

This chapter has been about aliveness as a central feature of the evolutionary story. We began with the light and heat of the stars, and we have ended with the divine energy manifested as an empowering sense of wisdom and enlightenment. Contrary to so many theories and speculations about a flawed and sinful world, the story of evolution seems to be pointing us in quite a different direction. To borrow from the Christian gospel: the light shines even in the darkness, and the darkness cannot overpower it. Whatever the hurdles along the way, there is light in the exploration. So let's continue to explore.

•

It is time to outgrow...

the fear-filled grip of mechanistic consciousness, rigidly clinging to the notion that creation is little more than dead, inert matter in a hostile, brutal, and flawed universe, where the blind forces of natural selection engage us in a battle for survival, and we end up ignorant of the mysterious life-forces that empower us from within and without.

It is time to embrace...

that wild, erotic power for creativity, embedded in the heart of the universe from time immemorial, evoking and sustaining life in a multifarious range of possibilities, revealing a depth of wisdom and purpose that we humans have scarcely begun to acknowledge or appreciate.

Part Three

RELATIONALITY

Relativity, quantum theory, and the gauge principle...are all based in one way or another on the point of view that the properties of things arise from relationships. —Lee Smolin

Chapter Five

The Divine as Relational Matrix

Nature and art are too sublime to aim at purpose, nor need they, for relationships are everywhere present, and relationships are life. — Johann Wolfgang von Goethe

We can truly know only that which we are not afraid to love, and we can truly love only that which we are not afraid to see. — Carter Heyward

THE CAPACITY AND URGE to relate are at the heart of the evolutionary process, and have been for time immemorial. This feature, more than any other, dominates the evolutionary story from the very beginning. Everything around us and within us is interconnected and is forever forging new links and connections. Relationality and interdependence are not just features of our universe; they form the heart and soul of what creation is all about.

Relationship, and the capacity to relate, we tend to associate with human beings, as in the case of intimate relationships. We use the word "relationship" more colloquially to describe various levels of friendship with other life-forms or even with a favorite landscape. We also use the word to describe our dependence on God. Predominantly, however, we consider relationships as being unique to human beings, and only thereafter do we apply the notion to other creatures and to other aspects of creation.

In the present chapter I propose quite a different understanding. I am suggesting that the capacity to relate belongs initially to the unfolding story of evolution itself, that it is a cosmic and planetary endowment before ever becoming a feature of human interaction. Consequently, we inherit our capacity and tendency to relate from the universe to which we belong, and our desire to relate always will feel incomplete and unfulfilled until we learn to appropriate anew the cosmic and planetary aspects of our relating.

World religions share many of these aspirations but give them expression within a context that fails to liberate their full potential. Because of the dualism whereby we set this world over against the next, the divine against the human, the sacred against the secular, religions postulate a God who relates closely to creation yet never seems be at home in it. I suggest that this projected sense of alienation describes a human rather than a divine way of seeing things. In evolutionary terms, the divine has never been absent or distant from creation and its unfolding. The divine is immersed in the evolutionary story at every stage of its unfolding trajectory. That, more than anything else, is what I want to explore in the present chapter.

Divinity Reconsidered

We begin by noting how scholars try to grapple with what often is described as the "God question." Classical theism operates on the basis of three dominant assumptions:

1. there is a God — contrary to atheism;

2. God is one — contrary to polytheism;

3. the one God is not to be identified with the world — contrary to pantheism.

Theologians and philosophers of religion also draw a distinction between theism and deism. Theism describes the God who is involved in the world and whose revelation is accessible through formal religion. Theism, in most of its expressions, is about a personal God, and therefore a God who deals in a special way with people. At best, the theistic God seems indifferent to creation at large.

Deism involves the notion of a supreme force ruling the world from without but rarely if ever being directly involved. Many scientists feel comfortable with this notion of God. Stephen Hawking (1988, 122) attributes the laws of physics to such a God and goes on to state, "These laws may have originally been decreed by God, but it appears that he has since left the universe to evolve according to them and does not now intervene in it." Richard Dawkins (1986) adopts a similar position, with echoes of Newton's God, who winds up the universal clock and then allows it to follow its own course. What keeps the universe ticking, therefore, is the driving force of natural selection. In this model, God is not involved in the world, but maintains a role of being an external but benevolent observer.

At various stages in Christian history, scholars grappled with the immanence of God in the creation and evolution of life. One of the more succinct statements emerged in the mid-twentieth century with the development of process theology. Pioneered by Alfred North Whitehead and his followers, process theology challenges the notion of a stable, unchanging, omnipotent, totally transcendent God, and suggests instead a God who is intimately connected with the unfolding process of creation and evolution. In the becoming of creation, the God-reality also takes shape and form; in the suffering and pain of evolution, God also suffers and struggles. (For further elucidation, see Griffin 1990; Palin 1989.)

The process position challenges the assumption that our God must always be a ruling, governing power above and beyond God's own creation. While allowing for a radical and creative freedom in God, it postulates that God is intimately involved in the E-mergence of creation, rejoicing in its achievements and suffering with its limitations. The "at-oneness" (read, atonement) of God with creation influences everything we perceive and understand about God and the divine involvement in the task of cocreation.

What conventional believers find unacceptable about the process position is the notion of a vulnerable God, allegedly at the mercy of capricious forces as are all the other creatures of the universe. If that is the God we believe in, then who or what is in charge? And what then is the ultimate hope in a world that seems so hopeless at times? If the Godhead itself becomes engulfed in that hopelessness, then what is the point in believing in God?

Evolutionary theology borrows liberally from process thought, proposing God's total involvement in the evolutionary process to be a primary conviction upon which everything is postulated. The divine cocreative power — a power toward relationality — has been at work from the very beginning, totally involved and affirming unambiguously everything that unfolds. Consequently, everything in creation is inevitably infused with the power of Spirit. All creation is innately spiritual. In human terms, it may not be perfect; in fact, it seems to be flawed in several senses. But for God, the imperfections and flaws do not seem to be a problem. The creative Spirit can work with limitations as well as with other creative possibilities.

If creation at large is fundamentally spiritual, then humans, in their essential nature, also are spiritual. This transparency to the power and giftedness of the creative Spirit may not always translate into constructive action or behavior. Endowed as we are with free will, we can usurp the Spirit-power in negative and destructive ways. But as a gift unconditionally bestowed on all creaturely reality, the Spirit-power is fundamentally benign.

Unknown to ourselves, and with varying degrees of self-awareness over several millennia, humans have been engaging with the power of Spirit in a vast range of responses and experiences. We have responded to the call of Spirit for much longer than formal religion is willing to recognize. Innately and intuitively, we are creatures of Spirit, and while we remain close to the empowering energy of the Spirit, especially as manifested in the interactive process of cosmic and planetary life, we know how to respond, and for most of our evolutionary history we have responded in a wise and responsible way.

By disassociating ourselves from the relational matrix of our cosmic-planetary origins, as we have tended to do over the past ten thousand years of patriarchy, we began to lose sight of our place in the grand scheme of things. Gradually, we broke lose from the cosmic-planetary web. We began to experience life as oppressive and alienating, failing to see that it was we ourselves who set the destructive process in place. We lost touch with the innate power of divine Spirit and began to postulate the need for an external divine ruler to set the whole thing right once more.

The new ruler that we began to envisage turned out to be an anthropocentric overlord (often represented by a king, or by a male warrior on horseback) with little or no relation to the cocreative Spirit that we had known for millennia. Gradually we lost (or rather, subverted) our innate capacity to cooperate and cocreate with Spirit-power. We cut ourselves off from the relational matrix. Intellectual rhetoric and physical prowess joined arms in conjuring up bombastic theories about an omniscient, omnipotent deity ruling everything from the safe distance of the heavenly realm. The internal sacredness of creation and evolution was virtually eliminated as the power of the external ascended triumphantly.

Wisely, John O'Donohue (1997, 14) reminds us, "If we become addicted to the external, our interior will haunt us." As we reclaim the evolutionary context of our being and becoming, Spirit-power invites us to come home once more. In our despair and confusion, we are unsure how to respond. We look to the wisdom of formal traditions, cultural and religious. But they convey all sorts of ambiguous, contradictory, and confusing messages. We seem to be loaded with baggage that weighs us down.

Yes, our interior does haunt us, all the more so as we reappropriate our evolutionary story and reconnect once more with the enlivening Spirit. Yes, this does feel like home. Intuitively, we know that we have been here before. At a more mystical level, some of us may have the graced experience of knowing that we really never left this place. Corporeally, we were banished outwardly, but spiritually, we remained connected inwardly. When all is said and done, we cannot destroy the resilience of the relational matrix and its divinely endowed power to hold all things in being.

Windows to the Relational Matrix

The relational matrix that holds creation in dynamic interplay has long fascinated the human imagination. Several myths, ancient and modern, bear evidence of this relational wisdom. On the other hand, scientific and religious dogmas tend to obfuscate the very mystery that they seek to illuminate. Science circumvents the mystery through excessive rationality, while religion does so by projecting all meaning to the external patriarchal Godhead.

Today, science often outpaces religion in reawakening access to mystery and deeper meaning. As scientists probe the microscopic world of subatomic particles, atomism is proving to be a theory that lacks coherence and conviction. The more we strive to break things down into "the ultimate building blocks," the more apparent it becomes that there are no isolated atomistic units. What we encounter is the flow of energy, sometimes as placid as a still lake on a calm evening, at other times as turbulent and destructive as a tornado. And that energy flow will manifest itself sometimes as waves, other times as particles.

There are other experimental moments in which we cannot really tell whether we are dealing with waves or particles. It might be both, or it might be neither. The most we can say is that we are dealing with "quantum fluctuations," and although they often seem fuzzy, random, and chaotic to the human eye, our intuition tells us that something of significance is going on that has ramifications that stretch far beyond the immediate context.

The bizarre world of virtual reality stretches even farther the influence and potential of relationality. This is not only about undiscovered powers of the human imagination to evoke things into being, but also about mysterious forces within the creative universe itself begetting new possibilities. And however random and unpredictable the whole thing may seem, the growing conviction of the scientific community is that all the dimensions are interconnected, even when things are happening across distances that can be measured only in light years (see Nadeau and Kafatos 1999). At the intuitive level, it may be this subtle awareness that fuels the passion for grandiose ideas such as "theories of everything" (TOES) and "grand unified theories" (GUTS).

Our new scientific insights are intertwined with a new vision for our earth and for creation at large. Ecology and cosmology enhance the relational understanding. Leonardo Boff (1997, 3) describes ecology as a knowledge of the relations, interconnections, interdependencies, and exchanges of all with all, at all points and at all moments. It is a knowledge of interrelated knowledges.

From the Greek root words *oikos* ("homestead") and *logos* ("knowledge"), modern "ecology" explores the detrimental consequences of objectifying nature and subjecting it to the functional analysis of divide and conquer. Nothing in nature can be understood in isolation. Pollute a local river, and you affect the quality of the air, the water, the plant life, the food chain, and the health of every creature that belongs to that bioregion. Interdependence characterizes every aspect of our environment, and only those who attend with awareness and wisdom can truly enjoy its benefits and blessings.

As we explore the larger cosmological landscape, the interrelatedness becomes even more compelling. We already have touched on our interdependence with the stars, our dependence on sunlight as the foundational nourishment of every life-form. Yet that same sunlight, if not shielded by the universe's own protective layers, can wreak havoc and destruction. The hole in the ozone layer is the consequence of human myopia, of a species trapped in the darkness of ignorance about the workings of the creation in which they are embedded. In our interdependent living we need to learn those skills whereby we can hold everything in creative balance and do justice to the multifaceted impact of our multilayered experience as a human species.

In both our upbringing and our education we innocently buy into a deadly perception of simplification. We deal with one thing at a time. We study every subject in relative isolation. We compete with and outdo every other, whether it be in the human or the natural sphere.

We are deprived of even the basic rudiments of what the relational mode is all about. We have a great deal to learn, and a sense of urgency prevails today to acquire this new wisdom.

Imaging a Relational God

Religion has several apertures into the relational matrix. Foremost among these is the ancient perceptions of the divine as (1) a form of Spirit-power that inheres in every aspect of created reality, and (2) a power for relatedness sustaining creation in an interconnected web of relationships.

Our sense of the divine as Spirit-power is very ancient and documented extensively by cultural historians, anthropologists, and some early Christian theologians (see Reid 1997). We recognized the power of Spirit in the fluctuation of seasons, in the rhythms of menstruation, in the energy flow of wind, water, and air, and above all in the cycle of birth, death, and rebirth.[7] We lived in awe and fear of this life-force, guardian of light and darkness, birth and death, creation and destruction. We invoked the divine Spirit in story and ritual, enamored by its closeness to us, and sometimes baffled and frightened by its destructive power.

Intuition and imagination governed our responses and informed our actions in our attempts to engage with the Spirit. Indications are that we felt no need to invoke the Spirit to come to us from some distant heaven; the Spirit was perceived as always being totally present. Our struggle seems to have been one of discernment on how to respond to the mutual engagement that the life-force seemed to invoke from us.

Our tendency to associate and sometimes identify the earth with the embodied presence of the great Spirit seems to have been one of our saving graces. Our symbiotic relationship with creation kept us attuned to the Spirit-power, but also, as modern science helps us to understand, it kept us congruent with the dynamic energies of the evolutionary process. As evolution worked out its interrelational dynamics, we worked out ours — very much along the lines suggested by Lynn Margulis (1998) in her theory of symbiogenesis. While we continued to engage with the relational matrix, we remained in tune with the divine, but also in tune with our own evolutionary destiny.

Not surprisingly, therefore, we would have appropriated relational images to enhance our understanding of how the divine creativity operates in the world. Some of these may have been quite anthropocentric — for example, mother or father images — but the focus on Spirit (referred to above) probably would have protected us from the more literal appropriations that emerged in later times. The imaging would have been more metaphorical rather than literal,[8] construing the divine as a relational life-force that permeates the whole of reality.

It seems to me that there is overwhelming evidence to suggest that humanity's oldest understanding of divinity is that of a relational benign energy that endows every aspect of the created universe. It is this ancient, profound, and often unarticulated experiential intuition that eventually becomes translated in the religious dogmas about God as "Trinity."

Our understanding of God in Trinitarian terms, a feature that characterizes several of the great world religions (not just Christianity), was not first evoked by religious creeds or creedal statements. Rather, it was the experience that came first; the dogma followed many thousands, perhaps even millions, of years later. Right back into the misty realms of antiquity, our ancestors, who were fundamentally spiritual in nature, had an intuitive awareness of the enveloping mystery. Insofar as this seems to have evoked a sense of everything being interconnected and interrelated, even then, in a primordial sense, faith in a Trinitarian God already was awakening. We have known and believed in such a God long before a doctrine of the Trinity was ever envisaged.

And this relationality, although often construed in a personal way and described in terms of personal relationships, embraces reality at a suprapersonal level. Personalizing divinity arises from our needs as human beings. It is the experiential context that provides the strongest and clearest sense of intimacy, connectedness, acceptance — all those qualities with which *we* wish to endow the divine life-force. Yet I do not believe that this is all projection, and sometimes our projections serve to highlight a deeper search for meaning. Paradoxically, our projections may reflect a deep desire to be rooted in a more authentic and meaningful existence.

Where the projections do become problematic and potentially dangerous is when they are employed to bolster the patriarchal will to conquer and control. Well intended though it may be at a conscious level, a great deal of the personalizing that we do around the Godhead is very similar to the reductionism that scientists tend to employ. We are seeking to quantify and verify an understanding of God that we can come to terms with, manage, and control. This is but a short step from subsequently using this newly acquired perceptual power to lord our supremacy over others, and especially over nature. Dogma can become the basis for the exercise of power and imperialism.

To one degree or another, all the world religions have fallen afoul of this misguided effort. And in nearly all cases it arises from cultural and mystical shortsightedness. We are now at a new evolutionary juncture when it may well be beneficial to reclaim the mystic within. The mystics, for the greater part, do not speculate about the relationality that they attribute to the divine. Rather, they are preoccupied with the actual relating, and they see no point in speculating about it. They are entranced with a relational sense of connectedness and meaning, within which everything has purpose and integrity. Things may not be very clear; indeed, it is the mystics, more than anybody else, who have bequeathed to us some of the most elaborate treatises on the darkness that often characterizes the spiritual journey. Real though that darkness is, it never clouds the foundational relationality that is the core perception and conviction of mystical consciousness.

Personhood Reconsidered

Our perceptions of the divine are faulty largely because our self-perceptions are deluded. We project onto the divine our notions of what we consider the person to be about. Patriarchy knows only one prototype: the autonomous, self-reliant individual who stands in isolation over against and superior to everything else in creation. Essentially, only males can fulfill this role, and consequently, the ruling God has to be male.

These patriarchal views have dominated Western consciousness for at least five thousand years, and they have been absorbed by much of human civilization under the colonizing influence of Western imperialists. Now they are in decline. The old monolith is breaking down, and millions all over our world are seeking new ways to understand the meaning and purpose of existence.

Many people feel confused and baffled, and they wonder how to embark upon this new wisdom. There are several valid starting points; many are reviewed in the pages of this book. Thus far we have focused on the cosmological, planetary, and ecological challenges of our time. We easily could overlook the personal dimension, but that, more than anything else, needs radical reassessment.

"Who am I?" continues to be a major philosophical question of our time. That question, however, is a great deal more than merely a philosophical one. It cannot be answered with the rational wisdom of a logical mind. Personhood cannot be reduced to either a biological or a metaphysical construct. Personhood is complex, evolutionary, unfolding, never complete.

Modern psychology defines personhood in terms of relationality: I am at all times the sum of my relationships. My uniqueness, what constitutes my deepest inner self, is not what makes me different from everybody else, in my isolated, autonomous integrity. Quite the opposite! I take my identity from the relational network from within which I unfold. This begins with my parents and the generative process through which I came into being, for which my parents are catalysts (biologically, culturally, spiritually) rather than initiators. Who I become at the various stages of my development is heavily influenced by my siblings, peers, friends, associates, and so on.

And the "sum of my relationships" is not just about people. There also is the cultural ambience of affect and influence, mediated through the creatures of the animal and plant worlds. Without these, my human growth would remain distorted and thwarted. There is an enormous range of environmental factors that profoundly influence my health and well-being, and central to all these is my relationship to the earth, which I inhabit, and the cosmos, to which I belong.

I do not have an identity apart from the relational context to which I belong. The mythical "lone ranger" battling it out on a lone island has fascinated humans for a long time, but it is a classical myth of patriarchal imperialism, a gross distortion of how humanity has existed and thrived for most of its time on planet earth. It is not in our aloneness that we come to authentic personhood, but in our capacity to relate. By the same token, a meaningful relationship with God does not arise from being an ascetical hermit, but from learning to relate lovingly and contextually.

When we appropriate a more authentic sense of what it means to be human, when we reintegrate the story of our humanity in its long evolutionary unfolding, we learn to deal differently with our human projections. This will affect our understanding of the divine and its role in our lives. The universe teaches us that all things unfold from within the relational matrix of creation, ourselves included. That, too, is where we need to begin our exploration into God.

What the evolutionary story highlights is not some patriarchal figure in a far-distant heaven impregnating creation with life, a perfect father inseminating with perfect seed for the propagation of life. No, the seeds of life and possibility come from within the evolutionary process itself. Our God is not a life generator from afar, but a power for relationship at work in the heart of creation itself. And the oldest understanding we have of that life-force is that of the creative, generative Spirit.

Many of our standard notions about personhood are inadequate. They belong to the culture of patriarchal imposition and have been validated in the name of the ruling "sky God," who entered the human story (possibly for the first time) about five thousand years ago. The evolutionary story reveals a very different understanding of personhood, born out of the creative process of the cosmos and planet earth, inspired and inspirited by the cocreativity of the divine Spirit. Relationality is at the heart and core of this identity, viewed from divine and human perspectives both.

The Jesus of Christianity serves as a primary model for this new type of human creature, embodying in our world an irrepressible manifestation of relational creaturehood. We will explore its significance more fully in chapter 8, but as the Christian scriptures indicate, it is in and through the power of the Spirit that Jesus operates. Even Jesus is subject to the influence of Spirit-power. For evolutionary theology, the activity of the creative Spirit is the foundational and enduring evidence of the divine at work in creation and throughout the entire story of cosmic, planetary, and human evolution. Reclaiming the primal and central place of the Spirit is at the heart of our exploration.

Revelation as Relationship

According to the Christian churches, the foundational truths of existence have been revealed to us by God in a unique and special way in the life of Jesus the Christ. Revelation is understood to embody and articulate depths of truth that the human mind never could attain. In the Christian faith, the concept of revelation has very clear parameters and frames of reference. Revelation comes directly from God, through Jesus, to human beings, mediated through a divinely inspired set of writings (the Bible), interpreted by a designated and approved body of scholars (theologians) under the patronage of church authority.

In the foregoing model, the course of evolution and creation at large cannot be sources of revelation, and several contemporary theologians consider this to be too narrow an interpretation. In their desire to embrace insights from the other great religions, they strive to enlarge the horizons of understanding (see Ward 1994, 96–97, 193). Scholars strive to move from an exclusive position, in which the revelation of Christianity is considered superior to that of other religions, to an inclusive one, in which the uniqueness of Christianity is upheld within a context of ongoing dialogue with other faith systems, to a pluralist position, which in its various renditions seeks an equality of all religions while safeguarding the uniqueness of each.

Doctrines of revelation tend to be preoccupied with claims about truth, particularly the absolute and indisputable nature of ultimate truth. John Haught (1993; 2000) shifts attention from the doctrinal focus to the experiential context, and this offers a whole new set of insights, ones that are particularly relevant to this book:

> Throughout the Bible, God's revelation is constantly portrayed in images of excess. This immoderate nature of revelation is a quality that our parsimonious human habits of religiosity find quite disturbing at times. Usually our expectations of how any conceivable revelation might confront us are framed in terms entirely too narrow to contain its superabundance. But it always spills over the upper limits of our apparatus for receiving it. And so we typically filter it out and shrink it down to our own size rather than embrace it in its fullness. (Haught 1993, 90)

Evolutionary theology strives to honor the fact that God has been at work in creation from the very "beginning," long before formal religion ever evolved, and therefore it postulates that creation itself is the primary and most basic evidence for the divine at work in the world. In the oft-quoted words of William Temple (1934, 304), "In the entire course of cosmic history there is to be found the self-revelation of God."

The conventional understanding seems to reserve revelation to the human sphere, something given mainly for humans and capable of being received only by humans. Evolutionary theology wishes to keep open the possibility that all forms of creaturehood (plant and animal alike) are dimensions of divine disclosure and can enlighten us in our desire to understand God more deeply and respond in faith more fully. Evolutionary theology is committed to a radically open-ended understanding of how the divine reveals itself in and to the world.

Evolutionary theology sees the story of evolution itself as endowed with ultimate meaning. The power of the meaning is not in answers, theological or scientific, but in the questions that forever irrupt in the human imagination. The fascination with mystery and prodigious cocreativity is the evidence that begets theological wonder. And the relational membrane that delicately but perseveringly holds the whole thing in being seems to be a crucial clue to divine involvement.

At the mystical level, the experience over several millennia seems to suggest that close involvement with creation itself, immersion in the daily cycle of being and becoming, and the ecological and biological processes of birth, death, and rebirth all evoke a deep intuitive sense of what we call the presence of the divine. Primal and tribal religion seems to have accessed this wisdom intuitively:

> It is often thought that the well-being and prosperity of the tribe depend upon the right relationships being maintained with super-sensory powers for good and ill; and they are maintained by the practice of rituals and by encounters with that super-sensory realm by trance-mediums. Religion is seen as primarily a social phenomenon. It is not chiefly concerned with the way in which a supreme God might be related to the whole world; but with the relations of particular spirits, gods, or ancestors to a specific tribe.... It is the continued good of the tribe that is the main concern of religious cults, and human beings are seen as parts of an interconnected spiritual realm which can assure such good. (Ward 1994, 61)

In our own time, there is growing evidence to suggest that creation itself, encountered in a receptive and reflective way, exposes the heart and soul to a sense of the divine. Sometimes this leads to formal religious commitment; on other occasions the growing awareness of the divine at work in creation may make commitment to a specific religion problematic. Some people who acquire a sense of God being at work in nature feel the call to respond by a deeper engagement in nature rather than attendance at church services. For others, the acquaintance with nature's exploitation and pain urges them to become more active in justice work.

Obviously, we are limited in how much "hard evidence" we can glean for this new understanding of revelation. But to those engaging with these fresh insights, accumulating such evidence is not a strongly felt need. Looking at the great achievements of Ice Age art, how can one avoid a tangible sense of divine cocreativity? As the psalms so often iterate, creation is awake with the glory of God. For much of our time as an ancient species we seem to have been acutely aware of the divine radiating through nature.

And the ensuing sense of the divine rarely seems to have been that of an external ruler on high. The prevailing image is that of a life-force working creatively and interdependently from within creation itself, hence the notion of the divine as a relational matrix. And in our recent evolutionary history, perhaps the outstanding portrayal of that relationality is the cult of the great Mother Goddess, who seems to have been extensively worshiped for much of the Paleolithic era.

This is a controversial subject, the evidence for which I review in a previous work (O'Murchu 2000). Ironically, it is the adversarial arguments denouncing the power of the feminine and specifically disparaging any notion of divine femaleness that provide compelling evidence for this ancient tradition. Leonard Shlain (1998) accumulates substantial evidence indicating that the patriarchal culture of the past five to six thousand years mounted an unrelenting attack on this ancient tradition. The strategy of divide and conquer is all too apparent in the fragmentation of the great Mother Goddess into several localized divinities (Boelen 1984; Leeming and Page 1994). And the subversion of ancient symbolism — for example, the serpent long associated with the creative power of sexuality and female wisdom — invokes anew a desire to reclaim that which has been snatched from us and demonized over many centuries.

As contemporary feminist writers highlight, the symbol of goddess consciousness is not so much about a historical figure that may or may not have been worshiped in the ancient past as it is about a set of qualities that humans have attributed to the divine over several thousand years (see Christ 1997). Such qualities include fertility, creativity, intensity of engagement, diversity of involvement, immanence in the cosmic and planetary processes, paradox (explored in chapter 6), and, above all, relationality. Contrary to the dualistic divide that requires the God of formal religion to be above and outside all created reality, the prevalent belief for much of human history is that God is immanent, all pervasive, and deeply involved in the evolutionary process.

Consequently, revelation may be defined as a process of unveiling in which both the meaning of the world and the meaning of God become more apparent at the same time. Along such lines, Peter Hodgson (1994, 132) writes,

> God is the light that illumines, the word that discloses, the reason that communicates, the love that cherishes, the freedom that liberates, the revelatoriness that reveals, the being by which beings are.

God is the event of world unconcealment by which new meaning and new possibilities of being are created.... God is neither an entity in the world nor an entity outside it but the revelatory-communicative-emancipatory event-process-power by which the world is.

Revelation and the Divine Eros

Revelation tends to be explained in cerebral terms. We think it through in our heads and use rational discourse to communicate its meaning. Once again, what we may need, in evolutionary terms, is the right metaphor rather than the right set of words. One of the things that the evolutionary story exemplifies with great clarity is that the coming forth of new reality (galaxies, planets, life-forms, etc.) often happens amid explosively volatile exuberance. When God creates, God seems to invest enormously excitable energy in the process of doing so. Hans Jonas's notion of the "cosmogonic eros" conveys something of this divine passion and pathos.

In popular parlance, the word "erotic" carries strong sexual connotations, frequently of negative import. The word conveys a sense of wild, ecstatic energy, sometimes giving the impression of behavior that may be out of control. But eroticism is fundamentally an energy toward relationship. In the words of Carter Heyward (1989, 187), "Although to some extent everyone's eroticism is distorted by abusive power relations (of domination and control), the erotic is the sacred/godly basis of our capacity to participate in mutually empowering relationships."

The erotic is a psychic connective tissue, sometimes described as a divine delirium. It is the energy of tender creativity that begets novel possibility. And it does not belong to the human and animal realms alone, but permeates creation in every sphere of life and evolution. Under the aegis of patriarchy, the erotic often has been distorted and even demonized. According to Hampson (1996, 172), "Yahweh formulates the code of eroticism between the two sexes as though it were a code of war." Distorted and subverted erotic energy frequently ends up fueling the strategies and implements of modern warfare (see Morgan 1989). We need to salvage what we have so desecrated and once more put it at the service of the larger evolutionary story, where it properly belongs.

Comparing creation to the female womb has resonances in a number of religious traditions. Creation is described as a primordial womb for being and becoming. From within that womb space the divine is forever pregnant with possibilities for new birthing. God cannot but birth forth. And in that very process, creation itself begets and gives birth too. This is what contemporary writers call "cocreation," with its corresponding notion of "coevolution." Everything creates and evolves in harmonious possibility — each species helps shape every other, and each is shaped by the others — often imbued with the paradoxical mixture of pain and exhilaration, achievement and loss, birth and death.

The relational God, who begets and sustains the entire process, predisposes creation toward novelty and relationality. Deep beneath the divisions and fragmentations imposed by patriarchal culture is an unbroken web of wholeness. For most of our time on earth, we humans seem to have worked creatively and dynamically with that relational matrix. Today, we hunger anew to reconnect. And that is our desire because it is precisely what our creative God desires for us.

In the present chapter I have reviewed what happens within the relational matrix as our universe and everything in it forever take shape under the erotic power of unconditional love. On the part of the divine creating force there is no brokering; everything is given as total gift with no conditions set down. Such is the outrageous generosity of the Originating and Sustaining Mystery, a proclivity that we witness everywhere in the created universe. The prodigious fecundity of our erotic universe mirrors the prodigious fecundity of our God.

The ideas and concepts in this chapter may seem very new, but in fact they belong to a deep and ancient tradition. But the purpose of this exploration is not to reconnect us with some long-lost golden age of human spiritual development. Rather, it is an attempt to honor the creative relational power of the divine manifested in the prodigious unfolding of life and to reclaim the genuine efforts of humans to respond to this divine invitation long before formal religion even evolved.

Despite our limitations and the barbarity that we often impose upon ourselves and upon nature, we are a people primed for relationship. There is much to suggest that we had it right for much of our time on earth, and there is hope that we can get it right again. We have a great deal of baggage to shed, particularly the false and misguided identity that has been imposed upon us in the name of the competition we need to survive, and the robust individualism with which we need to be endowed for that battlelike task. The new cooperative endeavor, the consequence of realigning our efforts within the context of the relational matrix, requires of us a different outlook and, qualitatively, a very different response. The evolutionary story reassures us that we can make that response, and the generous grace of our relational God affirms us in that hope.

•

It is time to outgrow...

the disconnections that seek to separate us from the spiritual and relational matrix through which we evolved and developed for several thousands of years, thus setting us free to leave behind those images and projections of the divine that foster destructive alliances with creation and with all other creatures.

It is time to embrace...

the inspirited and relational God, who impregnates creation from the very beginning, the divine life-force we have known, loved, and served long before formal religion was ever instituted, a God who reveals to us unlimited potentials for engagement, relationality, and enduring hope.

Chapter Six

Thriving on Paradox

And paradoxically enough, it is all that turbulence and fluctuation in the cosmos that does this, that gives all of nature's may be's and might be's a chance to become true. Danger and risk there is. But in its own tacit, latent way, it is as if the universe dreams big, promises big, and stands fully behind human hope.

—David Toolan

The intellectual appeal of cosmic pessimism is supported not so much by nature itself as by abstract mathematical representations that inevitably overlook the elusive complexity and indeterminacy that open the cosmos to a genuinely novel future. It seems entirely plausible that the universe of contemporary science is more congenial to promise than pessimism.   —John Haught

W E HAVE BEEN EXPLORING the relational matrix, the complex erotic landscape in which energy weaves in and out of an ever more variegated tapestry. Sometimes the emerging patterns are illuminating, often complex, and frequently baffling to the human mind. But the process endures, and not just under the impact of some mindless, brute force. The more we seek to unravel the whole thing, the less transparent it becomes to rational logic, but the more captivating it becomes to the creative imagination.

Thus far, our story is woven around the undulating patterns of birth, death, and rebirth. And horizons keep stretching. Whatever scientists claim about the second law of thermodynamics, the story of evolution celebrates possibility and novelty with an exuberant range of exploration and experiment. There is nothing in the entire story to suggest that cosmogenesis can be halted and that one day it will succumb to "the tyranny of entropy." Whatever else the future is about, it is full of promise; the horizon is aglow with optimism, not with pessimism.

"Unlike the previous static views of the world," writes Haught

94

(2000, 157), "evolution invites us to picture nature as the unfolding of a promise, a promise that has been internal to the universe from its inception." We need to keep a steady gaze on that sense of future promise, because in the present chapter, the plot of our story thickens. The grand expansion of previous chapters encounters the complexity of darkness, destruction, and cosmic violence. The story takes a new twist.

Contemporary cosmologists sometimes are accused of painting a rosy picture and bypassing or ignoring all the meaningless pain, suffering, and destruction that characterize our world at every level. We need to acknowledge and incorporate the dark side. It is a stark and frightening reality that often we explain away (rather than explain) in frivolous or oppressive fashion. We need to take the darkness seriously; we need to befriend its apparent meaninglessness, ambiguity, and horror. Even when it defies all our attempts at rationality, we must not run away. The further and faster we run, the more the darkness is likely to haunt us.

As we seek to unravel this baffling mystery, we note that the mainstream religions (especially the monotheistic ones) and the broad community of scientists have never been enamored with the concept of evolution. There are too many untidy bits to it, too many imponderables, too many issues that cannot be subjected to testable hypotheses. Both the scientist and theologian feel that somehow or other we should be able to describe the course of evolution as a straight line moving forward and upward, one that has a clear-cut sense of direction. Then we would know where we stand with it!

The legacy of Darwin explains a great deal. Darwin believed that the process of random mutation followed by selection and proliferation of the fitter variants necessarily would lead to a smooth, gradual evolutionary process. Since biology is driven by slow and small mutations, operating at all times and all places, how can the outcome be anything but smooth? For Darwin, and for subsequent generations of neo-Darwinians, the slow, gradual, predictable process became a linchpin of evolutionary theory. They named it "gradualism."

This neat linear view has been challenged on several fronts. I offer a few of the better-known works that propose an alternative way of reviewing the evidence. At the microlevel, Behe (1996) mounts a highly persuasive counterargument in his review of how our body cells evolve, illustrating that cellular mechanisms are irreducibly complex and can function usefully only when they are all simultaneously present, working cooperatively in a tightly integrated confederation; de Duve (1995) provides corroborative evidence, while scholars such as Laszlo (1993; 1996; 1998) and Eldredge (1999) adopt the alternative theory of punctuated equilibrium (the implications of which will be reviewed in the present chapter).

Because Darwin held such a cherished view of gradualism, apparently he also found it impossible to accept the existence of mass extinctions. Nor indeed could he appreciate the paradoxical contribution that such extinctions make to the unfolding trajectory of coevolution. That is a wisdom that belongs more to our time as we strive to reappropriate a more enlarged understanding of the evolutionary story.

The Punctuated Pattern

It is only in the latter half of the twentieth century that we seem to have come to terms with the E-mergence of planetary and cosmic life as a chaotic, irregular pattern with no obvious sense of direction. Thanks to recent scientific discoveries such as the theory of chaos (Gleick 1987) and the various theories of complexity (Lewin 1993), we are beginning to appreciate and comprehend that life in its great cosmic flow cannot be reduced to our linear and logical mental constructs. Nor will it cooperate with our human desire to reduce the whole thing to one neat equation.

The standard approach can be represented by a simple straight line (see diagram 1) moving forward and upward. Teilhard de Chardin seemed to favor this view, using the cosmic Christ of Christianity as the ultimate goal (the omega point) of the evolutionary process. On the other hand, Teilhard promulgated the notion of union through differentiation, which honors the more complex picture emerging from recent research.

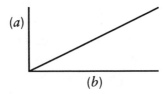

Diagram 1: The Model of Progression. *The (a) axis denotes increase in complexity, while (b) denotes duration across linear time.*

Direction and purpose are innate to this understanding. Both scientists and theologians warm to this model, but clearly it is at variance with the evidence that surfaces from the great story. It contradicts the trial-and-error philosophy of Darwinian theory, and on the grand scale, it fails to accommodate the massive gaps caused by the great extinctions. Nor does it explain those long epochs when, apparently, nothing was happening in the evolutionary unfolding of the universe.

This neat linear approach carries little credibility in our time. To reject a theory is one thing; to work toward a convincing alternative is another. In the case of evolution, the closed-model understanding of the universe, from both science and religion, meant that we did not really need a theory of evolution. In a closed worldview, everything is static and unchanging; quite literally, it is going nowhere, because there is nowhere for it to go. Therefore, rather than work for an alternative theory, evolution for much of the modern era became an esoteric concept that few serious scholar entertained.

Things began to change after Darwin's *Origin of Species* was published in 1859, but as already noted, the focus remained on organic, or biological, evolution only; the development of genetics over the next several decades reinforced that focus. Only in the final decades of the twentieth century did evolution, on the grand cosmic and planetary scale, come into its own. And the linear model was found to be seriously inadequate.

Scholars began to envisage the course of evolution in terms of great troughs of ascending and descending energies. Eldredge (1999), along with several other contemporary theorists, suggests that stability is the dominant feature of the evolutionary process; for long periods of time, things remain relatively unchanged. Then there is a gradual or sudden disruption with often lethal consequences for existing life-forms. The disruption can last for thousands and sometimes for millions of years, much longer than Eldredge acknowledges. At times it feels as if nothing is happening. Evolution seems to be in a state of total nonaction. Dare we suggest that it might be in state of contemplative waiting!

Scholars name it as the process of "punctuated equilibrium" (Eldredge and Gould 1972; also the cryptic résumé of Laszlo 1993, 96–97), a description that favors the human desire for a predominantly stable process, occasionally disrupted only for brief periods of time.

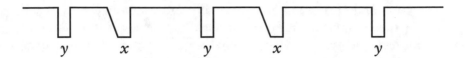

$$y \qquad x \qquad y \qquad x \qquad y$$

Diagram 2: The Model of Punctuated Equilibrium

In diagram 2, there are long periods of stability, which are punctuated by two types of disruptions, indicated by x and y. In the x breaks the decline is gradual, although time spans may vary from a few thousand to a few million years; in the y breaks the disruption is quite abrupt, as may have happened in some of the great extinctions.[9] This model avoids notions of direction and purpose, although scholars are beginning to use the phrase "a preferred sense of direction" (Haught 2000, 117; Laszlo 1998, 83), and many would agree that there is a movement toward greater novelty and increased complexity. The theory of punctuated equilibrium continues to cherish notions such as continuity and stability, but it does incorporate contemporary insights from chaos and complexity theory. And the unpredictability and irregularity of disruption is honored, although not explored in depth. Moreover, the prospect of novel forms and fresh possibilities always arises from the destructive disruption. The negative depletion seems to be a precondition for the release of fresh possibilities.

Diagram 3: The Cyclic Model of Creation and Destruction

In diagram 3, I outline a third option, which, while less precise, may be more creative and comprehensive in its attempt at intelligibility. It depicts the undulating process of creation (upward stroke) and destruction (downward stroke), explored by Swimme and Berry (1992). It is suggested that evolution unfolds according to a paradoxical pattern in which the forces of creation and destruction complement each other; it appears that we cannot have one without the other. In this model the time spans are not of great significance, and the essential unpredictability has appeal for quantum theorists from both the scientific and the theological realms.

There is also a religious rendering for this model as depicted in diagram 3. It has more of an Eastern spiritual flavor, suggesting that evolution unfolds according to a cyclic pattern of rest and activity. There are times of stillness, largely unobserved fertilization and gestation, and then, often suddenly, there is an exuberant outburst of life, frequently assuming an unexpected and totally new structure. Elegance, surprise, and creativity dominate the entire process.

It also invokes the notion of an oscillating universe, forever fluctuating between expansion and contraction. Although not popular among cosmologists in general, the idea continues to command attention. According to Mark Worthing (1996, 190), the oscillating-universe model does not have a great deal of support among physicists; yet it tenaciously remains an intriguing theory with some vocal advocates (see Paul Davies 1992, 50–55). Ironically, some scientists, such as Steven Weinberg, warm to it because "it nicely avoids the problem of Genesis." Once again, scientific and theological dogma become confusedly enmeshed.

The notion of an oscillating universe prevails, I suggest, because the symmetric, cyclic pattern is so fundamental to the great evolutionary story and to everything unfolding within it. Life recycles all the time, in a process that requires the dynamic of birth, death, and rebirth. It is the foundational mystery and, in a sense, the ultimate paradox.

The Baffling Paradox

Models 2 and 3 have one thing in common: they accept that destruction and violence are inherent to all evolutionary E-mergence. Moreover, the destruction seems to be an essential prerequisite for novelty and the emergence of new forms. New species tend not to evolve without the depletion or deletion of those that previously existed. Swimme and Berry (1992, 56) highlight its central importance:

> Indeed every invention of the universe having macrophase significance transforms the nature of violence and creativity. Violence, destruction, and disruption, on the one hand; creativity, synthesis, integration, on the other; these are multivalent words having distinct meanings for the galactic period, the stellar worlds, the elemental realm, the organic and the human levels.

The balance between existence and annihilation reached several critical junctures throughout the first five to ten billion years of universal life. We look at evolution's grand story and note massive gaps in our knowledge. The first stars evolved about twelve billion years ago; the Milky Way galaxy formed about five billion years ago. We know practically nothing about the intervening time, except for one thing: life evolved through some violently creative explosions, some enduring over millions of years.

In the early phase, all but one-billionth of the universe was annihilated. As Fraser (2000) indicates, everything that exists today is based on the survival of a tiny fragment of matter over the devastating power of antimatter. The star whose supernova explosion some five billion years ago gave birth to the elements that formed the sun, the earth, Mars, Jupiter, and the other planets wreaked havoc on the well-ordered galactic communities that previously existed (see Swimme and Berry 1992, 49).

From the human point of view, life in the vast regions of space-time is still a rather violent enterprise, and it would seem a rather wasteful one too. As Richard Feynman (quoted in Green 2000, 120) puts it, "Created and annihilated, created and annihilated — what a waste of time!" Yet apparently it has to be that way as a precondition for the creativity that begets so much else in our creative universe. In the closing decades of the twentieth century, Stephen Hawking and his coworkers began to suspect that black holes were not just about irreversible destruction; in some bizarre and not-yet-understood way, they also contributed to the emergence of life. (In another work, I explore the spiritual implications of this notion [O'Murchu 1997a, 124–27].)

Finally, in the 1990s, scientists in the United States (the Nuker team) and in the United Kingdom (at Oxford) began to identify supermassive black holes at the center of all galaxies, including our galaxy, the Milky Way. Research indicated that all the stars in a particular galaxy, although millions of miles from the black hole itself, are affected by it. And this led to the incredible discovery (still under investigation and review) that it is the supermassive black holes themselves that contribute significantly to the formation of both galaxies and stars (see Adams and Laughlin 1999; Musser 2000). What, in metaphorical terms, serves as the ultimate symbol of destructibility is now emerging as a primary icon of creative possibility. Surely, this is paradox in its profoundest sense.

There is no obvious answer to the baffling question "Who or what would have invented a crazy system like this?" Indeed, it even defies the logic and faith of the religious believer, because it also throws into disarray the widely accepted notion of the God of "intelligent design." Initially, it feels as if there is no meaning, no pattern, no point to the whole thing. Logically, it should have come to naught billions of years ago, but of course it hasn't, and the great imponderable is that it is unlikely to end in disaster in either the foreseeable or the distant future.

For evolutionists such as Laszlo, Eldredge, and Gould, this is not a crazy, random process. They describe it as a pattern: "Evolution produces, not isolated events, but repeated patterns which hold clues to how the process works" (Eldredge 1999, 5). It has a sense of flow to it. It is characterized by a degree of equilibrium that enables things to happen, and in some inexplicable way, sustains things in being after they have happened. The longer we work with this model, the greater the temptation to suggest that it has purpose written into it; at a very deep level, it seems to be impregnated with meaning. Thus, John Haught (1993, 150) writes,

> We know that the unfolding of cosmic evolution has not always been progressive, but this does not detract from its narrative character. For in all the great stories there are numerous dead ends and regressions;...there are long spans of waiting punctuated by brief but significant episodes of terror, victory, and defeat. Still over the long haul, the evolutionary story clearly displays a trend toward the emergence of more and more elaborate entities. Matter does not remain lifeless and completely dispersed, but gradually converges upon itself and evolves in the direction of more complex life and eventually consciousness.

To suggest that destruction and violence can contribute to life and to evolutionary E-mergence flies in the face of everything that we humans consider necessary for sanity and progress. Destruction baffles us, and we cannot stomach the helplessness of not being able to do anything to remedy or eliminate it. Destruction and suffering are our greatest enemies, ones that we would dearly love to get rid of. But alas, it is often our attempts to conquer the enemy that reinforce its ability to undermine us.

We fail to make a few important distinctions. What Swimme and Berry try to highlight is that the quality of destruction and violence is inherent to evolution itself. The ensuing destructability is neither good nor bad; it simply *is*. In fact, one could argue convincingly that in the long term it is always for a good outcome, assuming that we deem the growing complexity of evolution to be beneficial for future emergent possibilities.

There are several destructive outcomes in life and in nature that leave us with a distinctive sense of anomie and meaninglessness. Meaningless suffering abounds. What we humans need to face — yet another great paradox — is that it is we ourselves, and not nature, who are responsible for most of the meaningless suffering in the world.

We invent all sorts of ingenious plans and theories to exonerate ourselves, including the "cosmological anthropic principle" (Barrow and Tipler 1986), which basically states that life is intelligently designed to produce enlightened, conscious creatures such as us. The theory, intentionally or otherwise, ranks humanity above all other creatures that have emerged. And, implicitly at least, it suggests that we are the final outcome of the evolutionary process.

If we are the final outcome, with nothing else of a higher nature to evolve, then we are endowed with the wisdom and resources to resolve all of life's mysteries and riddles, especially the puzzle of meaningless suffering. Suffering is an aberration to be conquered and controlled. While religion claims to have the resources to resolve the mystery of suffering, science is convinced that one day it can rid the world of the phenomenon of suffering itself.

The Paradox of Human Suffering

We humans are largely blind to the fact that many of our attempts to diminish suffering actually exacerbate it and often render it even more meaningless. The Christian symbol of the cross, an emblem proffering hope and redemption, has been used to justify torture and oppression, crusades and witch hunts, scapegoating and victimization. Our record at reducing the suffering of humanity does not seem very enlightened; our record for dealing with our suffering earth is a great deal more precarious.

There are dimensions to this complex problem that we continually evade and ignore. Perhaps most serious of all is the realization that the meaninglessness of suffering is a human problem, not a natural, evolutionary, or divine one. In 2000, almost one thousand people perished in El Salvador when a massive earthquake tore through buildings, homes, and villages. People were baffled and confused, and many asked, "Why does God allow this to happen?"

It is understandable that people raise such a question and in the midst of their anguish and devastation turn to God for hope. Undoubtedly, their faith will offer consolation and strength, and even the very pursuit of the philosophical question — why did God allow it? — helps to invoke some sense of meaning in a tragedy that looks so meaningless. Looking to God for an ultimate explanation is not going to sustain faith or hope in the long term. This is not a "God problem." The earthquake in El Salvador was not an act of God. It was a geological, natural event; it was the earth releasing its pent-up energies, or perhaps realigning its internal structure. It was a purely natural event.

Even if we adopt the religious belief that God is at work in the cosmological creative process at every stage of its unfolding, it does not follow that God willed this destructive act with its impact on the people of El Salvador. The event belongs to the evolutionary dynamics of creation as a natural and supernatural process. As a natural occurrence, its meaning cannot be judged in the simple terms of it being bad or good. It is an integral dimension of the evolutionary process in which the dynamics of creation and destruction forever interweave.

We have nothing to gain by blaming creation or blaming God. The pain and havoc of the earthquake are not God's problem, but ours. If an earthquake similar to the El Salvadoran one happened in San Francisco or in Tokyo (cities regularly hit by earthquakes), most likely there would not have been a thousand deaths, perhaps not fifty or even five. Why? Because the Americans and the Japanese have the wealth and resources to build cities that can resist the impact of such an earthquake. And the El Salvadoran people would have recourse to similar resources if we — human beings — acted out of a more transparent sense of equality, justice, and fair distribution of those resources to which all earth's creatures have an equal right.

This is not a divine predicament; it is a human one. It is human greed, selfishness, and exploitation of resources that caused a thousand deaths in El Salvador. It is we humans and the oppressively unjust structures of our own making that are to blame for this catastrophe. And since it is we who created the problem, it is up to us to resolve it.

There is a great deal of meaningless suffering in our world, most of which arises from wrong ways of relating. Understandably, we look to the divine life-force to intervene and do something to set it right. In evolutionary terms, this notion of God making special interventions does not make much sense, either for creation at large or for the human creatures that inhabit planet earth.

The evolutionary story glistens with divine elegance. Transcendence is written all over it, even in its darkest hours. Unceasingly it points to the grandeur and intimacy of the divine. As far as the story goes, there never has been a time in which the divine was not present. The divine cocreativity is the heart and soul of the entire process, to a degree that makes talk about special divine interventions — as in the major religions — unnecessary and irrelevant. In evolutionary terms, the great religions are not about divine interventions or revelations. Rather, they probably were intended to be celebrations of God's involvement in the evolutionary process, perhaps statements of the process reaching a high point of development, as Teilhard de Chardin hinted in his several writings.

The notion — most highly developed in Christianity — that God had to intervene in a dramatic once-and-for-all reversal of humanity's plight says a great deal more about humans than about God. It reflects a phase of human evolution in which pessimism about the human condition and about humanity's own inability to modify it evoked a set of beliefs that may not be congruent with the bigger evolutionary picture of reality and God's creative role at the heart of it all.

The radical earthly and humanizing project of the new reign of God for which Jesus gave both his life and his death has been subdued and neglected for much of Christianity's two-thousand-year history. The emphasis on the death of Jesus overshadows the prophetic life of Jesus that made his death an inevitable consequence. The life of Jesus is an exemplary model of radical relationality that fosters creativity, equality, and justice in our guardianship of creation and its evolutionary process. Somehow we have lost a great deal of that radically inspiring vision, and correspondingly, the creativity of God is a neglected subject in our theological and spiritual scholarship.

Death and Resurrection: Christian or Cosmic?

Christians often wonder why Jesus had to suffer such a cruel, ignominious death before attaining the glory and freedom of resurrection. The Christian Gospels, and apparently Jesus himself, have no answer to this supreme paradox. It remains one of the great enigmas of the Christian faith, one that for some proves to be the ultimate incredulity in their belief in Jesus.

The evolutionary story suggests that the process of death and resurrection belongs first and foremost to creation. It is another way of naming the evolving cycle of destruction and creation. Because Jesus was endowed with a cosmic status, he was living out in his embodied presence the processes of cosmic evolution itself. According to this interpretation, the historical details are not important; it is the archetypal intent that merits primary consideration, not just for Christian theology, but also for a more creative understanding of the evolutionary process in its cosmic and planetary dimensions.

Something of this paradox arises in all the main religious systems, but nowhere as explicitly as in the Christian scriptures. There is no logical connection between the cruel, ignominious torture of Calvary and the archetypal breakthrough characterized by resurrection. We devote a great deal of scholarly research to the details of precisely what happened to Jesus in those final days of his earthly life. The evolutionary story favors the wisdom of the big picture over the desire for minute details. Assuredly, we need both, but in mainstream scholarship it is the grand scale of things that tends to be neglected, and this diminishes our capacity to engage more creatively with the elegance of divine life itself.

Written into the very fabric of evolutionary E-mergence, at the cosmic, planetary, and human levels, is this paradox of creation and destruction. The hub of the paradox is not so much the apparent contradiction as the largely incomprehensible connection in which the two aspects (destruction and creation) need each other in the service of greater life and complexity. In part, the logic seems to suggest that destruction is a precondition for new creation; undoubtedly that is true, but intuitively we know that this is only a partial explanation. And our intuition also tells us that we may never reach a full explanation on this one; the creative process will always be some steps ahead of us. The mystery and the paradox defy human rationality.

What, then, of the problem of suffering and the need for redemption? Fundamentally, suffering, depletion, and destruction are inherent to evolution, and if theology is to honor the evolutionary story and the divine creativity at work within it, then it must concede that the divine is at work also in this paradox. To state it more overtly, the evidence of evolution seems to suggest that God does not have a problem with the suffering and destruction that are innate to the unfolding process. We humans have a problem with it, but God does not. That is not to say that all suffering is meaningful at one level or another. Hidden, mysterious meaning covers a good deal of it; more of it is obviously horrendous and in no way could be willed by God — for example, the slaughter of almost one million people in Rwanda in 1994. In this latter case, the meaningless face of suffering, there is overwhelming evidence to suggest that it is caused by human beings, and not by the capricious nature of life, whether understood in secular or religious terms.

The basic issue here is not a theological, but an anthropological, one. We humans are unable to make sense of the meaningless suffering in the world. We postulate that there is an external cause to this suffering, ultimately requiring some type of external intervention to remedy the fundamental defect. For science, that external agent is humanity itself, in its controlling, conquering potential; for religion, it is God, however named or conceived. In both cases, I suggest, we are dealing with a great delusion. In the words of Carter Heyward (1999, 24), "The suffering rooted in evil is greatly increased by our collective failure to accept the suffering that is rooted in the incompleteness of God's creation."

We can transcend the delusion precisely when we choose to honor the prerogative and creativity of the divine as seen from within the evolutionary story in its total context. Let's begin where God begins in time, billions of years ago, long before humanity ever evolved, a God who will continue to beget life and possibility long after we have been outgrown by other evolutionary species. Let's then strive to honor and acccpt the paradoxical nature of the evolutionary process, with its baffling mixture of destruction and creation, but, in the long term, poised for possibility and creative breakthrough.

And we too are the beneficiaries of this same process of promise and new life. Yes, we are endowed with an altruism that can outdo the destructive impact of selfish genes, which, correctly understood, means the collective greed of the human community. But first we must reach a place of humility, honesty, transparency, and truth. From that place we can begin to admit that *we* are the propagators of most of the meaningless suffering in the world. It is we, not God, who have carved the planet up into rivaling factions; it is we, not God, who have invented warfare, genocide, biocide, starvation, and injustice; it is we, not God, who scapegoat innocent people to resolve our conscience. And at its worst we have committed all these atrocities not over the long aeons of our evolution, but in a most conspicuous way over the past eight thousand years of patriarchal hegemony.

Most of the meaningless suffering in today's world is caused by human beings. Even so-called threats — for example, global warming — are largely if not totally the result of wrong human interference.

As an evolutionary species, we have not always behaved like this. We never have been perfect, but we have been a great deal more benevolent — to our own type, to other life-forms, and to our home planet. Intuitively, we know how to do it differently, in a way that leads to healing and wholeness. We need to wake up and realize what we are meant to be about as an evolutionary species weaving an evolutionary story on behalf of the creation we inhabit.

The fact that we have gotten it drastically wrong for some eight thousand years is no big deal in evolutionary terms. Life will forgive us for that, and so will God. The daunting question is this: Will we forgive ourselves, abandon our destructive tendencies, and come home once more to an integrated, interdependent coexistence with the planet that we inhabit and with the cosmos to which we belong?

E-mergent evolution has so much to teach us, if we would only listen and strive to respond in a more enlightened and benign way. Before we can respond, we have a great deal of baggage to shed, especially all that stuff about scapegoating, blaming, conquering, controlling, crucifying, and paying homage to the warrior sky God. Instead we need to commit ourselves to the urgent task of healing and wholeness. We need to get things into perspective. And no greater wisdom is there at our disposal than the Holy Book of life itself, the story of our evolutionary unfolding.

Resurrection and Transformation

Yes, we are a resurrected people. Evolution has been telling us that since time immemorial. Resurrection is the mythical/religious name we give to the triumph of matter over antimatter, life over death, meaning over meaninglessness, cosmos over chaos. But it is also the name we give to that baffling transformative process that requires paradox — apparent contradiction — as an essential ingredient in every transformation, whether personal or global.

Death is not the consequence of sin; pain and suffering are not a punishment from God; alienation is not our birthright as a spiritual species. Consequently, as Carter Heyward (1999, 178) asserts,

> We ought not participate in a social or religious order constructed on the blood sacrifice of *anyone* for the common good. Nor should we worship a God who legitimates it. We should rather be struggling to expunge from our spirituality and politics the

patriarchal logic that such sacrifice is good for us or others. We must do this if we hope to be non-violent people. None of us, including Jesus, needs to be destroyed so that the rest of us can live holy lives.

Assuredly, not everything in our world is in harmony, and often we are overwhelmed by mysterious forces that push our sanity and sanctity to their very limits. But before we address these big questions, let's get our own house in order. Let's begin by resolving and dissolving all the meaningless suffering that we ourselves cause either directly or indirectly. Then the chances are that the other great paradoxes that baffle and confuse us will not seem that irrational anymore. We then will be in a position to understand with greater wisdom and equanimity the paradoxically creative Spirit who energizes the E-mergent miracle of our evolving universe.

Then, too, we are likely to be more at peace with the paradoxical enigmas of each day. With graced intuition we will be more at ease about the fact that death is a precondition for new life; we do not know why, but it is. Chaos is the fermenting ground for creative order; light is meaningless without the dark; pain and beauty have a strange familiarity; suffering awakens us into compassion. The evolutionary cycle of creation and destruction manifests itself in every realm of life and permeates every recess of our being.

We must learn to befriend paradox. The wise, self-organizing universe knows what it's about as it unfolds through the mysterious interaction of creation and destruction. We humans do not fully understand what it's about, and the accumulated scientific and religious knowledge of the past has not equipped us to deal more imaginatively with it. Despite all our conditioning, we can make a clean break — yet another reassurance promised to us as a resurrection people.

In the light of these reflections, we have a great deal to let go of and a great deal to embrace, but let's remember that this is not the first time in our long evolutionary story in which we have been stretched to infinity. We have been there before, and we survived it. There is every reason to hope that we will do so again.

•

It is time to outgrow...

our ignorance of evolution's paradoxical interweaving of creation and destruction, life and death, along with the perceptions and responses we have developed that inculcate in us an irrational desire to control rather than trust, to dominate rather than relate, to suffocate in fear rather than go with the flow.

It is time to embrace...

that quality of paradox that will enable us to explore and appropriate the mystery within which we live and move, especially the recurring cycle of birth-death-rebirth, thus equipping ourselves with the wisdom to engage our world in a more enlightened, compassionate, and justice-imbued way.

Chapter Seven

Boundaries That No Longer Hold

It is essentially meaningless to talk about a complex adaptive system being in equilibrium: the system can never get there. It is always unfolding, always in transition. In fact if the system ever does reach equilibrium, it isn't just stable. It is dead.
— Mitchell Waldrop

We once were made to feel secure by things visible, by structures we could see. Now it is time to embrace the invisible.
— Margaret J. Wheatley

SOME STORIES are very structured, others more malleable and fluid. The story that emanates from the atomistic worldview requires everything to be in a clearly defined state, at a specific time and in a specific place. But the quantum worldview, which underpins the reflections in this book, claims that things can be in several places simultaneously; but more importantly, when creativity is at its best, it is impossible to know precisely where, when, and how things are taking place.

For the atomists, those who try to uncover the meaning of life by breaking things down into tiny pieces, the story tends to focus on everything being perceived as isolated, autonomous, and constituted according to its own unique properties. A tree is a tree, a person a person, and a mountain a mountain. The boundaries are clear-cut; there is no overlap and there is no conceivable interdependence. Common sense alone indicates the limitations of this model. And it is no longer a case of stretching the boundaries so that a larger and more diffuse world can be included.

The very notion of a fixed, rigid boundary no longer makes sense at any level. Reality is perceived to be porous, fluid, and fundamentally open-ended. The critical issue is no longer boundaries that set limits, but horizons that often stretch to the realms of infinity itself.

In the present chapter I want to examine two boundaries in particular, ones that have been central to our understanding of reality for many millennia and continue to fascinate and engage many scholars of our time: time and space. These two boundaries, once considered to be absolutely unchanging, now are transpiring as among the most exciting and challenging horizons that engage the contemporary imagination. Both the scientific and the theological implications are substantial and far-reaching.

Knowing Where We Stand with Reality

As human beings, we have a strong need to know where things begin and where they end. Beginnings and endings characterize every feature of our daily lives. Anthropologists such as Mircea Eliade consider beginnings and endings to be primordial issues that have preoccupied the human mind from the start of time and feature in all the great stories known to humans. Hence, many of our religious ceremonies and ancient rites of passage are structured around key experiences related to beginnings and endings. Many of the great religions have special ceremonies to mark the beginning and end of human life.

Beginnings and endings are homely examples of the human need for structure. There are several others. On the global scale we have the boundaries of time and space; at the more local level we have evolved a vast array of social, political, and cultural institutions that enable us to structure reality in a way that gives us a feeling of order, harmony, and control.

Our human need for boundaries is so obvious as to defy question or inquiry. But in a book of this nature it requires reexamination, mainly because the evolutionary story requires us to envision life with greater openness, fluidity, and flexibility. What we have seen in previous chapters is an evolving universe characterized by unpredictability, surprise, paradox, and the novelty that is drawn forth by the power of the open-ended future. Assuredly, there are several physical, material, and even conceptual boundaries, but the energy that begets and sustains creation and everything in it is essentially formless, amorphous, often chaotic, and always creative.

In an attempt to come to terms with it all, we humans developed the two broad notions of time and space. They are useful constructs, and they were given absolute value and significance scientifically and religiously until Albert Einstein developed his theories of relativity, which demolished the certainty and clarity of our perceptual universe.

In the classical view of Newtonian science, time was something that existed in the world irrespective of all other objects or creatures. According to relativity theory, time is relative to an observer's perceptions, and measurements of time are affected by several extraneous factors. Although deemed to be a sophisticated conceptual theory designed to make scientific predictions, it does have some very basic applications to daily life. Most of us have experienced how time "drags" while we wait in the dentist's office; on the other hand, we speak of how time "flies" when we are enjoying the company of loved ones.

Strictly speaking, time is about control, about our need to be in charge. In terms of the past (or the present), we can exercise quite a lot of control, but not in reference to the future. Despite our best efforts to control it, the future will invariably surprise us. As indicated in chapter 2, evolutionary unfolding is governed by the allurement of future possibilities rather than by the constraint of past experiences. Yet we cling to the past, to what we claim has stood the test of time, to what is familiar, to what we think works best, although there may be substantial evidence that such is not the case.

We are victims of time because we misconstrue what time is really about: a human invention to control reality. And our desire for such control is so deeply ingrained and so fundamentally subconscious that we project our sense of time onto all forms of reality, including divinity itself. All the religions, even a nontheistic faith such as Buddhism, try to make sense of the divine presence in the world through human persons. The "founders" of the all the great religions were human beings, albeit unique and outstanding in human terms; many of the leading deities are depicted in human form; many of the emblems, such as statues, are distinctly human in design and form. The long evolutionary tradition of God being active in creation as a benign, all-embracing Spirit-force is largely ignored or by-passed. In this way, we end up with forms of historicism and literalism that are fundamentally idolatrous. Effectively, we reduce God to a time-contained capsule of our own making.

It is our insatiable desire for control that has made issues such as beginnings and endings so important for us. We need to know where things start and where they finish. We will trust the future only if we have some sense of where it is leading to. Much more important is our need to make sense of the past, because then we can figure out not only the meaning of the past itself, but also what is likely to ensue in both the present and the future.

Measuring Time

Our preoccupation with beginnings and endings largely relates to how we deal with time. The first successful pendulum clock was invented by Christian Huygens in the middle of the seventeenth century. The image of a clocklike universe operating according to mechanical laws already had been adopted by Isaac Newton, who postulated that God governed the world in clocklike fashion. The clock became a powerful symbol not only for managing and measuring time, but also for manipulating and controlling the movements of life and nature.

What did we do before the clock was invented? We measured time according to the rhythms of nature. We used the rising and setting of the sun to indicate the time of day. We used the seasonal variations of plant and animal life to determine the time of year. We used star formations to guide our sense of spatial direction. In this way, we were much closer to nature and to its inherently predictable and befriending wisdom. We lived in convivial dialogue with the surrounding world. Mystical rather than rational values governed our thoughts and actions.

As we began to objectify the world of our experience and view it as something to be conquered and controlled, time became a device of measurement. It takes a number of hours to achieve a task, a number of days to complete a course, and a number of years for a tree to grow. On top of that, we have devised a sense of history, in which we review and assess what happened hundreds or thousands of years ago. And when our sense of time fades into the ancient past, we invoke notions such as "prehistory" or "across the ages."

Measuring time in terms of the past is our favorite preoccupation. We know where we stand with the past. Things that have happened in the past feel more real, and things that have worked in the past we tend to repeat. We invest heavily in preserving and fostering the past, and our sense of time is more heavily influenced by the past than by the present or the future.

Both science and religion identify reliability primarily with the past. It is those things or beliefs that have "stood the test of time" that evoke our primary attention and concern. Questions of the future have scientific value only if they enhance the past, and they have religious value only if they build on the past and guarantee a more meaningful present.

Reflections on the meaning of time rarely do justice to the future.

Of all moments in time — past, present, and future — the future is what makes the difference. The future exerts a powerful influence on human behavior. In fact, largely unawares, we judge every situation in terms of future pull, allurement, or meaning. Quite rightly, Haught (2000) highlights the fact that there is no past apart from the future that it anticipates. Every past and every present moment has meaning in reference to the future that it seeks to bring about.

The direction of time does not belong so much to what we have achieved in the past as to the allurement of anticipation and possibility that the future evokes. We live for the future; we seek to create a better future. We want the future to be different from the past, and something deep within tells us that we can contribute to that difference. The story of evolution, although often construed as a narrative of past events, is essentially the outcome of a powerful pull toward the future, which evokes new vision for radically new possibilities.

What these reflections highlight is that time is something that we humans have invented. Time is not a neutral thing, and as Einstein's relativity theory asserts, there is no such thing as absolute time. We invent the sense of time. It is a device that enables us to feel in charge of what is happening in the universe we inhabit.

Despite our pragmatic preoccupation with the flow of time, there does awaken in the human soul a type of fascination with time, which occasionally transcends our desire to control it. This is particularly poignant when we reflect on deep and ancient origins. Let's review the standard scientific version, which growing numbers of theologians also espouse as they reflect on how it all began.

Both scientists and theologians tend to measure time from the moment of the Big Bang. A considerable number of scientists endorse the view of Augustine that the world evolved with time, not in time. In other words, time itself was invented with the Big Bang.

For several reasons, this is no longer a tenable position; in fact, it may be quite erroneous. Ever since the discovery of dark matter, we are confronted with the fact that ours may be only one of several evolutionary cycles that may have existed in the past and that could evolve again in the distant future (see Boslough 1992). Our universe may be a great deal older than we currently assume. There may well have been more than one Big Bang. And faced with this prospect, the eminent scientist Stephen Hawking suggests that it may now be more responsible (even more scientific) to think in terms of a world without beginning or end.

For fundamentalists in particular, this is a deeply disturbing notion. The major religions prognosticate an end to the world, an experience of cataclysmic change, a time for God's judgment, and an absolute declaration of God's supremacy over the world. These literal notions make little sense in the context of the great evolutionary story. We do not need to wait for a grand finale for God's "supremacy" to be declared or affirmed. As the psalmist declares, "Creation is aglow with the glory of God." God's supremacy already has been declared and proved to be indomitable right in the heart of creation itself. Respectfully, I suggest that God's supremacy is not the real issue; human supremacy is. And the basic problem may well be our reluctance to take seriously the God who cocreates with timeless ingenuity throughout the evolutionary process itself.

Time and Timelessness

We began this chapter reflecting on the meaning of time and our use of it as a measuring device in our attempts to make sense of reality. Our ancient ancestors, indeed right to up to a few hundred years ago, seem to have had a much more rhythmic appreciation of time and a more relational view of its operations. The flow of time was assessed by the seasonal fluctuations of sun and moon and by the keen observation of animal and bird behaviors. Long before it became a human prerogative to exercise control over nature, time was experienced *with* nature.

Against this background, some of Einstein's great insights take on added cultural and spiritual significance. Einstein suggested that we view time as the fourth dimension of a space-time continuum. Along with length, breadth, and depth, there is the dimension of time. Time belongs to our engagement with cosmic creation. When treated in isolation, it can become a type of cultural tyranny that distracts from the wholeness of our interdependence, alienating us from the sense of cosmic belonging within which we discover our true identity.

Scientists are particularly concerned about the "arrow of time" and its widespread acceptance in our daily lives. At the observable level, time follows the direction of entropy, from a state of wholeness to disintegration. The glass that breaks into pieces cannot reverse itself into being a whole glass again. At the observable level, irreversibility prevails, but not at the subatomic level of particle interaction, and this is what poses the agonizing puzzle.

As the glass breaks, atoms and molecules of the glass itself and those of the surface on which it breaks are shaken up and vibrate more rapidly. We know from particle physics that every interaction involving a pair of particles re-creates every conceivable option, including the original pair of particles. In this case, a reversible process has happened; it happens all the time at the subatomic level (see Davies 1995; Gribben 1999). And some theorists suggest that when the universe has run its course of expansion, it then will begin to contract until it eventually returns to its original state, thus repeating every known state of its long and complex evolution.

Many of these ideas are highly speculative, yet they do have a foundation in the subatomic world. They serve to remind us that reality is not as simple as we humans would like it to be, nor does it always function according to our rational logic. This is yet another invitation to maintain a sense of openness and transparency to deeper meaning. There is a timelessness to our world and to our experience of it that we cannot conquer or control. Our desire to master time may be one of the greatest delusions of our anthropocentric will to power.

And so while we continue to be fascinated by where it all started and how it all will end, we need to accept that the imponderables of beginnings and endings belong to a larger sense of mystery, the enigma of time and its illusive sense of direction, especially at the subatomic level. We do not have to resolve all these mysteries. We need to learn to befriend them, strive to understand with empathy and insight, and, in this way, remain more transparent to the awesome and baffling mystery writ large in the evolutionary story itself.

It is worth noting at this juncture that throughout the past few centuries, spiritual behavior, especially spiritual "progress," often was judged in terms of linear time. The longer you spent at prayer, the holier you became; and many religions prescribed specific prayers for certain times of day and for specific times of year. The success of the spiritual life was assessed in terms of time. Today, the emphasis tends to be on the quality of the experience rather than the duration of the exercise. And we give significantly more attention to spatial factors, such as the ambience of prayer places and times, body posture in prayer, environmental context, and group support structure.

"Space expands presence" is a phrase attributed to an unknown mystic of the Middle Ages. It verbalizes a great deal of what contemporary spirituality seeks to articulate. As we saw in chapter 4, space is about fullness, not emptiness. All space, whether global or local, is an invitation to look into greater depth, to the mysterious presence not immediately obvious to the human eye. The "presence" in the emptiness is vibrant and active, and it conveys a sense of aliveness. Space, not time, is what instigates the search for spiritual meaning in our time.

The Space around Us

The ancient Greeks speculated at length about the nature of space, and they developed geometry to help make sense of it. Greek cosmology maintains that the universe is finite and spherical, with the earth at the center of a system of concentric revolving spheres. Isaac Newton moved beyond the geometrical understanding; he was primarily concerned with the construction of mathematical laws of motion.

For Newton, absolute space in its own right, without relation to anything external, remains always similar and immovable. Space exists as something eternal and independent of all other realities in the cosmos. Einstein demolished this certainty, indicating that distance is not experienced identically by everyone and that on the cosmic scale it is affected by the power of gravity. Our perception and understanding of space became a much more modest affair.

There was also something of a revolution in how we understood the content of space. How are atoms propagated in space? What is the medium through which they travel? To solve these riddles, the Greeks proposed the existence of "ether," an intangible substance that filled the entire universe. By proposing that space and time are elastic and can change from one reference frame to another, Einstein was able to demonstrate that his theory of relativity rendered the ether superfluous. According to Einstein, space is empty.

However, the appearance of quantum field theory has retrieved the older conviction that space is full. We now believe that space is an immense sea of energy and that matter is merely a small ripple on that sea. Once again, we are confronted with another understanding of space.

It is precisely the quantum vision that opens up radically new perspectives on how we understand space and engage with it. Just a few hundred years ago, we erected massive buildings to store artifacts and books relevant to our accumulation of information. In the 1970s, we were able to consign all that information to a small object called a microchip. Information could be contained in a different space structure; indeed, the structure itself seemed to be becoming more and more spaceless.

Now in the twenty-first century, we can store the contents of not one, but several, libraries in mechanisms that are invisible even when we use powerful microscopes. We are into the world of nano-technology. A "nano" measures one-billionth of a meter, a minuscule entity that is widely employed today for several computer procedures. This weird new mechanism has a strange affiliation with the human body because the ribosomes that form molecules in the human body — for example, one amino acid — are of nano proportions. Indeed, when it comes to this new understanding of space, the strangeness of the outside world and the mysterious world within may be more similar than we heretofore have understood.

The Space–Time Continuum

In fact, it no longer makes sense to distinguish between the outer and the inner; both are dimensions of space-time understood as one continuous reality. And the reality that we encounter is bigger than our constructs of time and space, both of which are human devices designed to manage and control our world more effectively. Necessary though these constructs are at a commonsense level, if we are to be true to the evolutionary story that molds and fashions our world, we need to think bigger, contemplate more inclusively, and behave more creatively. In a world that takes evolution seriously, there is no room for Herbert Marcuse's "one-dimensional man," a robotlike creature excessively preoccupied with management and control. In evolutionary terms, we are primed for celebration, not for manipulation.

The space-time continuum is yet another reminder to us that our universe functions as an unified whole. Einstein pushed us toward the realization of a four-dimensional universe: length, breadth, depth, and time. Many among us have not yet come to terms with this new challenge. Meanwhile, wisdom rolls on at an accelerating pace, requiring us to grapple not just with a four-dimensional construct, but with something more akin to a ten-dimensional sphere. We are into the fascinating world of "string theory."[10]

Without entering into the complexities of its multidimensionality, what is intriguing about string theory is the imagery being adopted. Instead of an objectively identifiable point, the theory suggests that the fundamental realities of the universe may be compared to the vibrations that arise when we pluck something like the string of a guitar. "Superstrings" are postulated as strings of vibrating energy lacking any internal structure, perhaps as foundational to the material world as prokaryotes are to the world of organic matter, or as music is to meaning in our human experience (see Hayes 1994).

The musical metaphor has several historical precedents known to mystics, philosophers, and scientists alike:

> From the ancient Pythagorean "music of the spheres" to the "harmonies of nature" that have guided inquiry through the ages, we have collectively sought the song of nature in the gentle wanderings of celestial bodies and the riotous fulminations of subatomic particles. With the discovery of superstring theory, musical metaphors take on a startling reality, for the theory suggests that the microscopic landscape is suffused with tiny strings whose vibrational patterns orchestrate the evolution of the cosmos. (Green 2000, 135)

Other images arise in the creative mind. Always moving and oscillating, strings engage one another in a free-for-all dance, forming hoops and loops as they sway and bump and slide into one another in an upsurge of complex creativity. Not surprisingly, therefore, Ed Witten has renamed this recent exploration, opting for "M-theory" rather than string theory. The *M* can stand for "magic," "mystery," "membrane" (see Duff 1998, and the observations of Eisenberg 1998, 469 n. 102), or even "mother" to all other theories — what Green (2000, 386) describes as "a cogent framework for merging quantum mechanics, general relativity, and the string, weak, and electromagnetic forces."

In this revised version, particles are identified as matrices (not as numbers) — loops of strings and oscillating globules, uniting all of creation into vibrational patterns that are meticulously executed in a universe with numerous hidden dimensions, capable of undergoing extreme distortions in which the spatial fabric tears apart and then repairs itself. Might this not be a scientific version of the relational matrix described in chapter 5?

Some scientists are dismissive of these new ideas; others ridicule them, particularly since the conditions for reliable experimentation and verification have not materialized. I suggest that the real tension belongs to another level of reality. At the conscious, rational level, it all feels very speculative; however, what is driving the scientific imagination here is not rational logic, but a powerful subconscious mystical energy. The dreamer is outwitting the rationalist; the mystic is outstripping the scientist.

Speculative though these ideas might be, they help to open up that pervasive, subtle world of Spirit-power on which evolution thrives. And this is the deeper, spiritual realm that evolutionary theology must not neglect. Theologians in the closing decades of the twentieth century often alluded to "rehabilitation of the Holy Spirit." The role of the Spirit in the life of the church apparently had been neglected for some time. Little wonder, when the Spirit has been so seriously neglected in the evolutionary story itself.

Beyond the Boundaries

Almost in spite of ourselves, the relational matrix is commandeering our attention and allegiance. Nothing makes sense in isolation anymore. Rigid boundaries stifle rather than protect truth. Whether it be the illusive nature of the wave-particle duality, the seething vacuum of quantum potential, the vibrational resonance of strings, or the symbiogenesis within which cooperation outpaces competition — in all these cases and many others, the creative Spirit forces open new horizons, beckoning the human imagination to invent new concepts and fresh namings in our engagement with the evolving reality of our world.

In each and every case, the closed structure of previous atomistic models is broken open, and the fixed boundaries become porous and permeable. Progressively, as the boundary is stretched, its elasticity reaches breaking point; this is what modern scholars call "the edge of chaos," where boundary conditions no longer hold and we are embarking upon new horizons.

Reality in this new space behaves in a different way, or, more accurately, we perceive the behavior in a new light. It is no longer a simple procedure based on cause and effect, assuring a predictable and manageable outcome. Several outcomes may be happening at once, without a discernible cause-and-effect explanation. To the uninitiated, it seems chaotic and anarchic. It is only when we discover the patterns, rhythms, and relationships that things begin to make sense. And even if they do not make sense (to us), we realize that still they may be imbued with meaning; it's just that we have not yet discovered it.

Practically speaking, we still need boundaries, structures, and, possibly, institutions. I am not sure whether we need major institutions — political, social, or ecclesiastical — to handle reality in the new future that is dawning upon our world. At one time, information was contained and controlled within very definitive boundaries. Today, it is a commodity to which everybody has a large measure of access (and that may not always be beneficial), thanks to the creatively new networks through which it is transmitted and accessed on a global scale. Although many of us rely on banks to facilitate access to money, money itself has become a medium of electronic communication accessible to all of us through networking facilities. Networks rather than major institutions are likely to dominate the interactive world of the future.

What is a network? It is another example of a relational matrix, with no obvious hierarchy and a minimal structure that facilitates a whole new set of relationships. It is another chapter in the evolving story of our autopoietic universe, wherein self-organization veers more toward communal interaction than toward hierarchical order. It is further evidence that loose, flexible forms, even though chaotic and anarchic at times, have a particular appeal to our time, not because these are more fashionable, but because the consciousness of this time requires them as the means through which we engage with the world in which we are called to be creative participants.

What consciousness am I referring to? Obviously, it is not human consciousness on its own. I am alluding to the consciousness that surfaces today from many unexpected and unexplained sources. Perhaps it is the power of the Jungian "collective unconscious," which many claim is extremely volatile in our time. Or perhaps it is the collective energy of past evolutionary patterns, something akin to Rupert Sheldrake's "morphic resonance." Or perhaps it is the impending future, pulling us all across a new threshold where those of free and creative spirit will survive, but many others will succumb because of the lethargy and dead weight of the old consciousness.

Whatever the explanation may be — and all three of the preceding examples help us to name what it is — it is a driving force of our time whose influence none of us can escape. Ideas of this nature frighten some people and annoy others. They sound speculative and unsubstantiated. But if we take seriously the creative Spirit at the heart of the evolutionary process, then we must spare no effort to attune ourselves with the Spirit's wild, erotic energy, which shakes and disturbs our most sophisticated theories and requires us to reexamine even our most seemingly foolproof concepts and ideas. There is much to suggest that the creative Spirit is doing something amazingly original in our time, breaking asunder the encrusted forms of old and catapulting us toward new relational horizons, shattering our illusions and challenging us to new creative possibilities.

Can we respond appropriately? Can we see it through? And what, if anything, can we bring from our evolutionary past that will sustain and nourish us for this momentous challenge? A closer look at the evolution of our own species perhaps will help to illuminate the way forward. To that aspect of the great story we now turn our attention.

Meanwhile, let us note what the transition marked by the present chapter signals for us at this time:

•

It is time to outgrow...

our rational anthropocentric need to impose order, structure, and closure on every sphere of experience. Our fear of wild eroticism, of creative chaos, and of the radically new possibilities often condemns us to the imprisonment of our fretful imaginations, which then drive us to impulsive action and an irrational desire to dominate and control.

It is time to embrace...

horizons that stretch our minds and hearts to their very limits, trusting that the creative Spirit, who breaks down all rigid boundaries and barriers, will spearhead a new relationality in which we and every other organism will rediscover its true cosmic and planetary identity.

Part Four

EMBODIMENT

We live in a common sphere, a common space that makes all communication between creatures possible, a space which is in one sense our common body. —Denis Edwards

Chapter Eight

"This Is My Body"

The body is suffused with wild and vital energy. Essentially we belong beautifully to nature. The body knows this belonging and desires it. The human body is at home on the earth.
— John O'Donohue

How we image the human body plays a central role in how we image the world.
— Riane Eisler

THUS FAR OUR STORY has moved along the shady, mysterious porticoes of the subaltern world. We have explored the unseen realm of the quantum vacuum overflowing with bubbling energy, poised to explode into form and possibility. We have encountered a world of growing and developing organisms in which the domain of the living outpaces the forces that threaten extinction. We have stood in awe before the sheer grandeur of what we see and the puzzling questions that tease our imaginations into deeper appreciation of mystery. We have entered the dance in which everything is connected and interrelated, the relational matrix that maintains and nourishes the membrane of our evolving universe.

What does the survival of the fittest mean in a world of this nature? And who are these superfit organisms? I suspect that the fittest of all are those who do not "fight" for survival, but remain interconnected with the dance of infinite possibility, grounded in the inexhaustible love of the embracing Spirit of God. We are moving in the big realm of the big story. And we must not shy away from it, even though at times our engagement with it is couched in broad generalizations. For many of us, this may be the hardest thing about evolution: it is so vast and incomprehensible. Yet the wise and wonderful God made it that way, and also, I suspect, made us capable of engaging with it. But somehow we have lost the ability to wonder. The time has come to release once more the power of imagination.

Even in terms of our own evolution as a human species, it is amazing how much we have forgotten. Hopefully, the material of this chapter will help us to retrieve the lost treasures. We begin with something so elementary that readers may wonder why I give it attention. I refer to "embodiment," the fact that everything in nature has a body (of some type) and that we relate intimately with one another through bodily interaction. This is yet another major aspect of the neglected story of evolution. Indeed, the neglect of the body (as highlighted by scholars such as Raphael 1996) remains radically incomplete until once again we embrace the larger sense of embodiment that characterizes the evolutionary process.

The Body Demonized

In popular parlance, the body tends to be associated with human beings only. The bodies of other creatures — animals, birds, and fishes — although in some cases deemed to be of sacred and religious significance, were not ensouled in the same way as humans and therefore did not need the same care and attention. And in an unspoken way, it was assumed that all other embodied life-forms were there for the use and usufruct of the human species.

With the spread of Western imperialism and the insidious erosion of colonialism, some of the more benign religious attitudes toward the body — for example, in Hinduism and Taoism and in several indigenous religions — were largely suppressed. The Christian suspicion of and unease with the human body, especially the female body (see Daly 1978; Graham 1995), became a universal norm. Human embodiment was problematic, culturally difficult to manage and control, and religiously suspect as being prone to sin and evil. The body was considered to be a burden rather than an asset.

And things were not much better in our regard for the terrestrial body. In fact, some religions seem to suggest that that was the primary culprit. It lured people away from the things of heaven, immersed them in materialism and secularity, and distracted their minds from the things of God. But of course the problem was neither the terrestrial body nor the human body. The real problem was the dualistic mindset that divided everything into good and evil, spirit and matter, earth and heaven.

The human mind became inflated, and human ways of seeing things became distorted. We often attribute this development to the excessive rationalism propagated by René Descartes (1596–1650) and Immanuel Kant (1724–1804). Descartes's famous statement "I think therefore I am" affirmed that mind was all that mattered and that matter was essentially mindless. But this misapprehension goes back a great deal further, to what many contemporary writers refer to as "the dawn of civilization," about three thousand years before the Christian era.

"Civilization" is an innocent-sounding word that needs careful examination. In scholarly usage it refers to the development of writing and literacy in the Sumerian culture of the Tigris-Euphrates Valley around 3000 B.C.E. and to the accompanying development of the first urban settlements in what today we call the Middle East. These two features — literacy and urbanization — are widely considered to be the origins of civilization as we currently define the concept.

There is a dark side to this notion that many people do not seem to be aware of (see the timely and comprehensive critique of Shlain 1998). If 3000 B.C.E. marks the beginning of civilization, then automatically we are asserting that everything that evolved prior to that time — whether in the human, earthly, or cosmic spheres — is castigated as uncivilized, inferior, primitive, and barbaric. With one stroke of the patriarchal pen the creative Spirit of God is dealt a deadly blow, and the festering wound has cut deep into our embodied selves. The elegance of our long evolutionary story has been short-circuited, and so much of the Spirit's invigorating creativity has been consigned to pagan make-believe.

This is where the mind — the human mind — began to go mad. In one sense, insanity reigned thereafter. And perhaps it took something as barbaric as the twentieth century, the bloodiest and humanly most destructive on record, to bring us to our senses again and remind us that the project we call "civilization" has a dark and frightening side to it. By seeking to dismiss most of what our evolutionary story has been about, history has left humanity isolated and bereft on a lonely island of self-immolation.

Peter Brown (1988) traces the history of the usurpation of the human body in early Christianity and suggests that what happened between the times of Constantine and Augustine has had negative fallout with ramifications that have lasted to our own time. From a Christian point of view, this is a comprehensive and informed analysis, but once again it is a limited perspective. This is not just a Christian deviation; its roots penetrate into the abomination that we humans created when we tried to suppress the story of our existence over thousands of years prior to Christian times. And that misguided understanding is not just about demonizing the human body; it affected all forms of embodiment, organic and inorganic alike.

A great deal has been written about the demonizing of the body, particularly the human body. It is important to attend to this research to highlight how much needs to be retrieved and rehabilitated. In the present work, I will leave most of that to the initiative of my readers and suggest that they consult the extensive documentation already available on the subject. I wish to devote the rest of this chapter to the work of retrieval because that, more than anything else, is what the evolutionary story requires of us at this time.

The Body in Context

As indicated in previous chapters, Spirit-power is the driving force of the evolutionary process, the deep secret to unraveling the evolutionary story. But creative Spirit on its own comes to naught. It is a central paradox of evolution that Spirit comes to birth in matter, and without the material universe it remains not merely hidden but, in a sense, paralyzed. Spirit needs matter as the expressive medium of its prodigious creativity.

Spirit reveals its creative power in every dimension of universal life. And within that broad amorphous landscape, embodied form seems to be of special significance. In common usage we apply the term "body" to biological organisms, but metaphorically we also speak of the terrestrial body, the body of creation, and Christian religions refer to the faith community (the church) as the body of Christ. These varied uses of the term suggest that we intuitively associate the body with something more than biological organisms.

Mainstream science attributes the capacity to be alive to organic bodies only. As indicated in chapter 5, the story of coevolution requires us to stretch our understanding of what makes things alive. Our ancient ancestors over several millennia considered the earth to be alive in a fully organic sense, and modern science grapples once again with this notion — for example, in the Gaia theory (Lovelock 1979; 1988). And the speculative exploration around the notion that the cosmos at large also is alive is likely to be authenticated rather than dismissed over the next few decades.

Embodiment therefore becomes a characteristic not merely of humans and animals, but of all organic life, and of the earth and the cosmos as a whole. Embodiment expresses not merely a set of biochemical characteristics that define life, but something more akin to psychic endowments or spiritual qualities. Primary among these is a capacity to relate and to connect interdependently; and from within this relational matrix, possibilities for birthing (replication) seem innumerable.

Although several mystical images are overly anthropocentric, they help to uncover deeper meaning. Of particular relevance here is this statement of Meister Eckhart: "What does God do all day long? God lies on a maternity bed giving birth" (frequently quoted in Fox 2000). God cannot but create; however, this divine initiative is not operated by some external agency, but by a cocreative process engaging creation's potential for creative expression. The body through which God gives birth is not some type of divine endowment, unique to the divine Spirit; no, it is the body of creation itself in its cosmic, planetary, and creaturely modes. Without the embodiment of creation, God's creativity would be jeopardized. It is through the embodied nature of creation that we encounter and engage with the living presence of God.

What is at stake here is not the limits of God's power, but rather, the contextual horizons of God's creativity. Evolutionary theology seeks to extend rather than limit the horizons of divine becoming. And it also endorses the Buddhist notion that we should not speculate unnecessarily about the nature of God. Our call in life is one of orthopraxy (right action) rather than allegiance to orthodoxy (right doctrine).

Religious speculation on how God operates from afar, above and outside creation, has not served creation well, and henceforth it is unlikely to provide us with an enlightened understanding of the divine at work in creation. What it achieves fundamentally is validation for the patriarchal right to rule and control, requiring a projected "sky God" as the supreme, unquestioned authority over everything that exists. That God, although strongly supported by the monotheistic religions, is an imaginative construct that makes little or no sense from the perspective of our evolutionary story.

The God of the evolutionary story is a life-force radically committed to creative, cosmic embodiment. God may be about many other things beyond this reality, but the major concern of evolutionary theology is that we take this dimension seriously. Contrary to previous times, it is not a case of understanding God first and then the world will make sense. Rather, the world (created order) is God's first gift and revelation to us, and also the most enduring. It is precisely when we become enamored with the elegance of the mystery at work in creation that we begin to discover a more enlightened way to apprehend the mystery and reality of God.

Body as Process

Before we can read creation in a creative way, we need to appropriate a more wholesome understanding of our engagement with the body. Whether it be the body of the earth, ourselves, or any other creature, our first assumption is that the body is a material entity contained in space and time. And although we attribute immaterial features to our embodied selves — for example, mind, spirit, soul — it is the material and physical form that preoccupies our attention.

The major religions confuse the picture even further in asserting that it is the spiritual aspect that endures, whether in a reincarnated sense or in an after-death realm; in either case, the material body comes to naught. Once again we are trapped in a classical dualism, with the spiritual dimension enduring and the material form condemned to nothingness. Ironically, corporeality does not disappear completely; in the theory of reincarnation, spirit reinhabits a body until total union with brahman is attained; and according to Christian belief, at the end of time we will be reconstituted in a glorified body.

Many of these religious beliefs are highly speculative and smack of the human desire to wrap everything up in a neat package. Embodiment, however, is anything but neat, and it ridicules all our efforts at mastery and control. Bodies are not things or objects; bodies are processes — porous, fluid, flexible, and dynamic. Although to the human eye the body — whether it be that of the cosmos, planet, or person — seems to be an observable and measurable object, it is far more mysterious, illusive, and indefinable.

A few simple facts illustrate what I mean. For every single atom of ordinary matter in the universe there are one billion light particles; matter is nothing but gravitationally trapped light. Although energy resides in matter, its creation and mode of operation are much more amorphous and illusive. For instance, the sun emits more energy in one second than humankind has consumed in the whole of its history. Each second, the sun transforms four million tons of itself into light. The body of the universe reveals an illuminating evolution: at four minutes it was as dense as iron; at eleven minutes, as dense as water;

at five hours, as dense as air. Ever since then, the body of the universe itself, and all embodied forms within it, require greater expanses of "empty" space in order to function creatively. What the evolutionary story demonstrates is that nonmateriality rather than materiality is what makes the difference to the successful unfolding of bodies.

The human body bears evidence of the same paradox. Two-thirds of the human body is made up of water, held in place by a skin capsule that is itself highly porous. To process food, the adult human body has thirty-five million digestive glands. Stomach acid is so powerful that it can dissolve razor blades in less than a week. The stomach produces a new lining every three days to protect itself from its own acid, which means that the lining must shed and regenerate about half a million cells every minute. Bone is one of the hardest and most resistant tissues in the body, and yet only 45 percent of its composition is mineral deposit; 30 percent comprises living tissue, cells and blood vessels, and the remaining 25 percent is comprised of water. Every seven years the entire body architecture is replaced with a new skeleton. (For other relevant details see Fox 1999, 69ff.)

Embodiment is not a noun, but a verb. It is a process forever unraveling and unfolding. What we observe externally is the gestalt within which an amazing transformation is forever taking place. When viewed in depth, it is nebulous and mysterious. In the human body, the whole thing is operated by our DNA, the mysterious nature of which begins to surface when we realize that if the DNA in an average person was uncoiled and laid out end to end, it would reach to the moon and back one hundred thousand times.

DNA is fundamentally about information. At the observable level, that is what the body is all about — a self-organizing, intelligent organism, but one that requires creative interaction with all other embodied forms for the release of its full potential. No bodily form makes sense in isolation. Interdependence is written into the very essence of embodied reality. Indeed, it is these two features — intelligence and interdependence — that provide the most generic clues to the meaning of our embodied existence in a corporeal universe.

The Spirit-force that has fueled evolution from ancient times is also the power that enlivens all embodied processes. Embodiment is the channel through which the creative and intelligent energy flows. And the interactive dimensions of that process largely point toward a growing convergence — a feature of the evolutionary story highlighted by the priest-paleontologist Teilhard de Chardin. While Teilhard envisaged that process coming to completion in the Christ of Christianity, I envisage one that remains radically open and probably of infinite duration. The desire to postulate an end point is a human need, and the evolutionary story is larger and more complex than the perceptual needs of the human imagination.

Embodiment and Personhood

In evolutionary terms, embodiment is a concept of central importance. It is also a concept that has been grossly distorted and misconstrued. Both science and religion fall afoul of the same anthropocentric reductionism, subjecting the body to a type of suffocating minimalism. In terms of the evolutionary story, the body cries out for recognition, for the rehabilitation of its creative and dynamic uniqueness.

In the dominant consciousness of our time, we tend to treat the human body, and hence human personhood, as the model for all forms of embodiment, and this is at the root of many problems in the contemporary world. Human personhood is a relatively late development in evolutionary terms, and that being the case, the human, properly understood, brings with it everything that had been transpiring over billions of years previously. By setting the human over the rest of creation, we in effect have aborted the human from the womb of its origin and consequently reconstructed an image of the human that is largely at variance with the cosmic and planetary background. Because of this cultural and historical displacement, we often are left feeling alienated and estranged from our true selves.

In a previous work (O'Murchu 2000), I challenged the notion that the alienation that we often experience is evidence that we are not in tune with God and with God's plan for our lives. I believe that our alienation is about our distance from creation, not from God. We need to rediscover what it means to be at home in the creation that surrounds us. After that, I believe that our relationship with the divine becomes a great deal more natural and transparent.

What has proved to be particularly destructive is the isolation and arrogance that we have adopted as human creatures. Humans, we think, stand alone outside and above everything else. In fact, we tend to view and understand humans as lone creatures. We consider individuality as the basis for identity and uniqueness. And we tend to overidentify our individuality with the external parameters of our physical bodies.

Human personhood is viewed as synonymous with its embodied expression. Consequently, the quantifiable dimensions of the body — physicality, sociability, emotional capacity, intelligence, and everything we are capable of achieving in life — are considered to be more real than aspects such as intuition, imagination, spirituality, and psychic endowment, which tend to be dismissed as vague and nebulous. We judge personhood very much in terms of what we can perceive and measure.

Once again we are haunted by the culture of the machine, with its underlying principle that the whole equals the sum of the parts; consequently, there is no more to anything (in this case, personhood) than what can be objectively measured and quantified. But this is largely a sixteenth-century development, and therefore only of relatively recent origin. Treating the human body in relative isolation as an organism in its own right goes back a great deal further, probably to the dawn of patriarchy, some six to eight thousand years ago.

Humanistic psychology has helped us to reclaim a quite different understanding of human personhood, one that belongs to a much more ancient strand of our evolutionary story. Relationality is the core element, just as it is for all forms of embodiment in our cosmos. It proposes that the essential nature of personhood belongs to the relational matrix from which each person evolves in a unique way; hence this statement: "Who am I? I am at all times the sum of my relationships." It is my relationships that brought me into being and enabled me to grow and mature; it is my relationships that constitute the deepest layers of my meaning and purpose at every moment of my existence.

Just as my relationships develop and change, so does each one of us as creatures who grow and evolve in an evolutionary universe. Some relationships will be more enduring, providing me with security and the ability to trust the world of my experience; others will be more diverse and fluid, awakening in me the capacity to learn, adjust, and re-create new possibilities. And the relational matrix to which I radically belong is constituted not just by human beings, but also by a vast range of other creatures, biological and natural, as well as by the planet that I inhabit and the cosmos to which I belong. In the words of John O'Donohue (1997, 65), "The human person is a threshold where many infinities meet."

It is my relationships that define my uniqueness and confer my identity. I cannot but connect relationally. The mythic Robinson Crusoe, the epic hero on a lone island, is a figment of our imaginations. Most humans cannot tolerate such isolation for long. We are designed for relationality, not for isolation.

Human embodiment, therefore, is not primarily a physical structure, but rather, a relational matrix for which the physical body is a permeable container. The essential essence of the matrix is that of a fluid, amorphous energy reservoir, another version of the quantum vacuum in which energy flow is transformed into excitations and fluctuations that cohere in emotions, thoughts, aspirations, and actions. Just as the human cell may be described as memory with membrane wrapped around it, so all embodied forms consist primarily of creative energy that materializes in a vast range of psychic, behavioral, and creaturely interactions.

Issues such as immortality and life after death now take on a radically new meaning. The apparent demise of the body in death is much more about transformation than destruction. Several forms of destructibility across the spectrum of cosmic and planetary life serve as thresholds for new emergence, that is, new relational possibilities. The major contradiction to this truth is the forms of destruction initiated by human beings; usually these are dangerously and irreversibly devastating both to us and to nature at large. When we forget the relational context of our existence, it is then that we are most likely to behave in irrational and destructive ways.

Issues concerning the human soul and the origins of biological life also can be viewed in a new light. The relational matrix to which we all belong activates our being and becoming through media and channels that cannot be reduced to exact moments of beginning and ending. The identity of each one of us is best construed as a continuum, an energy flow emanating from the greater fullness (the quantum vacuum) and transformed into a greater complexity (e.g., the relational matrix). That seems to be the way of all reality, and why should it be different for us, who also are an integral dimension of the great cosmic web of life?

The Body as Eucharist

The major religions deal with the issue of the body with a mixture of awe and trepidation. Ambivalence toward the created order also is quite widespread. The religions seem to encourage a type of indifference to the created world, assuming it to be safe in God's care and therefore of no major concern to human beings. The religions seem to regard the human body as superior to every other created reality, including the planet and the cosmos; even animals get little attention from the great religions except for their use and value to human beings. By disassociating the human body from its earthly and cosmic ambience, the religious systems are in danger of misconstruing the meaning of the body at every level of existence, while also underestimating the interdependence on which all forms of embodiment thrive.

In the faith systems of several indigenous peoples we encounter rites of passage, many of which situate the body in the larger context of creation and celebrate both its creativity and potential destructibility in that context. And some of the richness of these ancient rituals has seeped into the mainstream religions. We encounter it particularly in what Christians call the Eucharist, the rite of passage around the sacred celebration of food, variants of which we find in every major religion with the notable exception of Islam.

The Christian Eucharist is a rite of thanksgiving, the enactment of a sacred meal in which the participants believe that God is present to them in a truly embodied way. A transformation of the bread and wine takes place, often referred to as a consecration, or in the Catholic church, an act of transubstantiation.

Our contemporary theology of the Eucharist has several interweaving strands. First, there is the notion of Eucharist as a sacred meal in which Jesus is truly present as he was at the Last Supper, at the postresurrection meals, and at the several other moments of table fellowship that we read about in the Gospels. Second, the Eucharist symbolically reenacts the sacrificial death of Jesus at Calvary; in other words, the salvation made possible in a unique way in the death of Jesus becomes available each time we celebrate the Eucharist. Third, the ongoing salvation of Jesus made available through the Eucharist has to be mediated through a specially ordained person, a priest. Fourth, the Eucharist has a special significance for the formation and nourishment of Christian community; each parish is considered to be a eucharistically based community. Finally, for many people, the Eucharist is a sacrament that they feel obliged to attend to fulfill their duty to God and to procure God's help for their ultimate salvation.

The Eucharist also is meant to be a celebration. This is a good place to begin if we are to make the sacrament more accessible to people. The people gather as a body, affirming their mutual relationality, which itself has been activated by the embodied God who they believe has called them together. In the word of life that is broken open the people give voice to their shared story of struggle and hope. The gifts that adorn the table — the bread and the wine — are the gifts from the body of the earth itself; in the offering and receiving of sacred food we encounter anew the closeness and reassurance of our embodied God. And this is no mere cozy huddle for comfort and affirmation; its primary goal is to empower the people to go forth and participate more dynamically in embodying new life at the heart of creation itself.

The Eucharist is a supreme moment of cosmic, planetary, spiritual, and human embodiment. All the elements meet as one in a ritual engagement from which nobody, for any reason, should be excluded. Radical inclusion is at the heart of every eucharistic enactment, subversively modeled by the Jesus of Christianity, who welcomed everybody to the eucharistic table, including those who were totally prohibited according to the religious rules of the day: tax collectors, prostitutes, and sinners.

There is a profound evolutionary connection with every eucharistic celebration, which often is overshadowed by the role assigned to the priest in the Christian tradition, and by his equivalent in other faith traditions. According to the official rite of celebration, the changing of the bread and wine in the Eucharist does not happen through the power of the priest, but by the invocation of the Holy Spirit — the "epiclesis." And eucharistic theology requires a second epiclesis to be enunciated after the consecration of the bread and wine, beseeching the creative Spirit to transform the hearts of all those who are about to receive the consecrated food so that it will nourish them to become more proactive in their commitment to justice and right relationships. That same Spirit-power which enlivens, animates, and sustains everything in creation is also the heart, source, and inspiration of every eucharistic celebration.

The Eucharist acclaims and celebrates unashamedly the radical relationality that characterizes every form of embodiment, from the cosmic to the personal. And it also pronounces that God is totally at home in the immediacy of that encounter; stated in the affirming assertion of Sallie McFague (1993): God loves bodies! God is present precisely in the moments of intense bodily encounter, whether in the erotic passion of sexual embrace, the intensity of human intimacy, or the inexpressible wonder of childbirth; God is also present in memorable moments of being at one with nature, the expressionless bond in which people of grief can be united, or the mysterious unity that brings people of every race, creed, and color around a eucharistic table. In all these situations and in many more besides, God is at home and radically present to us. Words may fail to say how, but the heart has its wise and unspeakable intuitions.

The Christian theologian may feel uneasy because I have moved into eucharistic reflections without first considering the embodied presence of Jesus as a historical person of the past and an incarnational influence in the present. From an evolutionary point of view, I suggest that the Eucharist needs a fresh articulation in the context of an alive creation that is forever responsive to God's allurement. Every Eucharist is a profound affirmation of the prodigiously nourishing God who wants to see nobody excluded from the table of cosmic abundance. God overflows and so does God's creation. In a word, that is what eucharistic celebration is meant to be about.

And nourishment is intimately linked with bodies. All bodies need sustaining nourishment and cannot thrive without it. God's body, the cosmic and terrestrial bodies, along with the vast range of embodied forms that populate creation, all meet at the eucharistic table. Yes, it is about sacrifice — in the literal sense of the word "sacrifice," which means "to make something sacred." In fact, what really happens is that we draw forth the innate sacredness of all things and unite as one body in proclaiming the prolific goodness of our nourishing and sustaining God.

•

It is time to outgrow...

the patriarchal alienation around the body that has haunted us for at least the past five thousand years. We have demonized the human body, focusing on instinctual drives and sinful tendencies; we have exploited the earth body, objectifying it as something that is there merely to be conquered and controlled; we have largely forgotten the cosmic womb from which we and every species evolves. Little wonder that we feel so lost and lonely!

It is time to embrace...

the essential embodied nature of all life — personal, planetary, and cosmic alike. All embodied forms coexist interdependently and are the primary vehicles for the manifestation and transmission of the creative power of Spirit. Embodiment is the primary realm in which creative transformation takes place, and we witness that in a unique way in eucharistic celebrations.

Chapter Nine

Humanity's Rightful Place

We have lost our sense of what it is to be human. We have lost our sense of where the deep roots of humanity lie, and hence we have lost touch with the source of our own efficacy as personal and moral agents.
— Danah Zohar

Our principal task as humans is to live in the universe. In a superficial sense of course everyone lives in the universe because we're all physically here. But in an intellectual or spiritual or emotional sense, most of us live elsewhere. This is indeed a strange situation, but it is a deformation that humans have succumbed to over and again throughout history.
— Brian Swimme

I F THE STORY we have been tracing was condensed into a book of a thousand pages, humanity would appear for the first time on page 994. In terms of the earth community, we are very recent visitors, and unfortunately we have not fared very well in integrating with the other creatures that were here before us and that now share the resources of the planet with us.

We have fared even worse when it comes to the cosmic community, the greater totality to which we all belong. But do we belong? And how could we ever hope to belong until we appropriate the sense of embodiment that we explored in the last chapter? How often do we think in terms of belonging? There are few indications that we give serious thought to this foundational aspect of our human existence.

Cosmologically, scientifically, and theologically we can rightly claim that in us, humans, creation becomes conscious of itself. We are not the only creatures through which this is happening, but our facilitation of this process certainly is unique and would seem to be more sophisticated than other creatures are capable of achieving. But we seem to be largely unaware — in fact, distinctively ignorant — of the cosmological, evolutionary task that we are meant to be about. We seem to have little understanding of what it entails and a shockingly inadequate sense of the interdependent relationships that make it all possible.

In cosmological terms, we are a very young species, one that is still finding its way about in the universe, still learning the language for the story that we are called upon to narrate. Even our role and purpose on planet earth are far from clear. Elisabet Sahtouris (1998) suggests that in evolutionary terms we are still at the adolescent stage, often acting like self-preoccupied, moody, belligerent teenagers. She goes on to suggest that evolution is pushing us into becoming young adults, and that our current crisis is that of a cosmic/planetary life stage. We are experiencing a major transitional disruption between carefree adolescence and the growing awareness that we are being called into a more adultlike responsible and creative way of being in the world.

Coming home to ourselves and to our true identity is one of the great evolutionary and spiritual challenges of our time. And perhaps the most authentic way to engage with that task is to embrace the story as it unfolds in current paleontological and anthropological research. Like the greater story of the cosmos and the planet, the human story is still very much in the process of discovery. But from what we do know, we can glean the broad outline, the unfolding overview, and the pattern that continues to unfold amid tremendous creativity, breakthrough, and enigma.

Our Beginnings

We humans are curious about the origins of our universe; we are even more fascinated with our own beginnings and the various stages through which we as a species have evolved. These are extensively documented by scholars such as Richard Leakey (1992), Steven Mithen (1996), Chris Stringer and Robin McKie (1996), and Ian Tattersall (2000), and will not be described in detail here. My concern is to highlight aspects of our great story that in themselves raise questions of ultimate meaning and hence become central considerations for an evolutionary theology in our time.

Currently, the oldest dating for a creature believed to be genuinely human, although externally resembling our ancestral primates in several ways, is that of 4.4 million years ago. That ancestor has been named by White, Suwa, and Asfaw (1994) as *Ardipithecus ramidus* (*ardipithecus* being the genus name, which means "ground ape," and *ramidus* meaning "root," to honor its Ethiopian source of discovery).

We are describing apelike creatures, possibly walking upright, thriving, it would seem, in an open tropical environment of eastern and southern Africa (having abandoned the forests to varying degrees), and in the evolutionary process of beginning to develop larger brains. Although apelike in appearance, sometime between four and five million years ago these creatures evolved unique human attributes. Indeed, the reputable scholar Richard Leakey believes that from the moment our ancient ancestors adopted bipedal locomotion, they were effectively human in the full sense of the word.

Our next major evolutionary step is that of *Homo erectus,* dated around two million years ago, a species popularly known for its ability to walk and run upright. But we now know, on much more reliable evidence, that humans walked some 3.6 million years ago.[11] What characterizes *Homo erectus* more than anything else is the sophisticated use of tools and the creative adaptations made through the innovative use of hand and mind. Already, two million years ago, we were behaving as creative, innovative creatures. A sense of being engaged with the surrounding creation is clearly in place, hence the appellation *Homo ergaster* (the human worker), commonly used in the relevant literature. Creativity is built into our very makeup. It is a vital clue not just to our survival, but also in the search for meaning that we have pursued for at least two million years.

Modern humans belong to the branch known as *Homo sapiens,* which first evolved about two hundred thousand years ago. Although African in origin, the first fossils were discovered on the Indonesian island of Java by Eugene Dubois toward the end of the nineteenth century. Some of the better fossils were discovered in the Olduvai Gorge in Tanzania and at the Koobi site in Kenya. What truly makes *Homo sapiens* a wise creature, as Tattersall (1998) intimates, is an innate ability to live convivially with the rest of creation. The wise human and the wise earth formed a subconscious alliance to work interactively. Each brings out the best in the other. Nature had been doing this for billions of years; humans then did it for thousands of years. In our time we seem to have lost this symbiotic relationship, and arguably we are the poorer for it.

All indications are that *Home sapiens* felt at home on the earth, a habitat to be exploited but not altered, and not there to be conquered and controlled, as agriculturalists subsequently would do. *Homo sapi-*

ens held creation with a sense of reverence and awe, the most poignant evidence being the creative adventure of Ice Age art, covering a time span of at least twenty thousand years.

Homo sapiens went through two main phases of development, the archaic and the modern, the former dated between 120,000 years ago until 40,000 years ago, and the latter associated with Upper Paleolithic culture, dated approximately from 40,000 B.C.E. until 10,000 B.C.E. The archaic phase usually is referred to as the age of the Neanderthals, who inhabited a wide area of eastern Europe and developed a culture characterized by cave dwellings, extensive use of fire, personal ornaments, and well-made stone implements — creative features that scholars tend to underestimate, as noted by Wong (2000).

Paleontologists have long argued about the origin and role of the Neanderthals in the evolutionary ladder. It generally has been assumed that they were the real ancestors of ancient *Homo sapiens,* who broke the link with the initial African origins and laid the foundations for modern Western humans. Scholars now are moving away from this view, suggesting instead a separate origin for the Neanderthals within Europe itself, and indicating that their rather abrupt ending is marked by the invasion of Europe by (African) *Homo sapiens* sometime between ten and twenty-five thousand years ago.

Western scholars tend to exalt the role of the Neanderthals and inadvertently use this information to enhance Western, European imperialism. As a result, the African origins of humanity often are sidetracked, even ignored. As I will indicate in the next chapter, the rehabilitation of our African origins is a theological and political appropriation of enormous significance. For far too long we have undermined or ignored our African heritage.

The Neanderthals have their place in our evolutionary narrative, and while they do enhance our development as a species, their contribution is relatively modest compared to other aspects reviewed in this book. We have exaggerated the Neanderthal contribution because it endorsed Western self-interests. The time is ripe not just for a rebalancing, but also for a reclaiming of the bigger story. Theologically, the time has come for honoring what the creative Spirit of God has been doing in and through our story, rather than focusing more explicitly on those aspects that feed into our human urge for imperial control.

Human origins continue to be a field of intense and intriguing study aided particularly by modern scanning devices and more ready access to the growing body of genetic biotechnology. From the information at hand one detects an enduring sense of unity amid great diversity. Continuity features strongly in the human chain, whether we trace it back to the original *Homo erectus* or to the *Homo sapiens* species of two hundred thousand years ago. Biologically, and not just culturally, we very much belong to one family, characterized by great age and an intriguing story of cultural exploration.[12]

And ours is a story not just about survival. In fact, we seem to thrive in those conditions in which survival is precarious and uncertain. Time and again we have adjusted to changing weather patterns, social dislocation, threatening environments, and exploration of vastly new experiences. Somehow, it cannot be reduced to the survival of the fittest, because even the "fittest" also took it on the chin at times. The will to live goes much deeper than that precisely because it is also a will to meaning characterized by a sense of purpose that transcends some of our best-known theories and outwits the pessimistic views upheld by a number of evolutionary theorists.

Creativity and the Evolution of Language

Humanity's story is tainted and distorted. The emphasis on our flawed nature, our fallen condition, and our primitive behaviors casts a gloomy shadow over an enterprise that for most of its evolutionary trajectory evidences some incredible ingenuity and breakthroughs. We humans have survived harsh external conditions as well as several internal upheavals. The will to meaning and our capacity for innovation and creativity have seen us over many an evolutionary hurdle. The sadness of our time now is that we have largely lost touch with this innate creative potential.

The development of spoken language, some one hundred thousand years ago, is only one of several creative breakthroughs that characterize our human story. This has been the subject of intense research, much of which has taken quite a new sense of direction in recent times. For a long time, scholars have held the view that human beings, unable to speak, were deprived of both imagination and creativity. In other words, it was language itself that released within us the capacity to be creative and symbolic. Many scholars consider our species, prior to the invention of language, to have been basically nonhuman.

Some recent studies, acknowledging our potential for creativity dating back several thousand, perhaps even a few million, years, challenge the prevailing view. Long before language ever evolved in its contemporary form, we humans communicated with each other, with our universe, and with the greater life-force in a nonverbal fashion that had its own deep sense of connectedness and the capacity to liberate a sense of meaning and purpose.[13]

Darwin claims that language first evolved as song, and then as speech. Subsequent to Darwin, the discoveries of Dax (1836), Broca (1861), and Wernicke (1874) laid the foundations for our modern theories of neurophysiological structure and provided the first opportunity to investigate the underlying biological structure of language.

Donald (1991, 16–17) suggests three transitions in the unfolding of human language:

1. From episodic to mimetic culture, culminating in successful tool making and in socially coordinated activities such as hunting, maintaining a seasonal home base, and using fire. Although verbal language was not used at this stage, real human communication took place.

2. From mimetic to mythic culture, culminating in the emergence of speech and language. In Donald's words, "Mythic culture tended rapidly toward the integration of knowledge. The scattered, concrete repertoire of mimetic culture came under the governance of integrative myth. The importance of myth is that it signaled the first attempts at symbolic models of the human universe and the first attempts at coherent historical reconstruction of the past" (p. 267).

3. From external symbolic storage to theoretic culture, leading to the development of the earliest alphabets, grammar, structure, logic, rationality, writing, and electronic communication, and leading eventually to what Donald calls "visuographic invention and the resulting growth of external symbolic memory media." (For an alternative view of this third stage, see Shlain 1998.)

In conclusion, Donald (1991, 2–3) writes, "The modern human mind evolved from the primate mind through a series of major adaptations, each of which led to the emergence of a new representational system. Each successive new representational system has remained intact within our current mental architecture, so that the modern mind is a mosaic structure of cognitive vestiges from earlier stages of human emergence."

Human language is a great deal more than a "representational system," whether viewed as an adaptation of animal forms or as some unique emergence from within the human species itself. In evolutionary terms, language itself seems to have been evolving from within creation at large. Every sound of nature anticipates the sounds that humans eventually make through their spoken words, and this in itself does not suggest that our speech is the final outcome of nature's desire for self-expression. The great story of evolution is forever inventing new ways to tell the story that underpins all other stories. Human language is one such outcome.

David Abram (1996) provides one of the most perceptive and creative outlines of this development. Put simply, his argument goes like this. For millions, if not billions, of years, the universe exudes a repertoire of sounds: the swishing of wind flow, the rustling echoes in foliage, the crushing echo of sea waves, the gurgling of rivers and streams, the explosive bang of thunder, the purring and bellowing of animals, the chime of bird song. As a human species, we have assimilated those sounds over the millions of years of our evolution, until eventually the assimilation reached what we might call a critical threshold, and we ourselves breathed forth unique sounds, at first various attempts at protolanguage and eventually verbal speech itself.

According to Abram, the oldest known alphabet (of the Hebrew language) in its original form contained no vowels. Consonants were used in conjunction with the air we breathe. Subsequently, the role played by breathing was replaced by the invention of vowels, but initially our ability to communicate with one another emerged as a type of symbiotic relationship with our capacity to respirate. Our speech needed the oxygen of the universe to be truly comprehensible.

Abram goes on to suggest that the transition to written form would have followed a similar pattern, again with nature providing the original inspirational forms. Humans for thousands of years would have observed the various designs and patterns in the world around them. The rich symbols of nature, full of fractal elegance, in time evoked in the human spirit a desire and a need to sketch, to draw, and eventually to write things down. We learned to script our experience because the world around us encouraged us to do so.

Contrary to the commonly held view that we became intelligent and capable of symbolic expression only after the development of spoken language, a distinctive switch in emphasis is emerging in our time. It is expressed most clearly in Deacon (1997), who postulates that language is a highly sophisticated symbolic system that could have been developed only by a species that itself had a profoundly integrated sense of symbolic endeavor. Prior to language, we were not a barbaric, primitive species; on the contrary, we had been for thousands of years a species transparent to mystery and capable of symbolic and spiritual engagement.

A Spiritualized Species

Our current understanding of language acquisition, with its complex symbolic repertoire, invites us to reappraise the spiritual dimension of human evolution. The capacity to engage with life at a symbolic level automatically opens the windows of perception and feeling, shifting us into transcendent territory or what Rudolf Otto called the "numinous." We begin to think and talk about questions of meaning and issues of ultimacy. We aspire to higher ideals and seek to link with that "something beyond" that impinges upon our daily reality. This quality of engagement with life we normally describe as "spirituality," a topic that has gained a new popularity in our time (see Zohar and Marshall 2000).

In previous works (O'Murchu 1997b; 2000), I explored and countered the widely accepted view that spirituality in human life is impossible without religious belief. In the past, the dominant view claimed that one had to follow a religion before one could be considered spiritual in any true sense. Formal religion as we know it today is about five thousand years old, dating its origins from the rise of Hinduism in the third millennium B.C.E. Spirituality, on the other hand, has very ancient roots in our evolutionary story.

When our prehistoric ancestors gathered around the fire some six hundred thousand years ago, they already were engaging in spiritual behavior. Fire symbolized light, energy, and warmth. It forged connections with the energy that characterized the creation around them. It provoked questions — preverbal, at that stage — about the meaning of life. The circular formation around the fire is likely to have led to dance movement. Dance is believed to be the most ancient form of religious ritual known to humankind. We danced our prayer and worship for thousands of years into our deep ancient past.

It is impossible to suggest when we humans moved from a subconscious to a conscious understanding of what we are about. Undoubtedly, it was a progressive unfolding, but it may also have been characterized by those sudden upsurges that occur frequently in the evolutionary story. In spiritual terms, such a leap may have happened around seventy thousand (some say one hundred thousand) years ago, when we buried our dead with what seems to have been a conscious and deliberate set of customs and rituals. An understanding of a governing life-force toward whom the dead were journeying seems to have been widely held. Moreover, humans felt that they could influence this divine life-force through their rites and rituals.

Another quantum leap of spiritual maturation seems to have accompanied, and may have contributed to, the great artistic explosion of Paleolithic times (40,000–10,000 B.C.E.). Scholars are deeply divided on how to interpret these cave drawings, with the various emblems and statuettes that have been discovered. The suggestion that humans across the populated world of the day worshiped a goddess figure for much of this era has generated an even more heated debate in academic circles (see the overview in O'Murchu 2000). Whatever the prevailing ideas about God were, this seems to have been an epoch in which humans lived in close harmony with their surrounding environment, and the evidence suggests that the close connection with nature contributed to the growing spiritual maturation of our species at that time.

Creativity abounded and manifested itself in several innovative artifacts, using the natural resources of the surrounding environment. Not surprisingly, therefore, humans came to a new appreciation of the earth's fecundity and fertility, leading to the birth of the agricultural revolution about ten thousand years ago. Cultivation of the land and exploitation of its immense resourcefulness brought human ingenuity and labor to new heights of engagement and expertise. There is growing evidence to suggest that women were the pioneering figures of this new development (see Eisenberg 1998; Eisler 1987), and their efforts may have been enhanced by the conviction that the earth itself was the embodied presence of the Great Goddess.

Meanwhile, an alternative wave of consciousness was evolving, the complex and unprecedented nature of which few understand even to this day. The land became subject to male domination and control. Fertility was streamlined and its feminine nurturance was subverted. Goddesses were expelled and replaced by warrior sky gods.

Steven Mithen (1996, 217ff.) attributes the rise of agriculture to two main factors: (1) sudden and dramatic changes in climate, and (2) a shift in population intensity requiring new food sources. A rather sudden rise in human population often is postulated as the primary motivation for a more proactive male role; adverse weather conditions may also have played a significant role. Whatever the precise reasons were, male supremacy quickly came to the fore, assuming modes of expression around power and control. To counteract the adverse weather conditions and procure extra food for the expanding population, it appears that the new male caste aggressively exploited the land's productive potential. This led to the acquisition and control of land, tribal rivalries, and power struggles that are all too familiar even in our own time.

Land became an object for human use and exploitation. It also became the subject for greedy acquisition. In a short time, the male warriors fought over sections of land and resolved their disagreements by setting up specific divisions and boundaries; the foundations were laid for what later became the nation-state, and warfare was developed so that states could defend and protect their respective territories.[14]

Most disturbing of all, the conquering heroes invoked the gods from on high to bless their efforts to set the world in order and salvage creation from the dangerous erotic energies of feminine power and female leaders. Inflated by their own self-aggrandizement, the power-hungry males set out to conquer and control even the gods themselves. Thus, formal religion came into being, the last ingenious stroke of the masculine will to power.

Spirituality had been subverted but not eroded. The power of the goddess had been subdued but not eliminated (see Christ 1997). The new sense of power and patronage, popularly named as "patriarchy," was to reign supreme for some ten thousand years. There are several indications in our time that it is breaking down and as a sociopolitical system is no longer capable of serving the best interests of either humanity or creation. It is against this background that we foresee a decline in formal religion and a renewed search for spiritual meaning in this time of major transition.

The Triumph and Tragedy of Civilization

Homo sapiens is a clever but not always wise species. Much of the time we get it right, but sometimes we get it drastically wrong. And occasionally, when we think we are on course, it is precisely then that we are seriously missing the mark, which, interestingly, is how the concept of sin is described in the Christian Gospels. Such has been our plight for the past ten thousand years — an era lauded as being the age of civilization, when we gradually abandoned the barbarity of our ancient past and came to terms with this strange world we now inhabit.

The development of agriculture is a pertinent example. Prior to that time, we were predominantly a hunter-gatherer species, not ruthless and barbaric, as is often intimated, but cognizant and respectful of the earth's ability to sustain and nourish us. With the onset of agriculture, human health deteriorated on several fronts. According to Cohen and Armelagos (1984), the onset of agriculture brought with it a surge of infections, a decline in the overall quality of nutrition, and a reduction in the average length of life.

Agriculture set the stage for a new relationship with creation. For much of the time it was neither benign nor beneficial. The power to conquer and control became the supreme value. And with the building of the first cities, and the simultaneous skill of writing, initially developed in the Sumerian culture of the Tigris-Euphrates Valley, humankind felt a sense of control over nature that it had never previously known. That high point in human evolution we subsequently proclaimed to be the dawn of modern civilization. Scholars often allude to it as "the rise of modern civilization" or "the beginnings of civilization."

And with that declaration we dismiss and even demonize everything that went before. The elegance of our African emergence, the innovative sleight of hand uniquely characteristic of *Homo ergaster,* the awesome discovery of fire and the spiritual awakening hailed by *Homo sapiens,* the unprecedented artistic upsurge of Paleolithic times — all these and so much more are denounced as primitive, barbaric, uncivilized, prelogical, and pagan. Even to this day we consider the rise of civilization to be a development of the past five thousand years. This arbitrary date is not so much about unique breakthroughs in our evolutionary story as about the human will to power absorbed in its own narrow vision.

Ironically, it is at the height of our so-called civilized status that we became a distinctly barbaric species. Why? Largely because we set ourselves up as the ones who could conquer and control creation, and in that process we began to rupture the womb from which all life is begotten. Not surprisingly, therefore, we sought to subvert, even eliminate, everything to do with the worship of the goddess. The tragic consequences are haunting us today, and faced with this demise, we are a species often overwhelmed with a debilitating sense of fear and alienation.

Our so-called civilized world has developed several outlets to vent our anger, fear, and sense of estrangement: marketing, consumerism, competitive sport, competitive education, drugs, pornography, evangelical religiosity. They help to keep us sane in our madness. Typically, they soothe our inner pain and our outer alienation, but they never will help to identify or resolve the fundamental problem.

At root, our angst is not about our humanness; it is about the deprivation that ensues when we cut ourselves off from the womb of universal life. We are so anesthetized from our deep, ancient story that effectively we do not know anymore who we are or what we are meant to be about in the world. In the words of Swimme (1996, 45), "What is needed is a transformation from the form of the humanity of today into forms of humanity congruent with the ways of the universe."

For most of our 4.4 million years on earth we did not experience creation as strange and alien. Nor is there any substantial evidence to show that we felt a need to conquer and control the whole thing. The symbiotic relationship, imprinted in our genes and deep in our individual and collective psyches, pushed us consistently toward interrelatedness and interdependence with our surrounding world. That has been the primary experience for most of our time on earth; that has been the major part of our evolutionary story.

Civilization involves a huge cover-up propagated by those seeking power for themselves. And it is from this addiction to power that the worst violence erupts in our world. Raymond Dart, describing many of his skull finds in southern Africa, suggested that in our protohuman, apelike condition we were a predatory species endowed with a very violent streak. Many scholars support the notion that we are innately a violent species and have been for time immemorial. I contend, however, that here we are dealing with projection rather than verified fact.

Initially, scholars took Dart at his word. His observations agreed with the long-held view that we were indeed a species prone to violence. Eventually, the evidence was challenged, and new research revealed that the punctured skull marks were those of other attacking birds and animals. We have long assumed that the earliest hominoids were hunters who killed at random and even slaughtered their own species in defense of territory or to resolve conflict. We now know that in many cases humans were the hunted (by animals) rather than the hunters, and the violence frequently attributed to humans actually arose from vulnerable exposure to other attacking creatures. One wonders how many more conventional ideas need fresh exploration.

Humans and the Evolution of Consciousness

Our evolutionary story as a human species needs to be retold in a whole new light. Our conventional wisdom is a muddle of confused perceptions. A fundamental flaw is engendered by the way we humans set ourselves above and apart from the rest of creation. We place so much emphasis on our difference that the links to the bigger story become tenuous and unable to sustain us meaningfully in our collective growth and development. We have a great deal to retrieve, to re-member, and to make whole once more.

The disconnected links impoverish us in our earthiness, in our sense of embodiment, and in our capacity to relate. But most serious of all, they undermine our psychic connections with the wisdom that imbues creation's vitality. In the emerging awareness of our time, that wisdom often is described as "consciousness." In one sense, that may well be the dimension of our self-identity that has been most neglected. Without it, our capacity to grow into that fuller sense of our humanity that evolution requires of us will be seriously jeopardized. How we engage, understand, and appropriate this consciousness is the major topic of consideration in the next and final section of this book.

Meanwhile, I conclude with these reflections on the E-mergence of our own species:

•

It is time to outgrow...

the stifling and self-limiting understanding that we have imposed upon our evolutionary story whereby we highlight our weaknesses and deficiencies in the never-ending battle with the forces of nature, which we also construe to be fundamentally flawed with imperfection and sin.

It is time to embrace...

our entire evolutionary story of over four million years, and to take seriously the explosive and at times paradoxical creativity of the divine at every moment of that evolving process. We are an interdependent species within an interdependent universe, endowed uniquely for the release of self-conscious awareness throughout the entire spectrum of the divine-human creative process.

Chapter Ten

Incarnation: African Style

A map of our past is the pathfinder to our destiny. Thus if we misread the map of our past or consult an incorrect map we will misdirect our efforts in shaping our future. —Nokuzola Mndende

It is impossible, in the African mind, to separate the salvation of human beings from that of the universe.... The Christ is viewed as clothed in the whole cosmos in the act of incarnation.
—Lisa Isherwood

NOBODY CAN DOUBT any longer where our species was born. Africa is the indisputable cradle of humanity.* Africa is where the human story begins, and when Africans tell stories about the ancestors, they touch very deep chords, a type of primal resonance that is very ancient indeed. And the ancestors that inhabited the African continent for possibly four million years before dispersion to other parts of the planet were already a highly creative species. We have to remove many layers of prejudice and racism before we can come to truly appreciate the elegance and creativity of our evolutionary origins.

Our African Origins

There is virtually universal acceptance among paleontologists and anthropologists that Africa is where human evolution began and that it is also the location in which humans survived and thrived for most of their time on earth. Two schools of thought have prevailed. The first, known as the multiregional approach, claims that the initial emergence

---

*In recent years I have worked with African people in the east, west, and south of Africa. The impact of Western oppression is still strongly felt among African peoples, but in more recent times Africans also feel that they have been abandoned by the West; one is left with a sense that they feel not just abandoned but betrayed. It seems to me that the betrayal is not just political and economic, but also historical and cultural. I hope that the present chapter, in however small a way, addresses that reality. Africa is so central to our evolutionary story as a human species that it is inconceivable that we could ever forget or abandon it.

out of Africa happened about two million years ago; thereafter, the original Africans became Inuits, Aborigines, Neanderthals, and so on. In the process, they lost their sense of being African and took on other cultural identities, meanwhile evolving into one predominant species known as *Homo sapiens*.

The second dominant approach claims that all human evolution, up to and including the *Homo sapiens* stage, happened in Africa, and that humans emerged from Africa for the first time only about ninety thousand years ago. Initially they spread into southern Asia (about sixty thousand years ago), then into Europe (some forty thousand years ago), and eventually down through the Americas (from Asia). If this theory is correct, then the widely held assumption that the Neanderthals (who initially evolved in Europe some 150,000 years ago) are the ancestors of modern humans is false; rather, they are a type of evolutionary cousin whose extinction was marked by the arrival of *Homo sapiens* in Europe some forty to fifty thousand years ago.

The second approach, while not conclusive (see Wong 1999), wins the approval of most scholars today. Whichever version is correct, what is being highlighted in both theories is the central role that Africa plays in our evolutionary story. Africa, and all it stands for, is imprinted in the inner soul of every human being. Africa is the cradle of the human species. Culturally and spiritually, we can never hope to reclaim our true identity until we reappropriate our African origins and the consciousness that unfolds with it.

And that consciousness is not just about evolutionary beginnings. Africa is where we first walked upright; the ancient footsteps are still visible in Tanzania (see Agnew and Demas 1998). Africa is where we first used our hands and minds to fashion tools and create ancient art. It is in Africa that we first lifted our hearts and minds to the embracing sense of divine Spirit. It is in Africa that we discovered fire, speech, and spirituality. Africa is a museum of the human spirit, a treasury of all that is sacred and dear to the human heart.

Incarnation Reassessed

It all began to happen about 4.4 million years ago. A new evolutionary impetus reached another critical threshold, and humans joined the diverse creaturely community. We were, and continue to be, very similar to the other higher mammals. And yet we were unique. We had a capacity to think and reflect, and to think about the fact that we could think, in a manner that was different from other creatures. Whether we had that capacity from the very beginning is, in a sense, irrelevant; it was there in nascent form, and it may have been appropriated in a more conscious way than we often assume.

And what was the divine power doing at that time? Was the creative Spirit at work in this evolutionary breakthrough, and if so, what does it tell us about the divine? Religious believers of all creeds claim that God has been fully at work in creation from the very beginning and is uniquely present at each evolutionary stage. Contrary to so many fundamentalist religious traditions, the evolutionary sciences point more to a God at work within the evolving process than to one who stands outside, guiding it all from some type of a distant royal throne.

So, if the divine energy is cocreatively involved in full endorsement of what is evolving from 4.4 million years ago, then this is where we encounter incarnation for the first time. In its basic sense, incarnation means God coming in the flesh of humanity, fully entering into that embodied condition, blessing and affirming all that is happening to it, and using it thenceforth as a means for bearing witness to the presence of the divine in the world.

Everything that Christians claim was happening to our humanity in and through Jesus had started 4.4 million years ago. God was fully at work then. God was not withholding any divine power or creativity, keeping some in store until Jesus arrived.

In God's eyes there is nothing deficient, incomplete, or flawed about the creature that evolved in eastern and southern Africa 4.4 million years ago. That creature was not perfect, and never has been since then, but one gets the impression that that has not been a problem for God. Humans have made it a problem for themselves and project their unresolved anxiety onto God, postulating a creator who births imperfect, sinful creatures so that they may benefit in due course from this same creator rescuing them. Perhaps, we need to deepen our understanding of the doctrine of original sin to accommodate this bigger picture.

Because our limited, imperfect condition is a problem for us, we assume that it should also be a problem for God. However, just as God does not have a fundamental problem with the shortcomings and paradoxes of creation at large (see chapter 6), neither is there a problem for God around "the human condition." What is problematic for us humans is the very material that the divine can use for all sorts of creative transformations. If we humans were perfect, then the divine creativity would be thwarted.

From the perspective of evolutionary theology, we must honor what God is about in the evolutionary process. We must heed and honor the divine unfolding at every stage and phase of the story. Otherwise, we are in danger not merely of undermining the meaning of evolution itself, but also of construing God according to the idolatrous projections of our own making. In our desire to make God the ultimate explanation of everything that exists, we proffer a solution that is more about our human longings than about the creative and mysterious potential of the divine. And that also inhibits our ability to see God at work across the aeons of evolution; we end up restricting the divine creativity to the realm of formal religion, a minuscule time span of five thousand years.

When we honor the evolutionary story, we encounter the big God at the heart of it all, but also the God of radical, intimate closeness, energizing, befriending, empowering, and affirming us at every stage of the way, truly the image of the birthing and nurturing mother. The meaning of the divine comes alive in a whole new way when we honor what the divine has been about, and still is, in every moment of evolutionary grandeur.

What, then, happens to Jesus (and, we could add, to the Buddha, Krishna, and all the other incarnational figures that populate world religions)? In that very question one hears echoes of the human need to protect Jesus against evolutionary insight, and I suspect that that fear is not of God. It is a human fear and in itself betrays something of the anthropocentric preoccupations that we carry around in religious belief and the convictions that are rooted in formal religions. Hampson (1996) and Heyward (1999) make some astute observations on this topic.

Christianity and the other formal religions that prevail today all evolved within a few thousand years of each other, indicating something of a major shift in spiritual consciousness. Could it be that what we are witnessing here is a divine affirmation of all that humanity had achieved throughout the previous four million years of evolutionary growth and development? Could it be that Jesus (from the Christian point of view) is a representative of humanity at a new evolutionary threshold, affirming humans in what they have attained over time and embodying in his own life and ministry guidelines for the next evolutionary stage?

Consequently, the Christian understanding of incarnation is not just about a coming of God in the flesh of humanity, but also about the transformation of our biological condition into one more transparent to the power of spirit. This is a recurring theme in the Gospel of John: the Jesus who is about to depart so that a new blossoming of the Spirit can happen (see John 16:7). Does the incarnate Jesus represent humanity at the height of its biological evolution, celebrating and affirming all that has transpired through the human species over the 4.4 million years and now inaugurating a new evolutionary wave in which the power of spirit rather than matter will come to the fore?

This is a significantly different way to understand the life and ministry of Jesus, but one that is quite congruent with the vision of the kingdom of God proclaimed by Jesus, especially in the Gospels of Mark, Matthew, and Luke. It does not deny the traditional understanding, but the focus shifts from the radical redemption wrought through the death of Jesus to the radical affirmation of life proclaimed in the vision of the kingdom. And this is not merely an affirmation of human life, but indeed of everything that has awoken and enhanced life across the entire spectrum of our cosmic evolutionary story.

The Spirit of Africa

At this point, the reader may be wondering what all this has to do with Africa. The Africa we know today is a torn, tortured continent, brutally exploited by outsiders, especially from the West, and internally paralyzed by ethnic and tribal tensions. Africa, more than anywhere else on earth, bears the scars of "man's inhumanity to man." Its long and profound history, especially its human evolutionary story, has largely been disowned, and its ancient spiritual inheritance condemned as pagan and primitive. Today, Africa, more than any other part of the planet, exemplifies the broken, battered body of Christ and of humanity. And it is not God, but humanity itself, that needs to render an account for such mindless self-torture.

The suffering that we have imposed and continue to perpetrate has taken a cruel toll on the soil of Africa, the rituals of Africa, and the relational matrix of the African people. By reviewing these three aspects — the soil, the rituals, and the relational matrix — we begin to see how integral the African experience is to our ongoing growth and evolution as an E-merging species. We begin to realize the healing that needs to take place, the reconciliation that needs to be activated, and the new socioeconomic policies that need to be put in place not just for the benefit of Africa, but also for the well-being of the entire planet.

The Soil. Inhabiting the open spaces characterizes the African people over many millennia. Although today we find massive urban conglomerates in Africa as elsewhere in the world, the African people have lived in close harmony with the soil of the earth. Long before the European-based agricultural revolution, Africans had explored the land and its resourcefulness. The seasonal rhythm of sowing and reaping; the elemental giftedness of wind, rain, and moisture; the fruitfulness of trees, plants, and shrubs; the healing properties of soil and plant — all these have long dominated the African consciousness.

Africans know their soil. They know it intimately and they love it. And their sense of interconnectedness with the soil is what has long endeared them to planet earth. Often, in the face of adverse weather conditions, Africans have coped with remarkable ingenuity, arguably with greater success and resilience than under the impact of Western development, which often is gauged to the needs of Western consumerism rather than the good of the African people.

The soil of Africa is saturated in sacred history while at the same time being rich in mineral resources. It is worth treating these two images simultaneously. In both cases, the exploration (and exploitation) is largely done by Westerners. Paleontologists and ethnologists have had a heyday in Africa, especially in Kenya, Ethiopia, Tanzania, and South Africa. Much of this information about our historical past, extrapolated from some of the poorest countries in the world, comprises a richness almost beyond value. And generally speaking, scholars have shared their discoveries generously, placing their insights at the service of those pursuing deeper intellectual, cultural, and spiritual understanding of our ancient story.

Sadly, this is not the case with the mineral wealth of Africa. Here we witness some barbaric exploitation whereby the mineral resources of several African nations are almost totally under the control of Western corporations. This is one of the great global scandals of our time. If African people had full recourse to their own mineral wealth, not only would they be free from the awful burden of international debt, but also they would have the wealth to feed and educate themselves on par with Western nations.

The dark cloud of imperialism still haunts Africa. The land and natural resources have been seized, vandalized, and desecrated. And while the political imperialists have departed, the economic headhunters remain. Meanwhile, the land of Africa has been carved into nation-states (which many contemporary Africans cherish over and above their common African identity), and the African people themselves, mesmerized by Western patriarchy, divide and alienate further into some ferocious tribal and ethnic rivalries. Our ancient ancestors who walked and roamed the one earth — the one Africa — feel alienation deep in their very souls. If those who protect our birthright are so alienated, it is inevitable that the rest of the human family also will be beleaguered and bewildered.

The Rituals. Africa is renowned for its rites of passage. Every major life experience and several social and seasonal events are celebrated with elaborate ritual, especially with dance, movement, and esoteric behavior. Some of these rituals are considered to be very ancient, often passed on from one generation to the next. Many are religious in nature, but most have been dismissed (by Western missionaries) as archaic and pagan.

How did Africans develop their sense of ritual? Who taught it to them? Nobody taught it to them. They developed it themselves. In other words, *we* developed ritual ourselves, because deep down we are creatures of symbol, imagination, and spirit. We cannot survive meaningfully without ritual and ritualistic celebration. And we have both the capacity and the intuitive wisdom to develop and explore ritualistic behavior, variously described in other cultures as rites of passage or as sacraments.

When the missionary Vincent J. Donovan (1989) worked among the Masai people of eastern Africa, he detected in their native rituals parallels for all the Catholic sacraments. In other words, the sacraments were there before he and his fellow missionaries ever arrived in Africa. I suggest that they have been there for a very long time.

The notion of sacrament did not begin with the Christian church, any more than the notion of meditation began with the great Eastern religions. African people have known sacramentality for thousands of years, long before formal religion every came to be. And they have pondered and discussed the mysteries and paradoxes of life long before the Vedas, the Bible, and the Koran were written. And for aeons before priesthoods were developed, shamans of both genders facilitated ritualistic experiences.

Not everything in African ritual is necessarily wholesome and good. We are dealing with some powerful energies in which light and darkness always prevail. Elements of sacrifice and bloodletting often reach preposterous proportions; male domination and control of rites of passage often victimize and oppress women; fear and ignorance rather than liberation for life often ensue. (These same criticisms can be made of many Western religious practices.) What I am trying to highlight is the deeper meaning, at both the human and cultural levels. In this regard, the people of Africa have a great deal to teach the rest of humanity.

The Relational Matrix. Africans refer to it as *ubuntu* (see Battle 1997; Sparks 1991). Westerners regard it as lack of differentiation, a type of cultural enmeshment from which developed people have been set free. At its extremes it is the difference between individualism and community consciousness.

For African people, *ubuntu* basically means that I am who I am because of the community I belong to. The phrase *umntu ngunmtu ngabantu* literally means "a person is a person through people." My identity is intertwined with the larger family to which I belong. But in the African context, that larger family includes the dead as well as the living. The dead do not "go to heaven"; they continue to live among the people as guardians of tradition and morality.

Africans have a strong devotion to the ancestors. It is a type of spiritual relationship with all who have gone before. How far back it stretches is not really relevant. Space rather than time is the key guideline — perhaps another version of the space-time continuum? The ancestors inhabit the sacred spaces of the home, the village, and the environment, and they belong to the traditions, customs, and rituals of the people. They are another expression of the relational matrix from which everybody and everything take identity and meaning.

The interconnectedness and relationality that characterize many new developments in modern physics and cosmology are endemic to the African psyche. Nothing makes sense in isolation. It is not in our separateness that we become our true selves, but in our interconnections. True selfhood always is relational.

So it is, too, with the power of Spirit as understood by the people of Africa. Spirit-power is immanent in everything, especially in the soil, the trees, the animals, and the people and their ancestors. Africans do not draw a hard-and-fast rule between good spirits and evil ones; intuitively they discern a bigger and more complex picture than that allowed by our Western dualisms. Whether the spirit's influence is for good or for evil depends on a complex range of interrelated factors. Many Western missionaries have never quite grasped the depth and complexity of this vision.

The spirituality of the African people is complex rather than primitive. It is complex precisely because the African psyche carries such a long and rich history and because that history is so enmeshed with the evolving nature of the landscape itself. It is not a matter of simplifying this inheritance, but of interpreting it in a more holistic and informed way. Western rationalism — and this includes the traditional proselytizing of Western missionaries — is unable to discern, never mind comprehend, the deep richness of this ancient wisdom. Indeed, the Western and Christian attempts to "convert" the African people are what is now beginning to haunt not just the African people, but the Western missionaries themselves.

The Suffering Face of Africa. Today, Africa, more than any other part of the planet, represents the woundedness of creation and the unnecessary suffering inflicted upon so many species. Because of poverty, malnutrition, and disease, millions die prematurely every year. Millions also perish because of tribal struggles and open warfare. Meanwhile, the struggle for survival, for basic meaning, for some reason to keep on living, extracts a higher price for African people than for probably anybody else on earth. In a word, Africa represents the open wound of a world torn to pieces by injustice and oppression.

As already indicated, external forces play a major role. Systemic injustice is more rampant in Africa than anywhere else in our world. Globalization is eating away the heart and soul of the African people, placating them with platitudes of little or no substance. But when people are down in the gutter, they collude with anything that gives a semblance of hope and a promise of a better future.

Capitalism is the other wound in the African psyche. In a continent deeply immersed in the values of relationality, the competitive spirit of the West never can and never will offer meaning or hope. And this is where the external oppression in many cases has become a form of internalized oppression. Here we encounter the dark shadow of the African people themselves, no more complex than that borne by humanity at large.

Africans look to the West for hope, prosperity, resources, and a future to believe in. All too quickly they hanker after and adopt the values of Western commercialism, the false alluring promises, and the frightening patriarchal power that goes with the lure of gain. And as Africans become educated and begin to climb proverbial ladders, whether in the commercial or the ecclesiastical world, the ferocious competitive spirit of the West seeps into their very souls. In a short time they become more authoritarian and dictatorial than their oppressors ever were.

The power-seeking male, so dominant in African culture and endemic to it according to Africans themselves, does not belong either naturally or spiritually to the African landscape. The power structure is not just a feature of tribal culture that goes back over several millennia. No, it belongs to the shadow side of the agricultural revolution, even though that revolution in its popularly understood sense allegedly did not reach Africa until relatively recent times. The external expression may not have reached the African continent, but the underlying consciousness did, and it continues to exert a powerful and deleterious influence to this day.

Contemporary Africa is a complex conglomerate of several tribes, languages, religions, and subcultures. It is ravaged by fragmentation to a degree that makes it difficult for many Africans to appropriate a collective identity as one people. Politically and economically, the seeds of that fragmentation were sown during colonial times; culturally, it has deeper roots in the seditious forces of patriarchal domination.

While much of this chapter is an articulation of what we need to reclaim around the groundedness of our being that Africa represents, we cannot hope to achieve that integration until we deal with the painful shadow of "man's inhumanity to man" that Africa illustrates with serrating brutality. Africa bears in a unique way the unresolved strains and tensions of suffering humanity and the agonizing earth. We project onto Africa and its peoples the issues that we do not like in ourselves, and we make Africa and its peoples the great evolutionary scapegoat of our time. Africa is like a mirror reflecting back to us how horrible we can be to our own species and to our earth.

The scapegoating is painfully illustrated in the violence that we project onto Africans and black people in general. Racism is just one aspect of this complex set of projections, but it is underpinned by a more complex and dangerous set of perceptions. We regard humans, and Africans in particular, as innately violent and aggressive. And we attribute this violent streak to our long primitive history, represented to this day in the tribal behaviors of African people in particular. Here we encounter several false assumptions that require attention, modification, and correction.

Violence Reassessed

The violence often considered endemic to the human species is another misguided notion based on a spurious interpretation of our evolutionary story. It reveals yet again a distinctive ignorance about our ancient past, which, while not being perfect, was a great deal more benign and creative than is commonly recognized. We exhibit a strange and frightening fascination with violence, but frequently we misconstrue both its existence and its meaning in our world. Currently, the research of the French philosopher René Girard (1979; 1986) is considered to provide one of the most enlightening analyses of this phenomenon.

Girard's anthropology seems to be heavily influenced by psychoanalytical theory. Allegedly, we humans are creatures of desire, and to satisfy our desires, we seek various objects, often (always?) pursuing what others also desire. We imitate others in their desiring, and Girard calls this "mimesis." A culture of competition ensues, which Girard calls "rivalry," and this inevitably leads to "conflict." In this understanding of human nature, violence is more fundamental than desire itself.

To resolve the tension of perpetual desire leading to violence, humans have learned to channel the violence through victimization or scapegoating. Psychologically, we project the violence onto one person or object, but effectively this will ensue in mocking the victim and ultimately in exterminating it. Consequently, humanity is condemned to a state of perpetual warfare, and many of the traditional rituals of the African people are considered to be ways of containing and channeling this destructive energy.

To resolve this dilemma, Girard postulates, humans have developed systems of sacrificial violence in the great mythological and religious traditions of the world. Through these rituals the ultimate destructibility of human violence can at least be contained, perhaps even resolved. For Girard, however — and this is his appeal to Christian scholars in particular — it is only in the Judeo-Christian religion that the nature and power of scapegoating are both exposed and subverted, with the Jesus of Christianity serving as a supreme, redemptive scapegoat for all humanity. (For further elucidation, see Bailie 1997.)

Despite the fact that many scholars accept and endorse this argument, I am unconvinced that it makes historical sense. Its basic premise, that humans always have been a violent species, flies in the face of substantial paleontological and anthropological evidence. More perturbing still, Girard and his followers seem to endorse the unquestioned and naive assumption that prior to the age of civilization (the past five thousand years), humans were barbaric and brutal in their essential nature, and now still exhibit these unruly tendencies, especially in African cultures.

Girard, it seems, goes along with the ancient myth of the scapegoat as a nonresistant, nonviolent martyr who exercised a healing function, bringing a cessation or reduction to the violence in society. This follows the line of argument that claims that it is essential that one person should die for the people, and in doing so will take upon himself (or herself) the wrath of God and the guilt of the people, appeasing God and once more setting the people right with the God of retributive justice. It also justifies the bizarre behavior of suicide bombers, who feature strongly in the recent terror tactics of some Islamic militants. It seems to me that Girard is heavily influenced by the hero archetype that largely belongs to the Middle Eastern culture of the three to five millennia before the Christian era. I am not aware of any substantial evidence for its existence before 10,000 B.C.E.

The notion of sacrifice is another cultural and religious concept that needs to be reviewed in a larger cultural context. For most of our time on earth, we humans felt no need to offer sacrifices to pacify angry, demanding gods. That concept largely, if not exclusively, belongs to the patriarchal era of postagricultural times, when the priestly caste first evolved, claiming unique access to the divine (which, it seems, everybody was able to access in Paleolithic times). They developed sacrificial rituals to pacify divine wrath while ingeniously protecting the ruling power of the priesthood (or the tribe) itself. Stories such as the call to Abraham to sacrifice his son Isaac epitomize the faith of the true believer. As Delaney (1998) highlights, what is at stake here is not the child's sacrifice, but Abraham's unquestioned obedience to the ruling God of patriarchal power.

It is our inability (or unwillingness) to name violence for what it really is that makes violence such a virulent force in the world today. Violence and patriarchal power are inextricably woven. The world's leading superpower, the United States, is also the world's leading investor in armaments and in military capabilities; little wonder that the United States itself became the target of extreme retaliation on September 11, 2001. And the next superpower likely to emerge, China, is following the exact same strategy. Formal religion has been used extensively to validate the oppression that requires violence as an "instrument for peace." The story of Abraham has parallels in every major religion; ironically, it is adopted much more blatantly in Islam (see Delaney 1998, 162–85) than in the Judeo-Christian tradition.

The myth of human violence — the propagation of the idea that we are innately a violent species — is precisely what makes violence such a difficult issue to confront in a creative and responsible way. And this is particularly so in Africa, which has witnessed such horrendous suffering in the closing decades of the twentieth century.

In this context, Africa is not so much a geographical place or a cultural sphere of the planet. It is something more akin to a powerful symbol of the collective unconscious of humanity itself. Foundationally, the violence is not about the violent things that we do to others, but rather, the violence that we do to ourselves precisely because we have betrayed and aborted our African origins as a human species.

Our coming home to who we really are in evolutionary terms is not merely a cultural, intellectual, and spiritual notion; it has deep ecological and environmental aspects as well. We are a species with a great story that we have largely abrogated; our roots in the soil of Africa are largely shriveled up, and the consequences are painfully visible in the bodies of the malnourished and starving millions in Africa today.

To engage meaningfully and responsibly with our world, we need to reclaim the exploratory playfulness with which we walked upon the earth some 3.6 million years ago. We did not always get it right, but indications are that we embraced our planet with a sense of grace and care that we have long since lost. And that leaves us very much an alienated and dysfunctional species in the world of our time.

Utopia Revisited

To many readers, the material of this chapter will seem romantic and far-fetched. Giving special attention to one sector of humanity and to one geographical area of the earth is not likely to elicit much credibility among modern scholars of any discipline. All the more so since the region in question, Africa, is so full of problems and generally not considered to be a major force either on the stage of world politics or in the considerations that preoccupy the scholars of Western academic institutions.

Others will view my meanderings as a type of "new age" nostalgia for long-lost traditions and for ancient roots. I often am accused of seeking and exalting a golden age in some far-fetched idyllic world of bygone days. The more perceptive reader perhaps will detect my utopian aspirations. The story with which we engage in the pages of this book is a utopian narrative. It has, despite all its flaws and contradictions, an illustrious past; it has even a more promising future.

Much of this illustrious past belongs in fact to Africa, to its culture, landscape, and peoples, dating right back to some 4.4 million years ago. That ancient narrative is imprinted in the heart and soul of every creature that ever lived on this planet. Yet we have subverted, ridiculed, and demonized that story. And in the process of doing so, we have alienated ourselves to a severe degree, and never can we hope to become whole and wholesome people again until we reclaim what we have so destructively undermined.

I wish to conclude these reflections with some timely insights from the scripture scholar Walter Brueggemann (1993). Brueggemann claims that we are a species suffering form a crippling sense of amnesia, what feminist scholars call "forced forgetfulness." In large measure we have forgotten who we are, and what we are meant to be about as citizens of planet earth. The patriarchal will to power, channeled into Western colonialism and validated by Western religion, has left us with a grossly distorted sense of ourselves and our world.

In a South African newspaper, *The Star* (December 14, 2000), Max Du Preez reviewed recent paleontological research on humankind's origins in eastern and southern Africa and posed urgent considerations for his own people:

> The place we call home is actually where all humankind comes from. How privileged we are. So, why is it that we don't appreciate it? Why is it that most of our people don't even know this remarkable history?... On a more spiritual level: knowledge of this remarkable story should make us even more proud of our region, and clear away any doubts about the beautiful dream of an African renaissance. In this sense the African renaissance would be a renaissance for all humanity.

The African people have largely forgotten their unique story. Some would argue that we Westerners have robbed them of it. But in forcing the people of Africa into cultural and historical amnesia, we also have dismembered our own cultural and spiritual inheritance. We have lost sight of the embracing universe to which we belong, the planet that nourishes and sustains us, and the African context that informs our evolution and growth for over four million years. By ignoring the larger context to which we belong and forgetting our past, we have ended up moored to an insular existence of isolation and alienation.

Consequently, claims Brueggemann, we tend to treat everything as a commodity, an object to be conquered, controlled, and used to our consumerist advantage. We treat the universe as a mechanized object, and planet earth as something to be exploited and used for selfish gain. In our consumerist society everything is there to be consumed and exploited for financial profit; and when things no longer are useful, we discard them.

Today, the people of Africa often feel abandoned and discarded by the rest of humanity. Africa is not perceived as a land that carries the depth and greatness of our human story. No, it is seen as a commodity to be exploited to propagate Western imperial values, and when it no longer serves those needs, we tend to abandon and forget about it.[15]

So, the amnesia breeds a climate of commoditization, and both lead into what Brueggemann describes as a climate of despair. Hopelessness overwhelms us. We see it in the eyes and faces of African people — the women struggling to eke out some last vestige of nourishment from undernourished soil, the young men in droves sitting at the roadside waiting for somebody to offer them work, the health workers over-whelmed by the ravaging impact of HIV/AIDS. In the despair of the African people we see our own despair, which in fact is a deep form of self-inflicted alienation caused by our forgetfulness and exploitative attitudes toward the fruits of creation.

Brueggemann claims that there is a way out and a way forward, and it begins with the enormous task of "re-membering." He deliberately spells the word in hyphenated form to highlight the double task of reclaiming the deep memory of our evolutionary story, and in that process, putting back together again that which we have fragmented and destroyed, namely, the interconnected sense of universal reality, the one earth, now carved up into nation-states, warring factions, ethnic tensions, and gross exploitation of the resources of wealth and food.

When we engage with the creative re-membering, we quickly discover that relationality (Brueggemann uses the biblical word "cove-nant") underpins all reality, and this requires of us a whole new way of engaging with life at every level. Commoditization means treating everything in isolation; ultimately, nothing has value except in terms of its usefulness to those who conquer and control. Operating from the basis of relationships requires a totally different outlook and ap-proach, one that in fact is much more endemic to our species when we are more authentically grounded in our evolutionary E-mergence.

And when we learn to relate and to see everything in the context of relationship, then, says Brueggemann, we rediscover an enduring sense of hope. This is the only utopia worth striving for, because it is the only one that endures. And it is a utopia to which we are all entitled. As indicated in previous chapters, the goal of the evolutionary process itself unfolds amidst the horizons of promise that know no limits. As cocreative creatures engaging with our cocreative God, we are forever stretching the horizons of possibility. That is what we are meant to be about; that is what we were about for the four million years of our African existence. Indeed, were it not for that resilient sense of hope, often in the face of utter hopelessness, the African people long ago would have succumbed to debilitating nihilism.

Re-membering, relating, hoping — these are the dynamics with which we revitalize our true story as an evolutionary species. These words embrace our incarnational sacredness, first encountered and experienced in the land of Africa. These words convey that enduring spiritual vision that we have known in our being for those long millennia before the forces of Western "civilization" contaminated and corrupted our deeper truth as a human species. It is time for homecoming: to re-member, relate, and hope once more.

•

It is time to outgrow...

the crippling and stultifying dominance of Western imperialism that attributes ultimate truth to the rational, religiously validated rule of power, a force that has minimalized the unique richness of other times and cultures, particularly the African context, to which so much of our evolutionary and Christian story belongs in a unique way.

It is time to embrace...

the depth and breadth of our human story, particularly its rootedness in Africa, the ancient incarnational significance of that unfolding, and the justice response that it calls forth in our time as the people of Africa cry out for hope and meaning.

Part Five

CONSCIOUSNESS

We must assume behind this force [in the atom] the existence of a conscious and intelligent mind. This mind is the matrix of all matter. —Max Planck, accepting the Nobel Prize for physics in 1918

Chapter Eleven

Consciousness:
The Future of Evolution

For if the what of consciousness is that it is pure information in a meaning universe, the where of consciousness becomes alternatively nowhere and everywhere. In a universe that is infinitely interconnected, consciousness can be anywhere it wants to be.
— Michael Talbot

In the history of the collective as in the history of the individual, everything depends on the development of consciousness.
— Carl G. Jung

F OR THE REMAINING CHAPTERS of this book, the story is very much in the future tense, yet paradoxically, we will be exploring what may well be the oldest resource known to us and to all creation over ages past: the power of consciousness. The story becomes more esoteric and mysterious, and some may consider it vague and nebulous. It is reality's story plunging into depths that are new for our time, yet surfacing a wisdom that we have known for a long time indeed.

In both science and religion, humans are considered to be the apex of evolution, after which there is nothing else to evolve. Evolution reaches its culmination in the human spirit, and now it is up to us to make sense of what it has been about since the beginning, and where it is likely to move over future millennia.

Human intelligence is the key to unlocking the ancient past and the guide to creating the best possible future. And humans believe that it is they themselves who will create that future, not some divine intelligence behind the whole thing, and definitely not some undiscovered secret within the course of evolution itself. Here we encounter the human will to power in the grip of unrelenting desire for power. The slogan "Man is the measure of all things" still reigns with a stubborn resilience.

169

From the anthropocentric point of view, the secret wisdom behind all life is located primarily (many would say exclusively) in the human brain. No higher intelligence ever did, or ever could, exist. Over the centuries we have conceded that mind also exists, but since we could not figure out its precise role, we consistently relegated it to the realm of philosophy or to the sphere of psychological speculation.

In a sense, we did the same thing with consciousness. Several contemporary scholars, including many who would consider themselves to belong to the era of postmechanistic science, describe consciousness as if it were an exclusively human property; hence the description *human* consciousness. And we search for its unique location and site of action primarily, if not exclusively, in the human brain. (For a comprehensive overview, see Seager 1999.)

Things began to change in the closing decades of the twentieth century. Consciousness, its nature, function, and purpose, became the subject of extensive research. The anthropocentric preoccupation and the tendency to identify consciousness exclusively with human beings began to shift. A larger picture was beginning to unfold, vividly depicted in Hubbard (1998). It seems to me that it is consciousness more than anything else that is evolving in our time. That wise and intelligent energy that has driven E-mergence since time immemorial lights up our horizon, throwing all our paradigms into chaos and confusion and inviting humanity to a place we have never been before. We live in a unique evolutionary moment, and we urgently need to discern the meaning of what is unfolding within and around us.

At this stage the story being explored in this book takes a type of quantum leap. What is being described feels strangely familiar yet defies the conventional wisdom of our age. Consciousness is one of those concepts that have crept up on us unawares. Twenty years ago, consciousness was the province of philosophers and psychologists. Today, it is a central concept in a new vocabulary, a transnational dialogue, in which the precise meaning of words is not felt to be that important because intuition seems more readily available to larger numbers of people. So let's explore what people are seeking to express as they embrace this new concept.

What Do We Mean by Consciousness?

Consciousness has only one meaning in the English language. In the ancient language of Sanskrit, there are twenty meanings (e.g., *chitta* is the mind stuff or experiencing medium of the individual; *chit* is the eternal consciousness of which human consciousness is one manifestation; *turiya* is the experience of pure awareness without an object; *dhyana* is consciousness focused on an idea; *purusha* describes the essential nature of consciousness itself). The fact that this ancient language requires so many words to describe the phenomenon may suggest that our ancient ancestors understood consciousness much more comprehensively than we do today.

In tracing its recent history, many theorists follow Plato's idea that the mind begins as a clean slate (or a set of neurons) and is gradually filled with the ideas that arise from sensations or reflections. Biologically, it often is described as a vast assembly of nerve cells and their associated molecules creating mental behavior, of which consciousness is merely a side effect.

The dualistic position, separating mind from other dimensions of the human person, was adopted first by René Descartes and by several theorists since then. Descartes postulated two distinct entities: mind and body, one mental and the other material, the former comprising atoms, and the latter, psychons (John Eccles). Currently, Paul Churchland (1988), Francis Crick (1995), Daniel Dennett (1991), and Fred Dretske (1997) are among the most ardent defenders of the idea that mind (and consciousness) is nothing more than a function of the human brain. As such, it is governed by neuron behavior in which objective representations are sent scurrying through connectionist networks wherein information bits hustle between dendritic pathways — all creating what Dennett considers to be the illusion of consciousness.[16]

It was psychology, more than any other science, that brought consciousness into the limelight. Sigmund Freud postulated three experiences of consciousness: (1) what I am consciously aware of at any time; (2) what I can become aware of after reflection (preconsciousness); and (3) what I am unaware of but nonetheless influenced by in its inner power (the subconscious). The subconscious is what opened up a whole new debate on our understanding of the human psyche.

True to the scientific mind of his day, Freud adopted a strong deterministic approach. We could control the conscious and preconscious material (for the greater part), but we had no control over the subconscious, and for Freud, at least 70 percent of our behavior was influenced by the subconscious drive. Consciousness could not be fully understood, nor could it be controlled; and although confined to individual human behavior, it could not be reduced merely to brain functioning. Something more nebulous and elusive was at work.

One of Freud's earliest admirers also was to become his greatest critic: Carl G. Jung. He challenged Freud's determinism, his pessimistic view of human nature, and above all, his understanding of consciousness. Jung agreed to the human appropriation of the conscious mind in terms of positive and negative influence; the latter is broadly what Jung means by the "shadow." But at all times the individual mind or awareness is under the influence of the "collective unconscious." This was, and still is, Jung's most provocative and influential idea.

For Jung, the collective unconscious permeates the whole of creation. It is an amalgam of all the thoughts, feelings, aspirations, and ideas that have ever been experienced. It is a reservoir of spiritual, psychic, and mental energy, and it exists everywhere. We cannot escape its influence. We cannot change its past, but we can contribute to its future unfolding. For Jung, it is a type of divine energy that we access through archetypes, symbolic behavior, and ritual — predominantly through dreams, intuition, and imagination.

What Jung described so elegantly (considered to be wild, unsubstantiated fantasy by many scientists) met with a more subdued recognition by other scholars. Bertrand Russell in 1927 suggested that we consider "protoconsciousness" as a fundamental property of all matter, just like mass, charge, spin, and location. The biologist Julian Huxley suggested that we complement the external realm of matter with an internal realm of "mind." The philosopher Alfred North Whitehead invoked the idea of "panpsychism," propounded by Leibniz some two hundred years previously, claiming that consciousness pervades the universe and all its constituents — a view long cherished and endorsed by Hindu and Buddhist philosophers and highlighted in our time in the writings of the transpersonal psychologist Ken Wilber.

Already in 1925, Teilhard de Chardin, the Jesuit priest and paleontologist, adopted a new word, "noosphere," to describe what he called the thinking envelope of the earth, "multiplying its internal fibres and tightening its network; and simultaneously its internal temperature is rising, and with this its psychic potential" (Teilhard de Chardin 1964, 132). For Teilhard, the noosphere was not just a mental concept; it contained thought, emotion, mind, spirit, psyche, and, above all, the power of love.

That consciousness is a property of creation at large and not just an aspect of human life (or behavior) elicits substantial support from contemporary scholars. Physicists such as David Bohm, Amit Goswami, Nick Herbert, Brian D. Josephson, and Paul Davies, and the mathematician David J. Chalmers (1996) claim that consciousness belongs innately to universal life. It is not derived from anything else and cannot be reduced to anything more basic. For Chalmers (1996, 126ff.), consciousness is a fundamental feature of the universe, and that must be a primary consideration ("the first datum") in our study of the human mind.

Robert G. Jahn, former dean of engineering at Princeton University, and his colleagues at the Princeton Engineering Anomalies Research lab have proposed a model of the mind in which consciousness acts freely through space and time to create actual change in the physical world. Their research is based on experimental evidence, which forms one of the largest data bases ever assembled on the effects of distant intentionality (see Jahn and Dunne 1987).

The worldview espoused by quantum theory, especially the quantum holism characterized by several parts acting as an integrated whole (see Zohar 1991; Zohar and Marshall 1994), has uniquely affected our view of consciousness and even of human awareness. What for long we assumed (and many still assume) to be a commodity that belongs to an elusive part of the human brain, we now suspect has much more to do with some type of cosmic, global brain. Freeman Dyson (1979, 249) expresses it vividly:

> I think our consciousness is not just a passive epiphenomenon carried along by the chemical events in our brains, but is an active agent forcing the molecular complexes to make choices between one quantum state and another. In other words, mind is already inherent in every electron, and the processes of human consciousness differ only in degree but not in kind from the processes of choice between quantum states which we call "chance" when they are made by electrons.

As noted in previous chapters, the mindful, intelligent universe thrives on a sense of self-organization, which as yet we humans understand only poorly. It is in this capacity for self-organization that growing numbers of scientists concede the existence of consciousness as a universal quality. Paul Davies, who writes extensively on this subject, asserts, "Consciousness should be viewed as an emergent product of a sequence of self-organizing processes that form part of a general advance of complexity occurring throughout the universe" (quoted in Russell, Murphy, and Isham 1993, 155).

Consciousness, Wisdom, and Depth

For the transpersonal psychologist Ken Wilber (1998, 41), "Consciousness is simply what depth looks like from the inside, from within." Michael Talbot describes consciousness as pure information (see the epigraph for the present chapter). Elsewhere in this book I describe consciousness as the all-pervading energy of creation, underpinning the unending process of cocreation. Teilhard de Chardin (1959, 57) describes it as a psychic force, combining but also transcending the power of mind and spirit. Vague though it may seem, Wilber's description of "depth" is probably closer to the truth than all the other descriptions.

Consciousness is not something that can be measured, quantified, or reduced to neural, brain-based processes. It is not something confined to the human mode of being in the world, nor can it be identified solely with what many religions claim to be the unique quality of life after death. Consciousness transcends all the names and labels that we put on it. It does not belong to the sphere of observable material reality; however, it is structured within universal life, and evidence for it can be gleaned from several of evolution's creations.

It belongs to the realm of inwardness, or what many spiritual writers describe as interiority. Partly, it is characterized by the ordering or patterning made possible by information coding and information transfer. But it is much more than information, as popularly understood today. I suggest that "wisdom" is the more appropriate word to describe the process under consideration, one aptly described by Kurzweil (1999, 30) when he writes, "Order, then, is information that fits a purpose."

Wisdom is a notion seldom invoked in the scientific literature. Yet it may well be the most accurate and dynamic word to describe the ingenious self-organizing and self-sustaining dynamics upon which creation thrives. It gives expression to that subtle will to meaning that defies detailed analysis or comprehensive description. It alludes to something that is tantalizingly illusive yet persuasively real.

In exploring this nebulous, mysterious quality, we also need to attend to our descriptive language, acknowledging that our best efforts will produce only approximate explanations. To suggest, however, that wisdom *governs* the world may be a dangerous and misleading statement. It invokes an authority from on high, divine or otherwise, whereas the power of wisdom seems to emerge from within. It erupts from the depths, sometimes gently and unobtrusively, more times violently and even destructively, and at other times with a wild, passionate exuberance that can be exhilarating and frightening at the same time. Wisdom animates and awakens rather than governs as if by external force.

Wisdom is characterized by creativity and freedom. It seeks engagement and expression, but clearly it does not control the unfolding patterns. The Darwinian process of genetic mutation, conscious choice, and natural selection describes threads woven into wisdom's tapestry. And wisdom can hold the whole thing together, paradoxes and all, in an adeptly innovative symbiosis. We get a sense of what this means from the description of organic life provided by Margulis (1998, 9):

> Living beings defy neat definition. They fight, they feed, they dance, they mate, they die. At the base of the creativity of all larger familiar forms of life, symbiosis generates novelty. It brings together different life-forms, *always for a reason*. Often hunger unites the predator with the prey or the mouth with the photosynthetic bacterium of algal victim. Symbiogenesis brings together unlike individuals to make larger, more complex entities. Symbiogenetic life-forms are even more unlike than their unlikely "parents." "Individuals" permanently merge and regulate their reproduction. They generate new populations that become multiunit symbiotic new individuals. These become "new individuals" at larger, more inclusive levels of integration. Symbiosis is not a marginal or rare phenomenon. It is natural and common. We abide in a symbiotic world.

The memory through which nature remembers is one of wisdom's outstanding characteristics.[17] Nothing ever is lost or wasted. There is no annihilation, only transformation. Past patterns repeat but also change. Wisdom brings every past into the present and utilizes the cumulative learnings and experience to pave the way to the future.

But wisdom is not just about the past. In fact, its primary generating power may be the allurement of the future (see Haught 2000). Wisdom is forever seeking out new possibilities. The future draws it forth, luring it into the promise of eternal becoming. Wisdom knows no end goal, no final chapter, no closed worldview. It is radically open-ended, and this, more than anything else, may be its single most baffling and fascinating feature.

Already the reader may be asking, "Are you not effectively describing God and the power of the divine at work in creation?" Consciously and deliberately, I have refrained from any reference to the divine. It seems to me that creation is saturated in mystery, admittedly paradoxical in many aspects, and invoking God too quickly absolves us from having to grapple with the sense of mystery in its earthly and cosmic aspects. Science tends to exclude God, while religion often brings in God prematurely. In both cases we are in danger of bypassing the challenge to the human imagination to engage more directly with the meaning of life. By depriving ourselves of that task — to become more reflective and discerning people — we may in fact be undermining a more mature and adult faith in how the divine works in our world.

As a religious believer, I believe that God is involved in the evolutionary process. But God is not confined to the consciousness and wisdom that inhere in creation. Nor should we worry unduly whether or not God is the ultimate source and creator of this consciousness. My appeal is that we acknowledge it for what it is, learn to appreciate and understand its mode of operating, allow ourselves to be influenced by its ingenious wisdom, and engage with its dynamic awakening of ever new possibilities for the unfolding future of our universe.

Consciousness Evolving

One of the most engaging aspects of evolutionary theory today is the evolution of consciousness itself. We witness this in even a cursory glance at the growth of information and its accompanying technology. From the beginning of the Christian era up to the dawn of the scientific revolution (ca. 1600 C.E.), the "quantity" of knowledge doubled that of the previous three to five thousand years; between 1600 and 1900 it doubled again. It took only fifty years for another cumulative leap (up to 1950), and thereafter it began to accelerate in leaps and bounds to the present time, when we estimate that the information content of our world is doubling in terms of months rather than years.

Alongside the expansion of knowledge, we noted a parallel effort to store information. To scan just the past few hundred years, we witnessed a progression from museums or laboratories, where data was stored in material and physical form, to libraries, where information could be stacked in less space because it was now in written form.

We then invented microfilms to contain masses of information while simultaneously finding new ways of communicating it, first by means of television and subsequently the video boom. Then came computerization and the microchip (first discovered in 1971), which in itself can contain a whole library of information.

It is now clear that as information increases, the means for storing it, in physical and material terms, becomes progressively smaller. In nanotechnology, the smallest "chips" are totally invisible to the human eye. This trend of being able to do more with less matter is what we call "ephemeralization," a term coined by Buckminster Fuller and described in detail by Peter Russell (1992, 35ff.). In 1977, the American working population crossed a significant threshold. For the first time ever, over 50 percent of the workforce was involved in processing information. Prior to that time, their energy was devoted to making physical objects. Information rather than "production" is mostly what we work at today.

The information explosion happened in the closing decades of the twentieth century, although, I grant, its full impact is only now reaching large sections of humanity. What we are now grappling with is consciousness rather than information. We no longer are able to control information as we have done for several centuries. Often, youngsters in their teens are more versatile on and aware of many important issues than their elders were, are, or will be. Access to information is a major organizational, political, and ethical issue for our time. The power with which we were able to control information in the past is no longer viable. A major shift has taken place and will accelerate as we move through the new millennium, and at the heart of that shift is the power of consciousness.

Consciousness is what discloses to us a world of greater complexity, openness, fluidity, and creativity. It alerts us to the fact that things happen and evolve according to principles bigger and deeper than what we humans envisage. It highlights the meaning within and behind so many things that we thought were just outcomes of pure chance or random selection. It invites us to consider notions that tend to be sidestepped to many mainstream sciences: purpose, sense of direction, and meaning.

Consciousness invites us to revisit notions of an alive universe, a creative vacuum, energy rippling in vibrational strings and in quantum leaps and bounds — all characterized by unpredictability, radical freedom, and creativity. And it invites us to stretch all our definitions of what we mean by "life": not some isolated biological process that we can accurately define and describe, but rather, a symbiotic relational process that explodes with exploding stars but has been incubating since the dawn of time.

The big picture takes over — alluring and exciting, but so petrifying for those locked into the ideology of power and control. Power belongs to a small world, often unable to see or appreciate the larger reality that embraces us all. And it is on this larger scale that the revolution of consciousness and its evolutionary expansion are happening in our time.

In human terms, the shift seems unprecedented; in evolutionary terms, the territory is vaguely familiar. The power is no longer in human hands or, indeed, in human heads. We cannot control the explosion of consciousness as we controlled information in recent times. Already, with the invention of computers, this control began to slip away from us. But we were so locked into the anthropocentric will to power that it never dawned on us that a day would come when we no longer would be in charge of what was happening on our planet and in our universe.

It often is suggested that our ancient ancestors were at the mercy of cruel forces over which they had no control. This perception probably is what led to the development of patriarchal domination in the rise of male ruling classes from around 6000 B.C.E. We now realize that the image of the helpless primitive ancestor is very much a projection arising from the shadow side of our will to power. The things that we did not like about ourselves we projected onto a scapegoat that could not stand up and defend itself. But in time, truth tends to prevail. Now, the projections are being exposed for what they really are, and we are invited to revisit our ancient past with a more benign and perceptive mode of enquiry.

Homo sapiens for most of its evolutionary history seems to have been quite a wise species. What anthropologists often describe as enmeshment, or lack of differentiation, may now be understood as alignment to and congruence with the surrounding environment. Our ancestors often lived in a type of symbiotic alliance with nature, frequently in awe, sometimes in fear. All indications are that planet earth was not perceived as an object to be used, managed, and ultimately controlled. The planet itself was a type of living organism, in which life breathed as in the wind, moved as in the streams, and shouted as in the thunder. And within it (rather than behind it) was a life-force, transcending the created reality yet totally present to it in its every movement.

In this ancient scenario, that unity of consciousness, which many meditation movements today seek to attain, seems largely to have been in place. Nobody talked or preached about cosmic consciousness, because everybody lived within it. I understand that they would not have been aware of it as we are today. And therein lies the supreme contradiction of our time. We now have the awareness to name these deeper realities, but for the greater part we seem to be unable to live according to their principles. We are so conditioned by the anthropocentric will to power that we have seriously lost our bearings on the human, planetary, and cosmic levels alike.

Meanwhile, the triumph of consciousness continues unabated. We have contributed to this triumph, but it also has its own momentum. And at this critical moment, the crucial question is not, "How do we control it?" but rather, "How do we submit to its higher wisdom?" Many people cringe when they hear the word "submit." It sounds so passive; but most perturbing of all, it means that we are asked to let go of our power. And yet letting go of power is another misperception, because when we choose to engage with our planet and universe in a symbiotic relationship, we do not abandon power; rather, we rediscover it in a whole new way.

As a planetary, cosmic species, we belong to a reality greater than ourselves. It is our congruence with our planetary identity and our cosmic potential that bestow genuine power upon us, including the wisdom to befriend our human vulnerability. As long as we continue to set ourselves against or above the creation in which we are embedded, all that we will achieve is more sickness, pain, alienation, and meaninglessness. We set ourselves at enmity with the creation to which we belong. Ironically, we may be paving the pathways of our own destruction, and if we continue blindly on that route, not all the gods on earth or in heaven will save us from ultimate catastrophe.

Nurtured by Consciousness

What, then, can we do to advance or nurture the new consciousness of our time? To begin with, we need to shed the compulsive drive to dominate and control what is evolving in and around us. Something is transpiring in our universe over which we do not have control. Evolution is poised on a new threshold. The power of creative energy is endowed with gravity, buoyancy, and depth. A new wave of consciousness sweeps across the proverbial chaos of creation, birthing novelty and extravagant possibilities. Chaos abounds as old conventions crumble under the impact. We are the beneficiaries and witnesses of a new evolutionary revolution.

What we need to do is resource ourselves anew so that we remain open and receptive to what is going on around and within us. We need to rediscover that commodity so rare today: the ability to be still, to be at home with creative solitude. In this cacophonous culture of serrating jingle-jangle from without and psychic-turmoil bombardments from within, we largely are unable to listen to what is emerging around us. We do not know how to be present to this pregnant moment, and formal religion seems largely to have lost the secret of liberating the cosmic contemplative that lies dormant in every human heart.

Meditation is a timely resource, irrespective of whether it is specifically religious or not. Not only does it help to slow us down; more importantly, it brings us to an inner place of stillness, helping to center us within that which is truly real. It enables us to calm down all the external distractions that strain our senses and dissipate our spirit. It helps to situate us once more at the place of heart — within ourselves, yes, but also within the creation that surrounds us.

The meditative stance makes us more transparent to what is happening around us. We become more sensitive to what is emerging (at every level), more perceptive in our understanding, more discerning in our judgments, and more in touch with the struggle and pain of this transition time. From this more authentic space there awakens what Knitter (1995, 104–6) identifies as the "mystical-prophetic dipolarity" (common to all religions). This often launches us into a discerning place requiring some painful choices in terms of work, relationships, commitments, and economic and political reality.

True stillness never leads to a place of passivity. It drove the contemporary mystic Thomas Merton from a peaceful rural hermitage in Kentucky to the sprawling urban masses of Southeast Asia. The Spirit that speaks within is also the fiery force of passionate justice and right relationships. True contemplation nearly always encounters heartrending restlessness. Inner vision is perhaps the greatest change catalyst that the world has ever known.

And above all, it is from the depths of that inner resourcefulness that we become receptive once more. We begin to understand and appreciate the world to which we belong, and the invitation in that belonging is to come home to more sustainable ways of being in our regard for other life-forms and for the planet we inhabit. We begin again to comprehend the wisdom that is innate to all living things, the creation that is endowed with a potential for meaning and self-becoming. We realize once more that everything is held — and held irrevocably — in the embrace of a benign life-force.

Yet it is painfully obvious that all is not well in our world; indeed, many things are out of kilter. They are out of kilter because we humans are not attuned to who we really are. Only when we begin to change from within can we come to realize the ambivalent and destructive role that we play within the cocreative process of universal becoming. Truly, we are creation becoming conscious of itself — what a privileged role! But also, what an onerous responsibility that goes with it. And that is the crucial challenge that haunts us at this evolutionary moment.

With or without us, creation will continue to evolve; consciousness will continue to grow and intensify. The choice is ours to come on board or to continue being the belligerent species that ruptures the womb that nourishes us. Our ultimate choices will be determined by the quality and quantity of our own awareness, and our receptivity to becoming a more enlightened and benign progeny. Hopefully, the reflections of this chapter will urge us in the right direction.

•

It is time to outgrow...

our intellectual arrogance whereby we prize the human brain as the primary site of conscious awareness, reinforcing the mechanistic view that creation is without intelligence, merely an objective entity for our use and benefit.

It is time to embrace...

a universe exuding vitality and wisdom, consciously manifesting its innate power in the variety and diversity of all life-forms, our home planet being the connective tissue that links our human intelligence with the cosmic wisdom that endows the whole of creation.

Chapter Twelve

Consciousness and Globalization

The first principle of non-violent action is that of non-cooperation with everything humiliating. —Mahatma Gandhi

The patriarchal order is based upon worlds of the beyond: worlds of before birth and especially of the after-life, other planets to be discovered and exploited for survival, etc. It doesn't appreciate the real values of the world we have and draws up its often bankrupt blueprints on the basis of hypothetical worlds.

—Lucy Irigaray

I N THE 1960s Marshall McLuhan hailed the arrival of the global village and alerted us to the impending communications revolution that would break down the anonymity and distance of foreign places, peoples, and cultures. Our world would become small and intimate, and so it did. A new version of the story began to take shape. Young and old alike began to travel, visit other countries, and experience other cultures. News flashed across the globe at an accelerated pace, exciting us about the variety and wonder of the natural world and horrifying us at the starvation and poverty that ravaged the lives of millions of people.

We were undergoing a massive paradigm shift, but it caught up with us long before we caught up with it. Culturally, it was exciting and bewildering. Politically and economically, it was, and still is, knotted in perplexity. In the wake of the Second World War, nations in the West began to solidify their national identities, often focusing

---

*On my first visit to Asia, in 2000, I was both inspired and challenged by Asian theologians striving to integrate globalization into contemporary theological discourse. In conversations with K. C. Abraham in India and with Mary John Manzanan in the Philippines, I came to realize that the Western tendency to exonerate globalization is becoming one of Asia's greatest nightmares. Indeed, the future evolution of the two-thirds world and the critical justice issues that surface basically depend on how we address this urgent contemporary development. This is a complex global question that impacts substantially on the evolutionary story of our time.

on internal self-reliance and the ability to withstand international interference. And as the colonial grip began to loosen, initially on Asia and subsequently on Africa (with seventeen African nations obtaining independence in 1960 alone), pride in the autonomy and uniqueness of one's own nation became the cherished value of the day.

We witnessed that same national pride and the corresponding search for national identity after the breakup of the Soviet Union in the early 1990s, and more recently, that of Yugoslavia. The desire for national autonomy, and the worldwide emphasis on passports and visas, indicate that national boundaries are still sacrosanct and must not be transgressed.

The Rise of Globalization

Meanwhile, McLuhan's dream of the global village has proliferated in ways that even he himself never envisaged. While ordinary citizens continually encounter passport checks and national security, politicians and business entrepreneurs do trade and commerce on an international scale that transcends all national restrictions. The concept of free trade was purported to make commerce in international markets more open and available to all nations, but what it actually has meant is that the rich and powerful nations seek to dominate the transactions of goods and services. Free trade is anything but free!

And ironically, those who thought that they would benefit from such trade agreements are often its greatest victims, because in reality it is not nation-states that control trade, but transnational corporations. These are business conglomerates of the West that throughout the 1960s and 1970s began to monopolize world markets and now control key resources on a global scale. They are accountable neither to any single government nor to international governmental agencies. They are a law unto themselves. They are the cultural and monetary nightmare that McLuhan did not envisage, even in his most insightful moments.

In my travels, I note that theologians and social theorists based in the West tend to describe globalization in positive, even glowing, terms, whereas for those in the two-thirds world, it is perceived as the greatest threat of our time to personal, economic, and cultural sustainability. In fact, we are dealing with two different but related realities. Positively, we are encountering the new global consciousness, highlighted by McLuhan and several others over the past forty years, which now is being translated into the "new cosmology" that I have explored throughout this book. Negatively, we are encountering those global, international forces that ravage the national, financial, cultural, and personal resources not merely of the two-thirds world, but indeed of the entire planet.

I wish to honor the critical concerns of my sisters and brothers in the two-thirds world and use the term "globalization" as they do. In the colonial culture that prevailed up to the middle of the last century, countries deprived of their freedom and creativity knew who the oppressor was and yearned for the day when they could remove the yoke of that oppression. In most cases, the oppressor represented a particular country, usually European — for example, Great Britain, Portugal, Spain, or France. Today, the oppression is subtle and complex. It frequently is unclear who the oppressor is. The oppressive regime has no obvious national or political identity. The acquisition and the control of what traditionally were considered to be national resources are often robbed from the legitimate owners — not by the banditry of the black market, but by the piracy of TNCs (transnational corporations).

The TNCs have reached unbelievable depths of sophistication in today's world. They successfully circumvent national and international controls, taking their cues from "sites of information" that effectively are international in nature. International espionage rules the world today, to the advantage of the powerful and wealthy.

Globalization may be described as the long-term intensification of exchange and trade culminating in the penetrating explosion of capitalism that has engulfed the world.[18] It is the inevitable outcome of that process of commoditization named by Walter Brueggemann (as described at the end of chapter 10). Planet earth, and even the cosmos at large, has become a commodity to be conquered and exploited. And the conquering forces are no longer nation-states, but transnational corporations.

And the weaponry of this new warfare is information and marketability. National governments are unable to keep pace. National security fails dismally. In most countries it has lost a sense of control, not merely of the drugs trade, but of the massive exchange of resources that goes on not at checkpoints in ports of entry but through highly sophisticated media transactions. And nationally sponsored education programs fail to impart critical skills to engage with the information explosion in today's world; most education systems tend to concur with the agenda of the oppressors.

Advertising, too, is internationally controlled and is hugely influential in affecting values and choices. Even youngsters in the slums of Calcutta can rattle off the name-brand labels on the latest designer fashions. The media allure people to desire things that they do not really need and that are in many cases deleterious to health and well-being. But in a market-driven world, the prevailing conviction is "If it's there, I must have it." Market forces do not merely govern international monetary transactions; they have infiltrated every nook and cranny of planet earth.

At the sociopolitical level, we are facing a crisis of enormous proportion, and, as the Indian writer V. Arul Raj (2000, 41) notes, national governments seem incredibly complacent about it. The notion that our world is supposed to be governed by nation-states has become anachronistic, and in some cases almost totally irrelevant. Nation-states no longer control wealth or international goods; TNCs do. National governments no longer control consumer choices or values; TNCs do. TNCs are not accountable to any single government or to the international conglomerates put in place by national governments, such as the International Monetary Fund, the World Bank, and the G8; these agencies effectively are laundering facilities that enable the TNCs to do their work.

In the past twenty years, a major shift has taken place from the state to the market (see Korten 1995). Monetary forces, controlled internationally, dominate not just the financial, but also the political, landscape today. For instance, Mitsubishi and General Motors have larger economies than any single state in Africa, also exceeding the national wealth of Indonesia, Chile, Greece, and Denmark. Already in the mid-1990s, of the top one hundred economies in the world, only forty-eight were nation-states; the remaining fifty-two were TNCs. The nation-state no longer is in charge economically. (Indeed, one wonders if it is in charge in any sense!) TNCs dominate the economic world of our time.

With the shift from the state to the market comes the shift from labor to capital. Money no longer is seen as something we earn with the work of our hands. For over twenty years now, we have been making money out of information rather than from the production of material goods (that threshold was crossed in the United States in 1977). Today, money is bartered and valued in terms of financial deals that have to do not with "heavy industry," but with weightless transactions. Over 40 percent of the employees of companies such as General Motors,

Exxon, IBM, and Toyota are located outside the home countries of these corporations.

The very nature of work has changed dramatically, creating enormous personal and social dislocation. The TNCs, not national governments, dictate the location of key resources. Often, governments are forced to offer tax incentives and financial handouts to the strongest players in the global economy at the expense of welfare payments to the poorer categories of people. Contract labor is the order of the day, leaving many skilled people unemployed for long periods of time and eradicating several support systems related to benefits and pensions.

Predictably, the impact on the poor of our world — well over 60 percent of the human population — is horrendous. In the feudal world of the Middle Ages, the slaves were ill-treated, but the system wanted them; in the traditional caste organization, the out-castes were the victims of discrimination and abuse, but without their labor the society could not function. But in the culture of globalization, the poor are unwanted; they are a burden and a nuisance. Globalization is a conspiracy of the rich against the poor, and those who stand in the way of "progress" simply will be eliminated!

It is at this level that we encounter injustices of unprecedented proportion. Shocking though it is to realize, in a few short years from now the people of Ghana (in West Africa) may not be allowed to sell cocoa on world markets because it will not measure up to internationally established standards of the patented version. Nor will Caribbean bananas be tolerated, because they too will have been deemed inferior to a newly patented brand. Even the genes of human beings will have become a commodity to be exploited. It is estimated that over fifty patents have been taken out on the DNA of indigenous peoples. Domination and control will have reached dangerously new heights.

Social dislocation is another largely unnoticed direct consequence of globalization. Environments and habitats are disrupted, and people's basic coping skills no longer are adequate. Kalliath (1999, 126) describes the impact on his native India:

> Little wonder that India enjoys the dubious distinction of harboring the world's largest number of development refugees. These are people who have to leave their homes because the forests, grasslands, rivers, wetlands and coastal habitats were usurped "in the national interest" or became unusable because they were either

poisoned or altered beyond description. The development dream has turned into a toxic nightmare.

The more we unearth what is really going on, the more paralyzed and petrified we become. It is a disturbingly explosive situation, in the face of which cynicism abounds and a meaningful way out is difficult to conjecture. What is particularly disheartening is the subtle collusion of national governments with the forces of globalization, hence the widespread corruption in the political sphere itself.

On the one hand, we witness the myopic insularism of the so-called superpowers. The United States government, during the presidency of Bill Clinton (1992–2000), adopted a leading military, political, and economic role in several foreign nations. And yet over 50 percent of the members of the U.S. Congress never visited a country in the two-thirds world, and over one-third of the members did not even hold an international passport. On the other hand, there is scarcely a government in the world, developed or underdeveloped, in which parliamentarians themselves do not hold stakes in TNCs. Some of these people buy their way into politics; others accrue wealth and power through their involvement in politics. Corruption and sleaze are rife within national governments the world over. Against this background, the progressive disintegration of the nation-state indeed may be a blessing in disguise.

The Shift in Consciousness

The reader may wonder what all this has to do with our evolutionary story and the new theological insights that ensue from it. We are dealing with an issue of ultimate significance that requires a radically new strategy if it is to be confronted and addressed in a holistic way. Piecemeal solutions do not work anymore, and in fact have not been working for at least the past forty years. We are at a new evolutionary threshold, one endowed with almost incomprehensible depths of light and darkness.

We, as a human species, have been there before. We know what it is to be in crisis and on the verge of deep despair. And we have pulled through, thanks to a deep resilience within us, but probably more importantly, thanks to the universe and the planet we inhabit, which in their innate wisdom enabled and empowered us to make the needed breakthrough.

This time around the crisis is more complex. The forces imploding within us and exploding around us seem overwhelming at times. And our earth is badly bruised and broken. From an evolutionary point of view, there are several indications that we are on a slippery slope of self-destruction, in which case the wise earth itself will resolve our dilemma: it will make us redundant, probably through some type of global catastrophe, and replace us with a more seemly species. It would not be the first time that the Earth Mother consumed her own offspring to spare herself and us so much meaningless suffering.

And yet hope lives eternal. In either our present or in a transformed fashion, we could make a breakthrough. Even if we are destined for a cataclysmic end, it can only be to our advantage to learn to live in a more convivial and sustainable way. And there are indications that it is possible. The question is this: Are there enough wise and free people poised to seize the moment? In other words: Can we make the shift in consciousness that could make a substantial difference?

We encounter signs of hope in the least-expected places at the least-expected moments. For me, a significant one happened on July 20, 2000. I walked down a rather disheveled market street in the Malate district of Manila in the Philippines. Everywhere I looked, I saw signs for pawnshops. Indeed, the poverty around me was exceptionally real. But then a strange image began to register in my brain. Momentarily, I wondered whether I was just imagining something, but no, it was for real.

As far as my sight could stretch, I saw a serial sequence that went something like this: pawnshop — Internet services — pawnshop — e-mail service — pawnshop — Internet accessories — pawnshop — e-mail facility.... Two worlds sitting side by side! In one shop a person was exchanging items such as jewelry to eke out a subsistence living for perhaps another few days, while in the shop next door a sister or brother or son or daughter was sending an e-mail to some distant land.

Not many years ago, the poor of our world were deprived of food, medicine, clothing, education, and basic information. Today, millions are still deprived of food, medicine, clothing, and education, but *not* of basic information. Even illiterate people, who can neither read nor write, learn to operate computers, and apparently they are easily motivated to do so. Information has exploded into every home and homeland of planet earth. Recently, a missionary friend of mine working in a remote area of Angola in West Africa informed me of families who send e-mails to friends in Great Britain or the United States, but who do not have running water, adequate medicine, sufficient clothing, and, sometimes, enough to eat. Information has become the great social and political leveler in today's world.

Information is our strongest hope for a new future, for a new world order, perhaps the last vestige of hope if we are to survive the waves of change sweeping across the world today. Information unites people into a new worldwide network that we humans have never known before. Almost in spite of ourselves, we are being drawn into a new global identity beyond the forces of nationality, ethnicity, and religion that have separated us for far too long.

Intuitively we also sense that information is power, and this becomes the double-edged sword. It opens us up to a world of alluring possibility; it stretches our horizons of vision and hope. But of course, it quickly dawns on us that it is a brutal world of haves and have-nots with so much weighted in favor of those who already have. And this is where we encounter the unprecedented violence that we have witnessed in the past few decades.

This is the violence that has erupted in South Africa, sending shivers of fear down the spines of so many people within and outside the country. The South African people carry deep wounds and understandable bitterness from the barbaric oppression of the apartheid years. As several commentators have noted, the process of healing and reconciliation is likely to take several decades, if not generations.

But those same commentators often miss the subtle undercurrents, even when they are verbally expressed. The anger of young South Africans in particular is not about the atrocities of the past; it is the older rather than the younger generations that felt those most acutely. For the young, the anger and outrage are about the here and now, not about the past. This is the information-influenced generation. They see their contemporaries in other countries, including black people in other parts of the world, who have access to the latest fashions, food, and opportunities. They want the same for themselves, and they want it now!

This is a unique feature of the information-influenced generation. They want the goodies now. They are not prepared to wait. The suffering peoples in the two-thirds world feel that they already have had to wait far too long. Patience is in short supply in this information age. And this is not just an irrational, knee-jerk response. It is the power of the collective unconscious potently reminding us that we are one human family, to which those who hunger for more subconsciously add, "And if we are one family, then are we not all entitled to the available resources?"

The information age is here to stay. It is, and will remain, a dominant feature of our evolving story. The problem is that many people and several major institutions are not ready for it. We have been so immersed in the mechanistic consciousness of the past four hundred years and so preoccupied with trying to safeguard the governing power of patriarchy that we have been caught largely unawares. All the mechanistic paradigms are screeching to a halt, and those trying to control the power are angry and reactionary as the power keeps slipping from their grasp.

In October 2000, two powerful revolutions took place in our world, one in Yugoslavia and the other in the Ivory Coast in West Africa. In both cases, people by the thousands flocked into the streets of the respective capitals, Belgrade and Abidjan, forcing the ruling dictators to flee. A critical breakthrough happened in each case when the protestors took over the national television studios. The people were now in charge of the information power, and that is where the real power will be for the future.

The same month, October 2000, witnessed a national upsurge of discontent in Great Britain due to escalating fuel costs. Oil depots were blockaded by a random, unorganized group of aggrieved people. Gasoline supplies began to dwindle. The country was approaching a major national crisis, and attempts by the prime minister and the government to intervene seemed to exacerbate rather than calm the situation. The crisis was resolved when the protestors ended the protest. It had been one of the most effective mobilizations of people power that the country had known in years, and it gradually emerged that the secret of its success rested in the power of the mobile phone. The power inherent in information was once again in evidence.

But information per se is not the issue. We are dealing with something much more complex, holistic, global, and enduring. We are undergoing a massive shift in consciousness, globally and personally, of which information power is but one dominant manifestation. "Awareness" is a more generic word to encapsulate what is going on. Illiteracy, at one time the great barrier to progress and development, is no longer a barrier. People who are officially classed as illiterate in fact do gather enough basic information to be able to operate computers, and where words fail them, they rely on graphic images. The very thing that the education system is so poor at activating, the imagination, is what the information explosion has rehabilitated on a solid foundation. And with the imagination back in its rightful place, people begin to dream and conjure up several new futures. The imagination, as Jesus illustrates so powerfully, is one of the most subversive gifts with which we humans have been endowed. The imagination, more than anything else, gives the endurance and resilience to negotiate many an awkward hurdle. It also can be used for callous and sinister outcomes, as illustrated, for example, in the attack on New York City's World Trade Center on September 11, 2001.

Information, awareness, and imagination are among the most neglected spheres of our evolutionary story over the past few millennia. Now, they are revisiting our world with a vengeance. They quite literally are taking over, throwing all the old models into confusion, chaos, and disintegration. The will to meaning has not been so coherent and so forceful for a long time, but imbued as it is with powerful energies of light and darkness, it is as yet unclear whether it will see us through the crisis that characterizes our time.

Time is running out, and those who lead our world are running far behind. Our parliamentarians are sidetracked by the TNCs, over which they exercise little or no control. Nor do they have much control over the information explosion, which is outwitting the political forces even more handily than are the TNCs. As for the religions and the Christian churches, they are even more incapacitated than the politicians. So convinced are they that they already have the fullness of truth, that many have chosen to stand above and outside the world of reality. And growing numbers of people seem quite happy to leave them out there.

Consciousness and the Mysticism of Our Time

So, from an evolutionary point of view, a foundational question is this: "What are we to do with the information power?" How do we seize this moment for the benefit of humanity, the earth, and the universe? And do we need to reframe the question to try to make sure that we are asking the right questions? This is where theology enters — the science that claims to safeguard ultimacy as the goal and purpose of all our questions.

How do we learn to live with this evolving consciousness? How do we allow it to befriend us, to our own benefit as well as that of all other living organisms? How do we make the evolutionary leap that our time requires of us? These are weighty questions requiring a quality of response that we have not been prepared for. All over the world our educational systems inculcate a quality of wisdom that tends to be fragmented (we study different subjects in isolation), competitive (as in the exam system), cerebral and academic (excessively focused on brain development), and infiltrated in subtle ways with the patriarchal philosophy of divide and conquer.

Echoes of this insatiable desire to control and dominate sound in the opening sentence of William Seager's book *Theories of Consciousness* (Seager 1999, ix): "Recently there has been a tremendous surge of interest in the problem of consciousness." Why describe consciousness as a "problem"? For whom is it a problem? If we begin our analysis with the notion that consciousness is a problem to be resolved, then the chances are that it will be problems rather than possibilities that will dictate every stage of our exploration. Why not view consciousness as a reality to be explored rather than as a problem to be gotten rid of?

The exploratory pathway is new for our time, but we are the beneficiaries of some long-standing precedents that have served us well. Specifically, I have in mind the great mystical traditions known to all the religions and long predating the formal religions of the past five thousand years. Unfortunately, mysticism has a quite restricted meaning in our culture. In the popular mind it often is consigned to the secluded world of recluses and monastics; it tends to be portrayed as a wisdom that belongs to a different type of world.

Many of the great mystics were not recluses, and even if their lives were lived in relative seclusion, their engagement with reality was anything but unworldly. One of the unique features of mystical experience is the ability to rise above the several dualisms of our religious cultures, which tend to pit the divine against the human, the earthly against the heavenly, and the secular against the sacred. For the mystic, these are not dualistic opposites, but complementary realms that hold both the tension and the possibility of integration.

Karl Rahner once described mysticism as an "orientation to boundless mystery." His fellow Jesuit William Johnston (1978, 124) writes, "It is the mystic who really loves life and loves people and loves the cosmos and finds joy in all that is beautiful in the universe. He loves all but is the slave to nothing."

These two short quotations from Western sources highlight what Eastern writers describe in a much more profound and sophisticated way: the outcome of all mysticism is the experience of profound interiority at the heart of the cosmos itself. Mysticism is not about human abandonment into the arms of the divine, but about immersion in the divine mystery at the heart of creation. Sharon Welch (1990, 178, 172) articulates this earthly and cosmic integration with great clarity and conviction:

> Divinity is not a mark of that which is other than the finite. Grace is not that which comes from outside to transform the conditions of finitude. Divinity, or grace, is the resilient, fragile, healing power of finitude itself.... We participate in divinity as we participate in the beauty of humankind, as we rage against all that destroys the dignity and complexity of life. The ability to love and to work for justice is profoundly spiritual.

The mystic views reality writ large, but it is a largeness impregnated with depth. Unfortunately, various religions tend to appropriate this all-encompassing vision and reduce it to the ideological perceptions of some religious creed. In this way, the archetypal struggles of great mystics — the dark night of soul and senses — often are reduced to individual appropriations of the passion and suffering of Jesus. I suggest that they have a great deal more to do with transpersonal transformation, influenced, as it always is, by the divine birth pangs from within the evolutionary unfolding of the cosmos itself.

In our own time, the Brazilian theologian Leonardo Boff (1995, 161–62, 70) has written on this subject with remarkable lucidity, and he provides a helpful and timely description of the cosmic and planetary dimensions of mystical experience:

> Mysticism is life apprehended in its radicalism and extreme density. Existence is endowed with gravity, buoyancy, and depth when this is conceived and known appropriately. Mysticism always leads to the transcendence of all limits. It persuades us to examine other aspects of things than those we know and to suspect that reality is more than a mere structure concealing the realm of the absurd and the abyss, which can strike fear and anguish into our hearts. Mysticism teaches us instead that reality is where tenderness, receptivity and the mystery of loving kindness can triumph and are encountered as joyful living, meaningful accomplishment and a faithful dream....
>
> The mystic is not detached from history but committed to it as transformation, starting from a nucleus of transcendent meaning and a minimal utopian dimension which, in as much

as it is religious, enables the mystic to be more perceptive than anyone else.

It is in their ability to see with breadth and depth that mystics contribute to the transformation of consciousness. They keep us focused on the larger picture and challenge us to engage with the deeper questions. Cultural constructs, conventional ways of dealing with life, whether political or religious, whether scientific or theological, always will be found wanting by the all-seeing heart of the mystical vision. Even when ensconced in a religious context, the mystical vision always will try to break out and forge bigger connections. William Johnston (2000, 205ff.) claims that no one religion will satisfy the mystical hunger, and he goes on to make this suggestion:

> We must pool resources and insights so that together the great religions can offer the values of meditation, interiority, compassion, nonviolence, justice, peace, fidelity. Through cooperation in this great venture, sincere believers of all religions can form friendship and community; they can travel the path of union. (Johnston 1978, 78)

The path of union to which Johnston refers is still a deep aspiration of the human species. Innately, we recognize it as the pathway that we knew for most of our time as an evolutionary species, and with the breakdown of patriarchal ordering, it is rising up to engage us once more, inviting us to claim it once again as the way to harmony and wholeness.

This is what consciousness is about today. In one sense we as a human species have never abandoned the "path of union." How could we, when the universe itself never abandoned it? And so as we become aware once more of the essential oneness of all things within the great cosmic womb, and when our perceptions change under the influence of this revived awareness, then a new wave of consciousness challenges us to befriend creation in a more benign way and to promote the divine cocreativity with intensity of vision and clarity of purpose.

Outgrowing Our Alienation

Two forces command our attention at this time. In the popular imagination they are considered to be poles apart and radically irreconcilable, but in fact they are two manifestations of the same evolutionary outburst. One is called the "new cosmology" and the other is called "globalization," as described in the present chapter.

The former — the new cosmology — translates into a mystical and intellectual pursuit of a unity that predates and underlies all the divisions and distinctions that humans have made in their attempts to make sense of creation. Critics dismiss it as esoteric, "new age," falsely idealistic, and irrelevant to real people in a real world.

The latter — globalization — is an intensified and concerted human strategy to mobilize as rapidly and efficiently as possible the resources of the earth (and perhaps those of outer space also) so that we humans can really be in control; then, allegedly, we can enjoy a real sense of being at home in the world. This is a rational, anthropocentric movement, overtly atheistic for the greater part, but in fact powerfully fueled by a subconscious need to play God.

In a sense, these two movements are like two ends of a spectrum, represented by tiny human minorities. Consciously, they do not represent the vast bulk of humanity. Most people cannot comprehend the mystical vision of the new cosmology, nor can they obtain the gilded carrot held out by the promoters of globalization.

Subconsciously, we are dealing with two powerful archetypes. One represents the primordial light, which has a luminosity that is too intense for most people, and which is incomprehensible to many people schooled in formal religion. The other — globalization (as understood from the perspective of the southern hemisphere) — represents the primordial darkness of oppression, exploitation, reliance merely on material form, subservience of the weak to the strong, helplessness, and, ultimately, despair.

The polarization could hardly be more extreme and intractable, and because we are so ingrained in dualistic modeling, we are not prepared — intellectually, spiritually, or politically — to name and activate the possible links between these two worlds. And yet, they are two manifestations of the same fundamental aspiration, the same archetypal, ancient yearning: to be one with our planet again.

•

It is time to outgrow . . .

our dysfunctional relationship with creation whereby we pursue a ruthless and relentless exploitation of creation's resources to the detriment of the fragile earth itself and all the vulnerable creatures who inhabit it. Globalization is a misguided effort at befriending creation in its global status; the strategy of conquer and control seriously conflicts with the process of evolution itself.

It is time to embrace...

the awakening consciousness of our time, inviting us to reclaim the ancient mystical wisdom of the one earth and the one universe. A new universality characterizes our time. It is a cultural and spiritual breakthrough inaugurating new evolutionary thresholds inviting us humans to respond in a much more enlightened, creative, and cooperative mode.

Chapter Thirteen

Our Next Evolutionary Leap

We are in a stage of transition between the break-up of the ancient cultures and the birth of a new civilization. . . . A new structure has to be found and this will necessarily be universal, as we now belong irrevocably to one world.　　　　　　— Bede Griffiths

Evolution is no mechanical law, but a complex set of processes, sensitive and symbiogenetic, in part resulting from the choices and actions of evolving organic beings themselves. Natural selection is often said to "favor" this or that trait. But the nature that selects is largely alive. Nature is no black box but a kind of sentient symphony.　　　　　　— Lynn Margulis

ACCORDING TO CURRENT evolutionary theory, life is a fairly simple process of replication, mutation, and selection. It is an observable, quantifiable, and verifiable interaction of a genetic will to power creating form and structure that change at a slow, gradual pace under the influence of natural selection. Biological creatures, including humans, are fundamentally gene machines. For the greater part, we are at the mercy of our genes. They determine who we are and what we become. Whether we evolve or whether we do not is of no real significance; in fact, all this talk about evolution only complicates what is otherwise a fairly simple and comprehensive picture, cryptically described by Richard Dawkins (1995, 19): "Life is just bytes and bytes and bytes of digital information."

That is one version of the story: fairly basic and, some would add, fairly grim. Even among scientists, many opt for something more creative, imaginative, and capable of generating hope for the future. After Darwin, contrary to the mainstream interpretation of his ideas, other perceptions began to surface, focusing on life as an open, creative process. Chance and necessity are not about blind, mindless forces, but can be understood as the dynamics of freedom and possibility

197

that characterize an essentially creative universe. Nothing is rigid and fixed; everything is in process. Reality is like a dance; movement is fundamental and primary. What is structured is movement itself.

Scientists are popularly portrayed as being fundamentally atheistic in dealing with the big questions of life. It seems to me that this is quite a misleading allegation. For a growing number of contemporary scientists, their understanding of divine influence has shifted from the external, anthropomorphic engineer to an internal, dynamical process that requires a whole new way of discerning the meaning (religious and otherwise) of what is transpiring. Contemporary scholars such as Davies (1998), Goodenough (1998), Lovelock (1979; 1988), Margulis (1998), Nadeau and Kafatos (1999), Smolin (1997), and several others grapple admirably with this new interpretation of reality.

This book is an attempt to augment the new orientation, with particular attention to the narrative undercurrent of the evolving process. The new aspects being explored fall under three broad headings: (1) the universal dimension, (2) the planetary realm, and (3) a redefinition of the personal. In each realm, scientific and theological questions intermesh. In each case, we can explore the objective reality only when we choose to honor the ultimate horizons of meaning and possibility. In a unique way, the evolutionary story enables us to do that.

Honoring the Universal

Our story begins with the notion of the "creative vacuum," the reservoir of creative energy, imbuing the universe as pure gift of promise and possibility. Where the energy came from is a philosophical question that is no longer of primary concern. Energy simply *is* — it probably always has been and very likely always will be. What is of greater interest today is that energy flow happens better when a system is "far from equilibrium." Energy is characterized by movement, instability, and unpredictability. And it has an inherent will to meaning to make things happen. Energy is both self-organizing and essentially creative.

The shift in our understanding, from the equilibrium to the nonequilibrium state, is described by Smolin (1997, 199):

> The question of why there is life in the universe takes on a very different light in such a postulated nonequilibrium universe than it did in the old picture of an equilibrium universe. In the old picture, the existence of life is an anomaly, or at least an enormous

improbability, which thus can only be the result of a statistical fluke. In the postulated nonequilibrium picture, the universe remains permanently in a nonequilibrium state. Such a state is a necessary condition for life to exist indefinitely in the universe. We see that in this picture living things share in some ways, and extend in other ways, the basic properties of nonequilibrium, self-organized systems that seem to characterize the universe on every scale, from the cosmos as a whole to the surface of planets.

The fact that energy works best in the nonequilibrium mode does not mean that chaos and randomness become the order of the day. This is where a second key concept comes into play, "information." Information is what makes possible the emerging sense of order and pattern that facilitates creative movement and novel possibilities. Where does the information come from? Not primarily from our human brains, but from an alive universe that is innately intelligent, a cosmos that thrives on a preferred sense of direction (Laszlo 1998) toward complexity, novel possibility, and open-ended future.

The universe knows what it's about. The fact that it does not make sense to us humans, that it often baffles us to extremes and undermines all our theories and expectations, is not a problem for the universe; it is a problem for us. We, therefore, impetuously conclude that the universe does not care about us or about anything else; like the selfish genes, it too unfolds along its blind, mindless path.

But is a blind, mindless path likely to produce stars and galaxies, supernova explosions and quasars, planets and atoms, bacteria and photosynthesis, and creatures of such enormous diversity? Instead of viewing it all as mindless, why not work with the option that it is mindful? Not only would that make the exploration more productive and hopeful; it also would make it a great deal more exciting, energizing, and engaging.

We also need to transcend this fretful preoccupation with where or how God comes into the whole picture. Theologians seem to be nervously concerned with keeping God in, while scientists are desperate to keep God out. I suspect that God is bemusedly puzzled by our human reactions.

The unfolding nature of the universe itself is something that we humans are only beginning to understand. Today, thanks to the pioneering work of scientists, new discoveries abound, new insights proliferate, and new understandings impact upon our daily awareness.

The vastness and distance of it all frighten and excite us, as the notion of the divine did for our ancient ancestors several millennia ago.

The more we learn about the great story, the more we are challenged to reexamine so many dogmatic assumptions. And in a culture still heavily influenced by dualistic fragmentation, we tend to veer one way or another. We begin to grasp, however vaguely, that we intimately belong to the universal reality, and that without it our lives are devoid of true meaning. Alternatively, we retreat further into our anthropocentric alienation, adopting either an unenlightened distance from or an adversarial attitude toward that external object called the universe.

If we are to continue to evolve, we need to allow ourselves to be embraced by the evolving universe itself. We belong intimately and inseparably to creation in its universal scale, to the impregnating stardust that exploded within the cosmic womb itself. Our lives are daily warmed and nourished by sunlight. The bacterial symbiogenesis serves as a perpetual reminder that life is about cooperation, not competition. And the information encoded in the DNA of universe, planet, and person alike never allows us to opt out of the communication network of universal dialogue.

The universe is the great relational matrix that the religions identify as Trinitarian interconnectedness. The matrix is the unbounded realm of space and structure held in being and animated by the quantum vacuum. Potentiality and possibility are inscribed into the very tapestry of creation.

As we grow into deeper understandings, we will find ourselves marveling at the wonders within and around us. The growth of such wisdom cannot be arrested. However, there are formidable hurdles to negotiate before this wisdom can be accorded universal significance. The rational mind needs to embrace intuition and imagination; the anthropocentric will to power needs to learn the wisdom of nonviolence; we need to come home to a deeper awareness that everything within and around us is alive. These "conversions" will take time. From a human point of view, we may not have the time, and that is the supreme critical question facing humanity today.

Befriending the Earth

While science continues to illuminate the great mysteries of the universal realm, our immediate experience of creation is through our engagement with the home planet. It has been here for at least four billion years, and for most of that time it has been home to organic life. The earth is fond of life, to such a degree, in fact, that it is quite amazing that scientists ever could conclude that it is made of dead, inert matter.

It is equally bizarre that religionists from several of the great faiths could be so oblivious to the aliveness and creativity of the earth. Truthfully, of course, we do seem to have honored the sacredness of our earthly home for most of the time we have inhabited the home planet. There is much to suggest that it is only in the past five thousand years that we have seriously deviated from our intuitive sense that we inhabit a living organism from which we draw life and sustenance at all times.

This, I suggest, is where both theologian and scientist need to begin their exploration. The Gaia theory, initially developed by James Lovelock (1979; 1988), invites us to engage not with life *on* earth, but rather, with the life-form that *is* the earth. Our earth is not an object to be exploited, but a living organism inviting our dialogue and participation. Setting humans over against the alive creates a violent disparity not only with humanity, but also with our home planet. Our lives are largely devoid of meaning unless and until we inhabit a meaningful planet. In the planet's coming alive, we too begin to live fully. (For a more comprehensive treatment, see Primavesi 2000.)

Theologically, we also have to shed many "ghosts" from the past. Our earth may not be perfect, but that does not seem to be a problem for the Originating and Sustaining Mystery. Nor does it seem to have been a problem for humanity for many thousands of years. We belong beautifully to the earth. It is the alive, maternal organism that brought us into being, sustains us throughout life, and receives us back into the fertile earth when our lives have run their course. Death is not the consequence of sin in a sinful world. Death is both a natural and a supernatural dimension of life recycling its resources, not in a mindless merry-go-round that never goes anywhere, but in a process resembling a spiral, always moving to realms of greater depth as evolution begets new possibilities from the death and transformation of old forms.

Redefining the Human

We humans exhibit an enormous reluctance in acknowledging that the fundamental problem is about us, not about the universe or our home planet. Hence comes our general lack of interest in evolution and its story. Evolution puts us in our rightful place, but dare we acknowledge the consequences of being there? We resent anything that points to the fact that something other than ourselves is in charge, that we are meant to be a servant species at the service of a greater organism.

Evolution also threatens our power. We have set ourselves up as the masters of creation, and religion tends to validate this conviction. Evolution informs and assures us that the real mastery is within the intelligence of the unfolding process itself. Our call, and our responsibility, is to learn to flow with it. The power and the wisdom are in the greater reality; we have tried to usurp this power and make it uniquely our own. That is our great mistake — one that could cost us dearly unless we choose to change our outlook.

The outlook is not about power and control; it is about participation in the great cosmic adventure. We need to become playful once more — creative, imaginative, cooperative, and spiritually alert. With or without us, the adventure of evolution will continue. And it will not devour or consume us; we are much more likely to do that to ourselves, as scholars such as Leakey and Lewin (1996) and Ward (1995) indicate with graphic and disturbing detail.

We yet have to learn how to mobilize most effectively the greatest gift at our disposal: consciousness. As noted previously, our ability to reflect on our capacity to reflect seems to be our unique endowment. And this is not some special form of mind power or brain skill. Foundationally it seems to be a psychic form of endowment, one that facilitates a coherent and creative response across all the other dimensions of our personalities — physical, social, mental, and spiritual. Our uniqueness is about our psychic potentialities.

But none of our capacities as human beings can be activated in isolation. We need the stimulation, modeling, animation, and support of others (humans and nonhumans) if our potentialities are to be evoked in a meaningful and productive way. This is eminently true of our psychic powers. Initially they arise from within the cosmic (archetypal) and planetary sphere of our existence, and their maturation seems to flourish precisely when we invest our energies in reciprocal interaction. It is in our giving to life that we ourselves receive abundantly.

The conditioning of recent millennia has deprived us of that which seems to constitute the heart of our humanity: our ability to invoke the wisdom that comes from within. This intuitive, reflective, deeply contemplative wisdom does not begin with us. It begins with creation; more accurately, it first manifests itself in the evolving creative process. We detect its power in the inspirited, creative energy that we name as the Originating and Sustaining Mystery, otherwise called the divine life-force, or God. And what we need to remember is that for most of our earthly existence and evolutionary experience, that encounter with the enduring mystery happened in the context of our cosmic and planetary existence, not in some heavenly, otherworldly abode.

Today, the wisdom of our time, externally displayed in the information explosion and the vastly accelerated pursuit of knowledge, is pushing us rapidly toward new evolutionary horizons. For several decades now, researchers — parapsychologists, for example — have been exploring various advances in how we humans perceive and understand our world. Extrasensory capabilities manifest themselves with growing frequency across the human population today. This is disturbing and threatening to those committed to strategies of power and control. Consequently, the research and findings have been suppressed, and often ridiculed in a way that undermines serious consideration.

People's wisdom is outpacing institutionalized knowledge, while the wisdom inherent in nature itself is stretching human resourcefulness to limits previously unknown. The conventional ways of understanding — predominantly the scientific and religious ones — evoke growing suspicion and cynicism from the masses. We are still very much in the breakdown phase; intimations of the breakthrough are still vague and poorly defined.

Undoubtedly, the breakthrough will begin to surface in a range of strange and unexpected ways — life is bigger than logic! The global access to information via computers is an obvious one, breaking through the poverty trap that for so long has kept the informed and the uninformed apart; now, even the poorest peoples in the world are accessing information and making global connections on par with their contemporaries in developed countries.

Perhaps one of the most provocative prognostications is that of the "longevity revolution," explored by the cultural historian Theodore Roszak (1998). Within a short number of years the elderly population of the United States will numerically outgrow the youth population. Already, population growth in Europe is in reverse. Even in the two-thirds world, population growth is slowing down. People everywhere are living longer, thanks to improved medicine and health care. The world's population is beginning to grow old.

In a culture fixated on youth and youthfulness, this is not good news. It is particularly disturbing for market forces, whose advertising and propaganda thrive on the "innocence" and naiveté of youth. Now, with the world population growing older, claims Roszak, the value system will begin to change significantly as older people, exhibiting different needs and appropriating more sustainable and caring values, demand a different quality of public response. Instead of everything being geared to the survival of the fittest, the "survival of the gentlest" (Roszak 1998, 240ff.) is likely to become the governing norm.

World population is still growing, but by the year 2020, figures are likely to stabilize universally, and by the year 2050, Roszak believes, world population, currently running at 6.2 billion, will be closer to 4.5 billion. The aging process, of which so many people live in dread and which popular culture regards with contempt, may prove to be the strongest hope for the future of human evolution. It would not be the first time in the evolutionary story that the wisdom of Gaia outwitted all our expectations.

The Future

Ours is a benevolent creation, an adventure poised toward life and possibility. To the human eye, its dynamics often seem bizarre and crazy, destructive and outrageous. But viewed on a panoramic scale, it is endowed with resilience and nerve. And it seems to be in no hurry about getting there. It took billions of years for biological life to unfold. And there are aeons still awaiting us for many more wild and wonderful explorations. Whether we will be around to enjoy them depends, to some degree at least, on us.

It very much depends upon our ability to reconnect with life on the larger and grander scale. We belong to the relational matrix of cosmic belonging and planetary integration. Our lives are meaningless, in fact nonexistent, without these larger supporting organisms. They provide us with everything we are and have. Our lives are microcosms of the universal life-force.

What the next evolutionary steps are for our cosmos and our planet are issues on which we can barely speculate, but that there are more steps is beyond dispute. The cosmos will continue to bloom and flourish for aeons that the human imagination can scarcely envisage. The future of planet earth has been the subject of several ominous predictions, from both science and religion; evolution is likely to prove every one of them grossly inadequate. Even with the worst predicted scenarios, earth is likely to survive for at least another five billion years. (That should put to rest the doomsday prognostications of all the major religions.) By then, the human mind itself will have evolved significantly, so we are likely to come up with very different perceptions — assuming that we ourselves will still be around!

Roszak (1998) indicates that it is to the advantage of humans that they become much more gentle. I suggest that we also need to become a great deal more humble. Our arrogance creates incredible pain, suffering, and meaninglessness for both people and planet. It is such a ridiculous way to behave. We have been endowed with such a magnificent universe, such a creative planet, such a variegated community of creatures and life-forms — what is the point of this crazy competitive drive that we postulate as normality?

We belong beautifully to the earth and intimately to the cosmic web of life. Daily we breathe in the odor of sanctity that imbues creation. Our God walks with us in the garden of life, the Originating and Sustaining Mystery who is radically transparent for those who have eyes to see. We need a fresh approach to our theology of God, one that honors the mystery within which everything is held. The divine is written all over creation: the quantum vacuum, the supernova explosions, the recurring cycle of birth-death-rebirth, the process of photosynthesis — these and many more are the chapters of our primary scriptures. Divinity abounds, in and around us.

The promise of future possibility is guaranteed. In a sense, this is the ultimate gratuitous act of God, the core truth of what Christians envisage in the notion of resurrection. There is no closure to the future, and it seems that there never can be. The future is way beyond the profoundest thoughts, ideas, and speculations of the human mind. In our presently evolving psychic capacity we need to move more into an acceptance of the creative potentials of such a future instead of the futile exercise of trying to predict short-term outcomes.

We need to move from speculation to trust. We need to move from the compulsive need for human certainty to a trust in cosmic hope. We need to embrace the story in all its beauty, pain, and possibility. As we learn to flow with the story, we rediscover, time and again, who we really are. And hopefully, in time we will realize that it is the story itself that guarantees our identity at every step of the way.

Truly, we who tell the story belong intimately to the story. The story is the sanctuary in which paradox and possibility lie down together, and therein, we too find our home, our truth, and our meaning in life.

•

It is time to outgrow...

the anthropocentric desire to dominate and control everything that unfolds in our evolutionary world. By clinging to this desire, we undermine the planetary and cosmic context to which we belong. Thus, there ensues both for ourselves and the creation that we inhabit immense suffering, estrangement, and alienation.

It is time to embrace...

the cosmic and planetary context within which our life story and the story of all life unfolds. We belong to a reality greater than ourselves, and it is within that enlarged context that we will rediscover the benign and generic mystery within which everything is endowed with purpose and meaning.

Notes

1. I am grateful to my colleague and Teilhardian scholar John Woodcock for suggesting the notion of E-mergence and encouraging me to use it in this book.

2. It is scholars of neo-Darwinian persuasion, rather than those propounding the ideas of Darwin himself, who tend to be most dogmatic, and often antireligious, in their approach to evolutionary biology. It often is noted that Darwin concluded his *Origin of Species* with these words: "There is a grandeur in this view of life, with its several powers, having been originally breathed by the Creator into a few forms or into one; and that, whilst this planet has gone cycling on according to the fixed law of gravity, from so simple a beginning, endless forms most beautiful and most wonderful have been, and are being evolved."

Scholars such as Dawkins (1976; 1986) and, particularly, Dennett (1995) tend to ignore these spiritual sentiments. In Dennett's view, Darwin has irrevocably destroyed the credibility of religion, particularly that of the Genesis account of creation. Stephen J. Gould, who argues consistently for the need for an ethical (though not necessarily religious) value system, seems to adopt a rather evasive and manipulative approach to Darwin's apparent religious belief. Without formal acknowledgement, he quotes Darwin's final words from the *Origin of Species* (see above), but modifies the text so as to eliminate all references to "the Creator" (see Gould 1993, 79, 179, 217). Such a strategy will do little to promote creative and constructive dialogue.

3. In fact, Taylor (1996, 99) suggests, "Our capacity for appreciating artistic images dates back some three million years, to an Australopithecine-inhabited cave at Makapansgat in Southern Africa, where a pebble in an occupation deposit was found to look like a human face."

4. Edward P. Tryon was one of the first to suggest that the universe emerged as a fluctuation of the creative vacuum. Spontaneous temporary particles always emerge from the vacuum, from "nowhere"; consequently, says Tryon, our universe may simply be a fluctuation of "the vacuum of some larger space in which our universe is embedded."

Tryon bases his conviction on quantum field theory, in which it is postulated that every phenomenon that could happen in principle actually does happen occasionally in practice on a statistically random basis. Tryon's apparent contradiction between "nowhere" and "some larger space in which our universe is embedded" is reminiscent of Polkinghorne's observation that our assertion that nothing existed in the beginning does not automatically mean that nothing was happening. The quantum vacuum is a hive of activity, full of fluctuations, with an unceasing rise and decline of creative possibilities (see Polkinghorne 1989, 59ff.).

5. In contemporary physics this is defined as the lowest energy state of a system,

where the mysterious "zero-point field" manifests itself. Ervin Laszlo (1998, 180) offers the following description:

> The energies of this field appear when all other — more conventional forms of energy — vanish at the zero-point (hence the name). Zero-point energies are "virtual" energies: they are not the same as the classical electromagnetic, gravitational, or nuclear forces. Rather, they are the very source of the electromagnetic, gravitational, and nuclear forces of the cosmos. As such, they are the originating source also of the energies that are bound in mass: the particles of matter that populate the known universe. The technical definitions of the zero-point energy field that underlies the quantum vacuum indicate an almost infinite energy sea in which particles of matter are emergent substructures.... Though these particles are not observable, they are by no means fictional.

In the 1980s others began to adopt the idea of the universe emerging from a quantum fluctuation, notably Alexander Vilenkin. He developed Edward P. Tryon's ideas (see note 4 above) by suggesting that originally creation takes place through a tunneling process that determines the initial conditions at the moment of nucleation. The better-known models proposed in the 1980s are those of James Hartle and Stephen Hawking, suggesting a space-time universe but without boundaries. Using imaginary numbers, they eliminated the initial boundary condition (the point in time), offering an image like an inverted cone that is rounded rather than beginning at a specific point, with the three-dimensional wave fluctuation forming the only boundary.

In 1986 John Barrow and Frank Tipler (1986) also opted for the wave fluctuation origin, but situated it within an initial time boundary whence is set off a series of universes, which they describe as branch universes.

6. Since Darwin's time, several other theories about the origin of life have been explored. Hoyle and Wickramasinghe (1993, 4) represent those who favor the notion of "life from afar," drawing on astronomical evidence that points to the existence of vast quantities of complex organic molecules in interstellar space. The notion that life came to earth from outer space — Mars or elsewhere — in the form of already viable microbes is popularly known as the "panspermia hypothesis" (see Achenbach 2000). Davies (1998) reviews the research on the notion that life began inside the earth, several kilometers down in the solid crust, probably beneath the seabed. In a geothermal environment, so hot that one would expect it to kill off most organisms, scientists have discovered bizarre microbes still living in these scalding locations today. Currently, this is a subject of intense study by marine biologist John Delaney and his coworkers from the University of Washington (subject of a BBC documentary in November 1999).

7. This experience of the divine in the elements of nature tends to be described by historians of religion as "animism" — a generic concept often dismissed as nature religion or paganism. According to Raphael (1999, 44), animistic religion does not distinguish between animate and inanimate objects, but sees all things in nature as conscious and partaking of the same vital energies. This perception of the world has

been more characteristic of indigenous religion, but the rise of ecological conscious-ness has done much to make animistic worldviews more widespread in Europe and America.

8. This suggestion that humans appropriated metaphorical perceptions prior to literal interpretations is related to how we perceive the evolution of spoken language. I explore this topic in chapter 9, following contemporary scholars such as Deacon (1997), whose research refutes the long-held belief that we were able to think imag-inatively and metaphorically only *after* we learned to speak. As Deacon and others suggest, language itself, being a highly sophisticated symbolic system, could have been developed only by a species that was itself highly intelligent and capable of those imaginative potentialities involved in the use of metaphor, simile, allegory, and the like.

9. Evidence for the great extinctions has been reviewed by several scholars in recent decades (see the comprehensive studies of Donovan 1989; Leakey and Lewin 1996; Swimme and Berry 1992; Eldredge 1991; 1999). All the examples cited be-long to the past five hundred million years, namely, those unexpected (and largely unexplained) erasures in the biological line when large sections of the then existent life-forms were either eliminated or severely curtailed.

The five extinctions that have been identified are named as:

- The end Ordovician, 440 million years ago, which saw the demise of almost 60 percent of marine invertebrate genera.

- The late Devonian, 365 million years ago. It is believed that the catastrophic effects here were not so much on species as on the sheer biomass that died out. Around the world, tropical reefs vanished as most reef-building corals became extinct.

- The end Permian, 225 million years ago, dealing a fatal blow to the mammal-like reptiles that had ruled terrestrial life for 80 million years. Because of the movement of tectonic plates, bringing the continents together into the super-continent, "Pangaea," shallow coastal waters were significantly diminished, wiping out an estimated 96 percent of extant marine species.

- The end Triassic, 210 million years ago. Once again, marine invertebrates were the primary victims, with their populations reduced by well over 50 percent.

- The end Cretaceous, 65 million years ago, allegedly marked the end of the dinosaurs and other large reptiles, thus enabling the mammals to flourish.

These are considered to be the five big extinctions. Several others are known to have occurred, including what George Cuvier, in the early nineteenth century, described as "catastrophism." Jack Sepkoski and David Raup claim that such extinctions occur not at random, but approximately every twenty-six million years. They attribute this consistent regularity to Nemesis, a companion star of the sun, which periodically disrupts the orbits of asteroids and comets, setting a barrage of objects on a collision course with the earth. If one of these extraterrestrial bodies, such as a meteorite, hits the earth, there is likely to be mass destruction and the ensuing diminution of one or more species. What caused the great extinctions? Comets and meteorites have been suggested, as well as volcanic eruptions, all having the effect of blotting out sunlight by dust in the atmosphere. But these connections have not been proved. More likely are long-term climate changes, cooling, and glaciation — itself caused perhaps by continental drift toward the poles.

10. Twentieth-century science has been haunted by the search for a "grand unified theory" (GUT), one that would link together the four major forces of nature: gravity, electromagnetism, and the strong and weak forces. Einstein grappled long and hard with this idea. To realize this dream, we needed more than the four space-time dimensions of length, breadth, depth, and time. In the early 1920s, the Polish physicist Theodore Kaluza and the Swedish physicist Oskar Klein suggested that space-time might have a hidden fifth dimension. In 1962, Paul A. M. Dirac postulated that an electron might resemble a minute bubble rather than a point. In the late 1960s, Gabriele Veneziano, then a research fellow at CERN in Switzerland, revisited the work of the eighteenth-century Swiss mathematician Leonhard Euler, inspiring other scientists in the early 1970s to use Euler's "beta-function" to describe hitherto unknown interactions in particle physics, leading to the intuition that particles might better be described as strings than as pointlike objects. Finally, in 1974, John Schwarz, of the California Institute of Technology, and the French theorist Joel Scherk suggested that we replace the notion of atoms with that of "strings," fundamental entities 10^{-33} centimeters long and comprising ten dimensions.

Subjecting the new ideas to test and verification proved enormously difficult, and consequently, the novel idea was largely abandoned. In the 1980s, Schwarz joined forces with Michael Green, then working at Queen Mary College in London, and relaunched the idea of strings, now calling it "superstring theory." Meanwhile, Ed Witten, of the Institute for Advanced Study in Princeton, New Jersey, embraced the new vision and became one of its most ardent proponents throughout the 1990s. (For further details, see the very readable account of Green 2000.)

Bodies are made up of atoms, but atoms are not material things. Rather, they resemble an indefinable field of trapped light and energy flow. Fox (1999, 47) explains it rather vividly: "An atom is a vast region of empty space in which incredibly tiny particles called electrons orbit around a nucleus. Blow an atom up to be the size of the dome of St. Peter's basilica in Rome, and the nucleus would be the size of a grain of salt."

11. Among the many outstanding discoveries of Mary D. Leakey (wife of Louis and mother of Richard) was a series of human footprints at the Laetoli site of northern Tanzania; in fact, the footprints were first noticed by one of her associates, the geochemist Paul I. Abell. The footprints are those of an upright hominid and have been dated to 3.6 million years ago. For more information, see Agnew and Demas 1998.

12. It has been pointed out that two gorillas sharing a similar environment in either eastern or western Africa are genetically more divergent than a Canadian Inuit and an Australian Aborigine. The common chimpanzee of central Africa has three subspecies, which overtly look very similar. But genetically, these three chimpanzee "races" are almost ten times as different from each other as are the African,

European, and Asian divisions of *Homo sapiens*. In the words of Stringer and McKie (1996, 113), "We [humans] display remarkable geographical diversity, and yet astonishing genetic unity."

13. In fact, a dimension of our contemporary evolutionary unfolding may involve a reclaiming of this ancient capacity for nonverbal (or perhaps, supraverbal) communication. We often note in contemporary psychotherapy that a person finds it difficult to express in words what is going on within. When the client is invited to use some nonverbal mode — for example, clay, music, movement, or art — there often is a breakthrough, an inner connection and an externalization of an inner process that apparently words were unable to express.

14. The fact that many species of animal are territorial and sometimes fight and kill to defend their territories is an argument often used to explain human territoriality and to justify the aggression exhibited in early agricultural societies. As distinct from most species of animal, we possess a different quality of intelligence and we are endowed with free will. The link with animal behavior is no longer adequate either to explain or to justify human territoriality.

15. This is precisely what happened in Rwanda in 1994. The Belgian army turned a blind eye to what they knew was a dangerously explosive situation. Meanwhile, the UN was locked in a financial argument with the United States government on what price should be paid for helicopters for use in Rwanda. Everybody from the West seemed to know that carnage was imminent. They did nothing, and meanwhile, almost one million people were butchered.

16. Although the research on the brain as the location and source of human consciousness usually leads to a reductionistic, materialistic, and anthropocentric outcome, there are some notable exceptions. The higher-order thought (HOT) theory of consciousness, on which David Rosenthal (1990) is a leading authority, distinguishes between intentional mental activity (reflecting on the fact that I can reflect) and nonintentional states, namely, sensations (often described by the scientists as "qualia"). Rosenthal argues that consciousness in its primary meaning belongs to intentional mental behavior.

The British physicist Danah Zohar draws on the pioneering work of the neuroscientists Wolf Singer and Charles Gray, who showed that bundles of neurons all over the brain oscillate simultaneously at similar frequencies (about 40Hz) if they perceive the same object. These generalized oscillations (40Hz waves) in the human brain create a coherent pattern that transcends the abilities of any single neuron or localized group of neurons. This coordinated brain activity happens simultaneously throughout the whole brain. Zohar suggests that consciousness is an emergent property of these neural oscillations and may be understood as the force that enables many brain processes to function in unison in a coherent and creative way.

Zohar's research, along with that of the American neuroscientist Rodolfo Llinas (see Zohar and Marshall 2000, 67–90), augments the notion that consciousness forges a sense of unity wherein the whole is greater than the sum of the parts. This holistic quality in itself provokes us to explore consciousness as a dimension of life, including but transcending the human brain. The nearest that mainstream science gets to this approach is connectionism — how the brain's neural networks match various states of sensory consciousness — promoted especially by the neuroscientist Paul Churchland (1988).

17. Conventionally, we associate memory with the human capacity to remember from previous learning or life experience. Neuroscientists, assuming that memory is located in the human brain, devote a great deal of research on trying to locate the precise brain centers from which memory is activated; researchers adopting a holographic approach suggest that it is spread throughout the brain.

In the present work, memory is postulated as a much more elemental evolutionary quality that long predates human beings. I suggest that it is an endowment of creation's dynamic unfolding through which past patterns are invoked to enhance future possibilities, as explored in some of the groundbreaking work of the biologist Rupert Sheldrake (1988; 1991).

18. Allegedly, the G7 (consisting of the United States, Canada, the United Kingdom, Japan, Germany, France, and Italy), in conjunction with the International Monetary Fund and the World Bank, oversees the operations of transnational corporations. More accurately, the G7 facilitates the activities of the corporations, with the subtle but dominant agenda that capitalism and its values must be safeguarded and promoted. Consequently, Russia was incorporated into the G7 (now known as the G8), not as a token of goodwill and inclusiveness, but as a cover-up for the dismal failure of capitalism in the former Soviet Union. The culture of capitalism must not be seen to fail!

Bibliography

Abram, David. 1996. *The Spell of the Sensuous*. New York: Vintage Books.

Achenbach, Joel. 2000. "Life beyond Earth." *National Geographic* (January): 24–51.

Adams, Fred, and Greg Laughlin. 1999. *The Five Ages of the Universe: Inside the Physics of Eternity*. New York: Free Press.

Agnew, Neville, and Martha Demas. 1998. "Preserving the Laetoli Footprints." *Scientific American* 279 (September): 28–37.

Arul Raj, V. 2000. "Trojan Horse in the Global Village." *Jeevadhara* 30:39–63.

Bailie, Gil. 1997. *Violence Unveiled*. New York: Crossroad.

Barrow, John, and Frank Tipler. 1986. *The Anthropic Cosmological Principle*. Oxford: Clarendon Press.

Battle, Michael. 1997. *Reconciliation: The Ubuntu Theology of Desmond Tutu*. Cleveland: Pilgrim Press.

Behe, Michael. 1996. *Darwin's Black Box*. New York: Free Press.

Boelen, Jean Shinoda. 1984. *Goddess in Everywoman*. San Francisco: Harper & Row.

Boff, Leonardo. 1995. *Ecology and Liberation*. Maryknoll, N.Y.: Orbis Books.

———. 1997. *Cry of the Earth, Cry of the Poor*. Maryknoll, N.Y.: Orbis Books.

Boslough, John. 1992. *Masters of Time*. London: J. M. Dent.

Brown, Peter. 1988. *The Body and Society: Men, Women, and Sexual Renunciation in Early Christianity*. New York: Columbia University Press.

Brueggemann, Walter. 1993. *Texts under Negotiation: The Bible and Postmodern Imagination*. Minneapolis: Fortress Press.

Bruteau, Beatrice. 1997. *God's Ecstasy: The Creation of a Self-creating World*. New York: Crossroad.

Chaisson, Eric J. 2001. *Cosmic Evolution: The Rise of Complexity in Nature*. Cambridge, Mass., and London: Harvard University Press.

Chalmers, David J. 1996. *The Conscious Mind*. New York: Oxford University Press.

Christ, Carol P. 1997. *Rebirth of the Goddess*. New York and London: Routledge.

Churchland, Paul. 1988. *Matter and Consciousness*. Cambridge, Mass.: MIT Press.

Cohen, M. N., and G. J. Armelagos. 1984. *Paleopathology at the Origins of Agriculture*. New York: Academic Press.

Crawford, Robert. 1997. *The God/Man/World Triangle: A Dialogue between Science and Religion*. New York: St. Martin's Press; London: Macmillan Press.

Crick, Francis. 1995. *The Astonishing Hypothesis: The Scientific Search for the Soul*. New York: Simon & Schuster.

Daly, Mary. 1978. *Gyn/Ecology: The Metaethics of Radical Feminism.* Boston: Beacon Press.

———. 1998. *Quintessence: Realizing the Archaic Future.* Boston: Beacon Press.

Davies, Paul. 1987. *The Cosmic Blueprint.* New York and London: Simon & Schuster.

———. 1992. *The Mind of God.* New York and London: Simon & Schuster.

———. 1995. *About Time.* London and New York: Penguin Press.

———. 1998. *The Fifth Miracle: The Search for the Origin of Life.* New York and London: Allen Lane/Penguin Press.

Dawkins, Richard. 1976. *The Selfish Gene.* Oxford and New York: Oxford University Press.

———. 1986. *The Blind Watchmaker.* New York: W. W. Norton.

———. 1995. *River Out of Eden* New York: HarperCollins.

Deacon, Terence. 1997. *The Symbolic Species.* New York and London: Allen Lane/Penguin Press.

De Duve, Christian. 1995. *Vital Dust: Life as a Cosmic Imperative.* New York: Basic Books.

Delaney, Carol. 1998. *Abraham on Trial.* Princeton, N.J.: Princeton University Press.

Dennett, Daniel. 1991. *Consciousness Explained.* Boston: Little, Brown.

———. 1995. *Darwin's Dangerous Idea: Evolution and the Meaning of Life.* New York: Simon & Schuster.

Donald, Merlin. 1991. *Origins of the Modern Mind: Three Stages in the Evolution of Culture and Cognition.* Cambridge, Mass., and London: Harvard University Press.

Donovan, S. K., ed. 1989. *Mass Extinctions: Processes and Evidence.* London: Belhaven.

Donovan, Vincent J. 1989. *The Church in the Midst of Creation.* Maryknoll, N.Y.: Orbis Books.

Dretske, Fred. 1997. *Naturalizing the Mind.* Cambridge, Mass.: MIT Press.

Duff, Michael J. 1998. "The Theory Formerly Known as Strings." *Scientific American* 278 (February): 64–69.

Dyson, Freeman. 1979. *Disturbing the Universe.* New York: Harper & Row.

———. 1988. *Infinite in All Directions.* New York: Harper & Row.

Edwards, Denis. 1995. *Jesus the Wisdom of God: An Ecological Theology.* Maryknoll, N.Y.: Orbis Books.

———. 1999. *The God of Evolution.* Mahwah, N.J.: Paulist Press.

Eisenberg, Evan. 1998. *The Ecology of Eden: Humans, Nature, and Human Nature.* New York: Alfred A. Knopf; London: Picador.

Eisler, Riane. 1987. *The Chalice and the Blade.* New York: Harper & Row.

Eldredge, N. 1991. *The Miner's Canary: Unraveling the Mysteries of Extinction.* New York: Prentice Hall.

———. 1999. *The Pattern of Evolution.* New York: W. H. Freeman & Co.

Eldredge, N., and Stephen J. Gould. 1972. "Punctuated Equilibria: An Alternative to Phyletic Gradualism." In *Models in Paleobiology,* ed. T. J. M. Schopf, 82–115. San Francisco: Freeman.

Ellis, Marc E. 1997. *Unholy Alliance: Religion and Atrocity in Our Time.* London: SCM Press; Minneapolis: Augsburg Fortress.

Fox, Matthew. 1999. *Sins of the Spirit, Blessings of the Flesh.* New York: Harmony Books; Dublin: Gateway.

———. 2000. *One River, Many Wells: Wisdom Springing from Global Faiths.* New York: Tarcher/Putnam.

Fraser, Gordon. 2000. *Antimatter: The Ultimate Mirror.* New York and Cambridge: Cambridge University Press.

Girard, René. 1979. *Violence and the Sacred.* Baltimore: Johns Hopkins University Press.

———. 1986. *The Scapegoat.* Baltimore: Johns Hopkins University Press.

Gleick, James. 1987. *Chaos: Making a New Science.* New York: Viking-Penguin.

Goodenough, Ursula. 1998. *The Sacred Depths of Nature.* New York and Oxford: Oxford University Press.

Goodwin, Brian. 1996. *How the Leopard Changed Its Spots.* New York: Simon & Schuster.

Goswami, Amit. 1993. *The Self-Aware Universe: How Consciousness Creates the Material World.* New York: Tarcher/Putnam.

Gould, Stephen J. 1989. *Wonderful Life.* New York: W. W. Norton.

———. 1993. *Eight Little Piggies.* New York: W. W. Norton.

Graham, Elaine. 1995. *Making the Difference: Gender, Personhood, and Theology.* London and New York: Mowbray.

———. 1998. *Transforming Practice: Pastoral Theology in an Age of Uncertainty.* London and New York: Mowbray.

Green, Brian. 2000. *The Elegant Universe.* London and Sydney: Random House/Vintage.

Gribben, John. 1999. *The Birth of Time.* London: Weidenfeld & Nicolson.

Griffin, David Ray. 1990. *Archetypal Process: Self and Divine in Whitehead, Jung, and Hillman.* Evanston, Ill.: Northwestern University Press.

Hampson, Daphne. 1996. *After Christianity.* London: SCM Press.

Haught, John F. 1993. *Mystery and Promise: A Theology of Revelation.* Collegeville, Minn.: Liturgical Press.

———. 2000. *God after Darwin: A Theology of Evolution.* Boulder, Colo., and Oxford: Westview Press.

Hawking, Stephen. 1988. *A Brief History of Time: From the Big Bang to Black Holes.* New York and London: Bantam Books.

———. 1993. *Black Holes and Baby Universes.* New York and London: Bantam Books.

Hayes, Michael. 1994. *The Infinite Harmony: Musical Structures in Science and Theology.* London: Weidenfeld & Nicolson.

Hefner, Philip. 1972. *The Human Factor: Evolution, Culture, Religion.* Philadelphia: Fortress Press.

Heyward, Carter. 1989. *Touching Our Strength: The Erotic as Power and the Love of God.* San Francisco: Harper.

———. 1999. *Saving Jesus from Those Who Are Right.* Minneapolis: Fortress Press.

Hodgson, Peter C. 1989. *God in History: Shapes of Freedom*. Nashville: Abingdon Press.

———. 1994. *Winds of the Spirit: A Constructive Christian Theology*. Minneapolis: Fortress; London: SCM Press.

———. 1999. *God's Wisdom: Toward a Theology of Education*. Philadelphia: Westminster John Knox Press.

Hoyle, Fred, and Chandra Wickramasinghe. 1993. *Our Place in the Cosmos*. London: J. M. Dent.

Hubbard, Barbara Max. 1998. *Conscious Evolution*. Novata, Calif.: New World Library.

Jahn, Robert G., and Brenda J. Dunne. 1987. *Margins of Reality: The Role of Consciousness in the Physical World*. New York: Harcourt, Brace & Co.

Jantsch, Erich. 1980. *The Self-Organizing Universe*. New York: Pergamon Press.

Jantzen, Grace M. 1998. *Becoming Divine: Towards a Feminist Philosophy of Religion*. Manchester: Manchester University Press.

Johnson, Elizabeth. 1992. *She Who Is*. New York: Crossroad.

Johnston, William. 1978. *The Inner Eye of Love: Mysticism and Religion*. London: Collins.

———. 2000. *"Arise, My Love": Mysticism for a New Era*. Maryknoll, N.Y.: Orbis Books.

Jonas, Hans. 1996. *Mortality and Morality*. Evanston, Ill.: Northwestern University Press.

Kaku, Michio. 1998. *Visions: How Science Will Revolutionize the Twenty-First Century and Beyond*. Oxford and New York: Oxford University Press.

Kalliath, Anthony. 1999. "Globalisation: Colonization Perpetuation." In *Religion and Politics from Subaltern Perspective*, ed. Thomas Kadankaval, 114–42. Bangalore: Dharmaran Press.

Kauffman, Stuart. 1995. *At Home in the Universe: The Search for Laws of Self-Organization and Complexity*. New York: Oxford University Press.

Kaufman, Gordon. 1993. *In Face of Mystery*. Cambridge, Mass.: Harvard University Press.

Knitter, Paul F. 1995. *One Earth Many Religions*. Maryknoll, N.Y.: Orbis Books.

Korten, David. 1995. *When Corporations Rule the World*. West Hartford, Conn.: Kumarian Press.

Kuhn, Thomas. 1970. *The Structure of Scientific Revolutions*. Chicago: University of Chicago Press.

Kurzweil, Ray. 1999. *The Age of Spiritual Machines*. London: Orion Business Books.

La Chance, Albert. 1991. *Greenspirit: Twelve Steps in Ecological Spirituality*. Shaftesbury, Dorset: Element Books.

Laszlo, Ervin. 1993. *The Creative Cosmos: A Unified Science of Matter, Life, and Mind*. Edinburgh: Floris Books.

———. 1996. *Evolution: The General Theory*. Cresskill, N.J.: Hampton Press.

———. 1998. *The Whispering Pond*. Shaftesbury, Dorset, and Rockport, Mass.: Element Books.

Layzer, David. 1990. *Cosmogenesis: The Growth of Order in the Universe*. New York and Oxford: Oxford University Press.

Leakey, Richard. 1992. *Origins Reconsidered: In Search of What Makes Us Human*. London: Abacus Press.

Leakey, Richard, and Roger Lewin. 1996. *The Sixth Extinction: Biodiversity and Its Survival*. London: Weidenfeld & Nicolson.

Leeming, David, and Jack Page. 1994. *Goddess: Myths of the Female Divine*. Oxford: Oxford University Press.

Lewin, Roger. 1993. *Complexity: Life on the Edge of Chaos*. London: Macmillan.

Lovelock, James. 1979. *Gaia: A New Look at Life on Earth*. New York: Oxford University Press.

———. 1988. *The Ages of Gaia*. New York: Oxford University Press.

Macquarrie, John. 1966. *Principles of Christian Theology*. London: SCM Press.

Margulis, Lynn. 1998. *The Symbiotic Planet: A New Look at Evolution*. London: Weidenfeld & Nicolson; New York: Basic Books.

Margulis, Lynn, and Dorian Sagan. 1995. *What Is Life?* London: Weidenfeld & Nicolson.

Maturana, H. R., and F. J. Varela. 1980. *Autopoiesis and Cognition: The Realization of the Living*. Boston and London: D. Reidel Publishing Company.

McFadden, John Joe. 2000. *Quantum Biology: The New Science of Life*. London: HarperCollins.

McFague, Sallie. 1993. *The Body of God: An Ecological Theology*. Minneapolis: Fortress Press.

———. 2000. *Abundant Life*. Minneapolis: Fortress Press.

Mithen, Steven. 1996. *The Prehistory of Mind*. New York and London: Thames & Hudson.

Morgan, Robin. 1989. *The Demon Lover: On the Sexuality of Terrorism*. London: Methuen.

Musser, George. 2000. "The Hole Shebang." *Scientific American* 283 (October): 12–13.

Nadeau, Robert, and Menas Kafatos. 1999. *The Non-local Universe: The New Physics and Matters of the Mind*. New York and London: Oxford University Press.

Nelson, Paul A. 1996. "A Sensible God: The Bearing of Theology on Evolutionary Explanation." In *Facts of Faith and Science*, ed. J. M. Van der Meer, vol. 3, 169–97. New York and London: University Press of America.

O'Connor, Kathleen. 1988. *The Wisdom Literature*. Wilmington, Del.: Michael Glazier.

O'Donohue, John. 1997. *Anam Chara: Spiritual Wisdom from the Celtic World*. New York: Bantam Books.

O'Murchu, Diarmuid. 1997a. *Quantum Theology*. New York: Crossroad.

———. 1997b. *Reclaiming Spirituality*. New York: Crossroad; Dublin: Gill & Macmillan.

———. 2000. *Religion in Exile*. New York: Crossroad; Dublin: Gateway.

Palin, David. 1989. *God and the Process of Reality*. London: Routledge.

Peters, Ted, ed. 1998. *Science and Theology: The New Consonance.* Boulder, Colo., and Oxford: Westview Press.

Polkinghorne, John. 1989. *Science and Creation.* London: SPCK.

Prigogine, Ilya. 1997. *The End of Certainty.* New York: Simon & Schuster.

Prigogine, Ilya, and Isobel Stengers. 1984. *Order Out of Chaos.* New York and London: Bantam Books.

Primavesi, Anne. 2000. *Sacred Gaia: Holistic Theology and Earth System Science.* London: Routledge.

Raphael, Melissa. 1996. *Thealogy and Embodiment: The Post-patriarchal Reconstruction of Female Sacrality.* Sheffield: Sheffield Academic Press.

———. 1999. *Introducing Thealogy: Discourse on the Goddess.* Sheffield: Sheffield Academic Press.

Reid, Duncan. 1997. *Energies of the Spirit.* Atlanta: Scholars Press.

Robson, John M., ed. 1987. *Origin and Evolution of the Universe: Evidence for Design?* Montreal: McGill-Queen's University Press.

Rose, Steven. 1997. *Lifelines: Biology, Freedom, Determinism.* London and New York: Penguin.

Rosenthal, David. 1990. *The Nature of Mind.* New York: Oxford University Press.

Roszak, Theodore. 1998. *America the Wise: The Longevity Revolution and the True Wealth of Nations.* New York: Houghton Mifflin Co.

———. 1999. *The Gendered Atom.* Berkeley, Calif.: Conari Press.

Russell, Peter. 1992. *The White Hole in Time.* London: Aquarian Press.

Russell, Robert John, Nancey Murphy, and C. J. Isham, eds. 1993. *Quantum Cosmology and the Laws of Nature.* Berkeley, Calif.: Center for Theology and the Natural Sciences.

Sahtouris, Elisabet. 1998. *EarthDance: Living Systems in Evolution.* Alameda, Calif.: Metalog Books.

Schüssler Fiorenza, Elisabeth. 1984. *In Memory of Her.* New York: Crossroad.

———. 1994. *Miriam's Child, Sophia's Prophet.* New York: Continuum.

Seager, William. 1999. *Theories of Consciousness.* London and New York: Routledge.

Sheldrake, Rupert. 1988. *The Presence of the Past.* London: Collins.

———. 1991. *The Rebirth of Nature.* London: Collins.

Shlain, Leonard. 1998. *The Alphabet versus the Goddess.* New York: Viking.

Singer, Peter. 2000. *A Darwinian Left: Politics, Evolution, and Cooperation.* New Haven: Yale University Press.

Smolin, Lee. 1997. *The Life of the Cosmos.* London: Weidenfeld & Nicolson; New York: Oxford University Press.

Sparks, Alister. 1991. *The Mind of South Africa.* London: Heinemann.

Sri Aurobindo. 1939. *The Life Divine.* Pondicherry: Sri Aurobindo Ashram Press.

———. 1963. *The Future Evolution of Man.* Pondicherry: Sri Aurobindo Ashram Press.

Stringer, Chris, and Robin McKie. 1996. *African Exodus: The Origins of Modern Humanity.* London and Sydney: Random House.

Swimme, Brian. 1996. *The Hidden Heart of the Cosmos*. Maryknoll, N.Y.: Orbis Books.

Swimme, Brian, and Thomas Berry. 1992. *The Universe Story*. San Francisco: Harper.

Talbot, Michael. 1988. *Beyond the Quantum*. London and New York: Bantam Books.

Tattersall, Ian. 1998. *Becoming Human: Evolution and Human Uniqueness*. New York: Harcourt Brace & Co.

————. 2000. "Once We Were Not Alone." *Scientific American* 282 (January): 38–44.

Taylor, Timothy. 1996. *The Prehistory of Sex*. London: Fourth Estate Ltd.

Teilhard de Chardin, Pierre. 1959. *The Phenomenon of Man*. London: Collins.

————. 1964. *The Future of Man*. London: Collins.

Temple, William. 1934. *Nature, Man, and God*. London: Macmillan.

Toolan, David. 2001. *At Home in the Cosmos*. Maryknoll, N.Y.: Orbis Books.

Tryon, Edward P. 1973. "Is the Universe a Vacuum Fluctuation?" *Nature* 246: 396.

Van Ness, Peter. 1992. *Spirituality, Diversion, and Decadence*. Albany: State University of New York Press.

Ward, Keith. 1994. *Religion and Revelation: A Theology of Revelation in the World's Religions*. Oxford and New York: Oxford University Press.

Ward, Peter. 1995. *The End of Evolution*. London: Weidenfeld & Nicolson.

Welch, Sharon. 1990. *A Feminist Ethic of Risk*. Minneapolis: Fortress Press.

White, Tim D., G. Suwa, and B. Asfaw. 1994. "Australopithecus Ramidus, a New Species of Early Hominid from Aramis, Ethiopia." *Nature* 371: 306–12.

Wilber, Ken. 1993 [1977]. *The Spectrum of Consciousness*. Wheaton, Ill.: Theosophical Publishing House.

————. 1998. *The Eye of Spirit*. Boston and London: Shambhala.

Wong, Kate. 1999. "Is Out of Africa Going Out the Door?" *Scientific American* 281 (August): 7–8.

————. 2000. "Who Were the Neanderthals?" *Scientific American* 282 (April): 78–87.

Woolfson, Adrian. 2000. *Life without Genes*. London: HarperCollins.

Worthing, Mark William. 1996. *God, Creation, and Contemporary Physics*. Minneapolis: Fortress Press.

Zohar, Danah. 1991. *The Quantum Self*. London: Bloomsbury Publishing.

Zohar, Danah, and Ian Marshall. 1994. *The Quantum Society*. London: HarperCollins.

————. 2000. *SQ: Spiritual Intelligence the Ultimate Intelligence*. London: Bloomsbury Publishing.

Index

FOR JOE, MY SEEKER FRIEND:
"CREATION ITSELF IS THE PRIMARY
& MOST BASIC EVIDENCE FOR THE
DIVINE AT WORK IN THE WORLD."
D. O'MURCHU

EVOLUTIONARY
FAITH

CONGRATULATIONS ON YOUR
GRADUATION: AUGUST 9, 2014?

CONTINUE THE QUEST?

LOVE,
Uncle Bob M.